The Edge of Modernism

The Edge of Modernism

American Poetry and the Traumatic Past

WALTER KALAIDJIAN

The Johns Hopkins University Press

Baltimore

9   7   5   3   1   2   4   6   8

The Johns Hopkins University Press
2715 North Charles Street
Baltimore, Maryland 21218-4363
www.press.jhu.edu

Library of Congress Cataloging-in-Publication Data
Kalaidjian, Walter B., 1952–
The edge of modernism : American poetry and the traumatic past /
Walter Kalaidjian.
p. cm.
Includes bibliographical references (p.   ) and index.
ISBN 0-8018-8231-1 (hardcover : alk. paper)
1. American poetry—20th century—History and criticism. 2. Literature and history—
United States—History—20th century. 3. Holocaust, Jewish (1939–1945), in literature.
4. Anti-communist movements in literature. 5. Modernism (Literature)—United States.
6. Genocide in literature. 7. Cold War in literature. 8. History in literature.
9. Slavery in literature. I. Title.
PS310.H57K35   2006
811'.509358—dc22   2005006243

A catalog record for this book is available from the British Library.

In memory
Elizabeth Barron Kalaidjian (1922–2003)

Contents

Acknowledgments

My thinking for this book began in response to the graduate students in my "Literature and the Real" seminar at Emory University and to the participants in the trauma seminar that I led for the Modern Studies Association. In particular, I am grateful to Aimee Pozorski, Patricia King, and Diana Miles for what they taught me about reality. Through an Emory University Research Committee grant I had the opportunity to examine genocide survival testimony at the Zoryan Institute in Cambridge, Massachusetts. A number of talks given at the Modern Language Association, Modern Studies Association, American Studies Association, and the Association for the Psychoanalysis of Culture and Society as well as lectures at the University of Minnesota, Colgate University, and the University of Kentucky helped to refine the scope and method of this book. Earlier drafts of parts of this book appeared in *Modernism, Inc.* (2001), ed. Jani Scandura and Michael Thurston; *Marketing Modernisms: Fates and Fortunes of the Literary Text in Commodity Culture* (1996), ed. Kevin Dettmar and Stephen Watt; and *College Literature* (1997).

For advice along the way, I owe a debt of gratitude to Cathy Caruth, Deborah Lipstadt, Peter Balakian, Chris Lane, Elissa Marder, Charles Shepherdson, Rita Barnard, Rachel Blau DuPlessis, Cary Nelson, Gordon Hutner, Dale Bauer, and Caroline Betensky, among others. Special thanks go out to Willa, Andrew, and Ted, to Lisa Rosof, and especially to Pat Cahill who, as reader and companion, kept me together in the life of this writing.

In addition, I gratefully acknowledge permission to reprint the following:

Excerpts from *Selected Poems,* by Diana Der-Hovanessian, copyright © 1994. Reprinted by permission of the author.

Excerpts from *Sad Days of Light,* by Peter Balakian, copyright © 1993. Reprinted by permission of the author.

Excerpts from *Dyer's Thistle,* by Peter Balakian, copyright © 1996. Reprinted by permission of the author.

The Edge of Modernism

Introduction

Trauma of the kind that haunted twentieth-century modernity—total war, genocide, terrorism—has hardly been left behind in today's public sphere. Inaugurating the new millennium, the historic destruction of the World Trade Center drove home the violent stakes of contemporary globalization even as it signaled the persistence of modern social trauma in the new times of postmodernity. The urgency of coming to terms with trauma's relation to narrative, material culture, and society has never been more pressing. Since 1980, the year that the American Psychiatric Association defined Post-Traumatic Stress Disorder (PTSD), an array of psychological, neurological, legal, ethical, and cultural methodologies has complicated how trauma is represented in literary studies. Throughout the 1990s, trauma studies exfoliated through a cross-disciplinary enterprise that was as provisional as it was dynamic. Several of the key questions that emerged from trauma's relation to testimony remain site-specific, or "unique" to such singular events as the Holocaust. Other issues of comparative witnessing probe trauma's imprint across modern cases of genocide, the atomic bombings of Hiroshima and Nagasaki, rape and incest narratives, racial and ethnic antagonisms, not to mention the ontic sources of trauma that may well be rooted in the human condition as such.

What trauma studies has lacked, however, is the kind of searching metacommentary that would adjudicate among its several emergent logics, truth claims, intellectual strategies, and objects of study. That dream of totalization—the aim of mastering trauma's disciplinary field—is precisely what Dominick LaCapra has questioned in *Writing History, Writing Trauma* (2001). Discerning trauma's place in historical narrative, LaCapra distinguishes between, on the one hand, the documented, evidentiary truth claims of "objectivist historicism" and, on the other hand, the "radical constructivism" of critical historians such as Hayden White and Frank Ankersmit, who locate a deep structural affinity in the tropological rhetoric that historical and aesthetic narratives share.[1] Negotiating between historical reference and textual representation, however, reaches a certain limit in the wake of the Holocaust, where what can be verified in the facts of genocide will take one only so far in addressing their force, significance, and meaning. Coming to terms with this challenge entails a certain rapprochement between historicity and the literary. The risk in writing trauma lies in succumbing to a melancholic acting out of its original event. But as Judith Butler, David Eng, and others have argued, melancholic attachment to traumatic loss can also produce new modes of aesthetic and cultural representation, social identity, and political agency.[2] For his part, LaCapra accepts a certain "empathetic unsettlement" as a requisite for working through trauma without, however, confusing past and present, loss and absence, the experience of the other with that of one's own. In recovering traumatic memory, the ethical standard here would observe the limits of difference as such in sustaining what Kaja Silverman describes as "heteropathic identification."[3] Clearly, as Dori Laub, Shoshana Felman, Geoffrey Hartman, and others have argued, writing trauma demands an act of witnessing whose testimonial modes of inquiry and authorship unsettle the otherwise dispassionate, objective truth claims that traditionally legitimate disciplinary understanding.[4]

This book addresses a related challenge for contemporary trauma studies—namely, the issue of the cultural work that trauma effects across multiple publics. Traumatic events are routinely commemorated in material culture and preserved in institutions of memory: museums, galleries, video and film vaults, rare book collections, and manuscript repositories. Such sites of archival memory play an important if not determining role in mediating a society's lived relationship to history as such. Although archives do not literally produce civic voices, they nevertheless have a stake in preserving, reproducing, disseminating, and thus shaping what these voices say. The constitutive role of the archive's techniques and institutional practices of preservation, as Jacques Derrida has argued, "determines the structure of the archivable content even in its very coming into existence and in its relationship to the future."[5] Such archival practices do not just record but actively frame the terms of cultural discourse: what Michel Foucault characterizes as "the general system of the formation and transformation of statements."[6] Unlike Foucault, however, Derrida underscores the modern "Freudian impression" whose *mal d'archive*, or "archive fever," troubles the discursive formation, regulation, and totalization of contemporary *regimes du savoir*.[7] Thus, traumatic memory opens a certain epistemological crisis in the discursive regime of archival commemoration. As wound, disaster, catastrophe, and so on, trauma breaches discursive representation and eclipses thought itself.[8] Just as trauma's pathology poses limits to critical reason and disciplinary inquiry, it also ruptures archival memory.

Analyzing the unique conditions and effects of trauma, Sigmund Freud theorized a key difference between traumatic events and traumatic memory. Only the latter's deferred action (*nachträglichkeit*), he insists, constitutes psychical trauma proper, insofar as its memory "acts like a foreign body which long after its entry must continue to be regarded as an agent that is still at work."[9] What does it mean, however, for traumatic memory to have agency—"to act like a foreign body at work" in the modern archive? What are the consequences for civic subjectivity of that psychic labor, inflected as it is by the disjointed temporality of deferred action? Can one assume a civic voice prior to, or apart from, the psychic agency of such archived "foreign bodies" or must the former always already be worked through the latter? Such questions of how archived, traumatic memory bears on civic identification, nation formation, and other social modes of class, racial, gender, and ethnic orientation are further complicated by today's postmodern condition—a world increasingly defined by the mechanical reproduction and circulation of sign exchange in photojournalism, film, museum and gallery culture, academic and literary discourses, and the popular entertainment industry. It is precisely the susceptibility of such signifying elements to rearticulation and recoding that in the case of genocide, some argue, results in a certain routinizing, normalizing, and repressing of traumatic memory.[10]

In this vein, consider the resources and limits of conventional Holocaust representation in negotiating memory and the production of new subjectivities among multiple publics. In his recent history *The Holocaust in American Life*, Peter Novick writes that "one of the things I find most striking about much of recent Jewish Holocaust commemoration is how 'un-Jewish'—how Christian—it is. I am thinking of the ritual of reverently following the structured pathways of the Holocaust in the major museums, which resembles nothing so much as the Stations of the Cross on the Via Dolorosa."[11] In the U.S. Holocaust Memorial Museum, as Novick implies, various strategies of promoting audience identification with the camp deportees risk a certain implosion of the difference between then and now. As a scrupulously organized simulation, the museum offers a particularly intense encounter with the archive of modern genocide. Museum architect James Ingo Freed, a protégé of Mies van der Rohe, designed his 265,000-square-foot building interior to signify on the architectural vernacular of concentration camp design. The Hall of Witness, which forms the atrium core of the museum, employs steel-girded brick walls, a warped skylight, blind arches, catwalks, and tower motifs to recall the surveillance architecture and the bleak industrial look of the Nazi extermination factories. Making one's way downward through the three floors of exhibits arranged chronologically from 1933 to the present, the museumgoer confronts, among other things, the 1,600 photographic portraits of the Tower of Life commemorating the Jewish victims of Eishyshok, display cases featuring Jewish relics, Sonderkommando uniforms, Nazi paraphernalia, camp documents, thousands of shoes from the Holocaust victims of Majdanek, iron casts of crematorium doors, a railway deportation car, as well as documented images of atrocity scrolling out on the video monitors and viewer booths replete with headphones, multimedia computer touch screens, and so on.

Through a sustained immersion in the visual icons, artifacts, survivor testimony, and semiotic codes of the Holocaust generally, the museum urges arguably not just an understanding of its history but an imaginary identification with Jewish victimization. Novick, in particular, has questioned the efficacy of such traumatic identification and has shown that the Holocaust narrative of "Jew as victim" has had a complex ideological history of signification in American postwar culture. At times avowed and at others disavowed by American Jews, the cultural meanings of Jewish victimization have been inflected differently by the politics of U.S. realignment with Germany, Cold War anticommunism and the domestic Red Scare, by the Eichmann trial, American Zionism and the establishment of the State of Israel (1948–1949), the Six Day War (1967) and Yom Kippur War (1973), and later media events such as the global distribution of the NBC *Holocaust* miniseries (1978) and Hollywood blockbusters such as Steven Spielberg's *Schindler's List* (1993). In the face of such various messages and agendas, Novick concludes, "the desire to find and teach lessons of the Holocaust has various sources—different sources for different people, one supposes. Probably one of its principal sources is the hope of extracting from the Holocaust something that is, if not redemptive, at least useful. I doubt it can be done" (HAL, 263). Certainly, much of Holocaust representation has a didactic purpose that aims to teach us something significant about the past that will have value for our present and future lives. But does the archive's cultural representation describe a one-way street of pedagogic transmission? Does a bright line lead from the archive's didactic strategy to its intended modes of civic engagement?

Perhaps it might be more pertinent to question not just what people can learn from the Holocaust but, more to the point, what they have done with it: what kind of civic voices have they assumed from the psychic agency of its traumatic memory? In what ways, that is, do multiple publics interact with Holocaust memory? How do people recode and rearticulate it to other narratives of material culture?

How, moreover, are we—and who are we—to adjudicate the material culture of the Holocaust? Is there an ethicopolitical standard by which we can judge the "civic voices" of the Holocaust at home? By "home," I am not just referring to American culture in the postwar decades but also the sense of self-possession one assumes in being at home, everything that Freud pointed to in the word *heimlich* and its radical estrangement from what is precisely *unheimlich*. Poetic discourse affords, arguably, a unique and particularly concentrated medium for listening closely to the uncanny return of Holocaust memory as deferred action (*nachträglichkeit*).[12] Theodor Adorno's famous slogan that "to write poetry after Auschwitz is barbaric" tacitly assumes a temporality locating us "after" the Holocaust rather than within the deferred action of its unfolding event.[13] Nevertheless, postwar poems such as Anthony Hecht's masterful sestina "The Book of Yolek"—in sharp contrast to Adorno—bear witness to the uncanny return of trauma as deferred action across the generations of the Holocaust. Much of postwar Holocaust verse, as we shall see, similarly contests the foreclosure of Adorno's temporal framing.

More controversial still, it seems, is the comparative identifications poets such as Sylvia Plath have claimed between Jewish victimization under Nazism and women's place under contemporary patriarchy broadly conceived. Plath's comparative recodings of the Holocaust recover the obscure traces of women's domestic trauma that are not, as Laura S. Brown has theorized, "outside the range" of everyday life.[14] Until recently, of course, this criterion of being "outside the range of usual human experience" defined PTSD under category A of the *Diagnostic and Statistical Manual of the American Psychiatric Association,* and it was only dropped from the *DSM-IV* in 1994. Such feminist identifications of private and public trauma narratives, however, risk a certain trivialization of the unique historicity of the Holocaust, which in Cynthia Ozick's critique, threatens to reduce Jews to metaphors.[15] What are the chances and pitfalls, then, of crossing what is inside and outside the range of everyday life when one identifies the Jewish concentration camp survivor with the feminist survivor? Should we read Plath's appropriation of Jewish victimization as her "failure" to identify with the authorized representations of the Holocaust archive, or is that failure the precondition for recovering new forms of subjectivity in which the "foreign bodies" of repressed narrative and affective memory are more powerfully at work precisely because they have not been worked through? Indeed, so uncanny is Plath's repetition of issues at the heart of the modern "Jewish question" in poems such as, say, "Daddy" that her comparative identifications wholly elude contemporary critics, thereby pointing to what is, even now, a deep-seated narrative of repression in the American reception of the Holocaust archive.

Few poems, arguably, are so widely anthologized and so universally misread as Plath's "Daddy." Perhaps the most symptomatic blind spot in Plath criticism touches on her relation to nationalist narration. For her part, Plath insisted time and again on positioning herself as a writer of Germanic descent in relation to the Holocaust archive: "In particular," she made plain in her 1962 BBC interview, "my background is, may I say, German and Austrian . . . and so my concern with concentration camps and so on is uniquely intense."[16] It remains, however, a curious symptom that Plath's own nationalist self-positioning is consistently disavowed in her American critical reception. Thus, Edward Butscher would not be the first or last to elide Plath's German ethnicity in resisting the Holocaust in her writing: "There is no way," he writes, "that the poetry of an American girl writing from the remote perspective of the 1950s could ever capture the actual, brutal reality of the Holocaust."[17] Similarly, Al Strangeways' important essay "'The Boot in the Face': The Problem of the Holocaust in the Poetry of Sylvia Plath" interprets "Daddy" as an expression of "American interest in individualism."[18] Even as discerning a critic as Jacqueline Rose reads the poem's feminist emancipation in nationalist terms. Plath's exorcism of and liberation from the father, Rose argues, leaves the "paternal body in bits and pieces spreading across the American nation state."[19]

Beyond this American nationalist claim on Plath's poetic identity, her Holocaust verse more radically goes to the heart of the "Jewish question" as it touches on German identity. More than her postwar critics, Plath seems to understand what is at stake in claiming a German positionality in the post-Holocaust epoch. On the one hand, Plath's poetic avowal of a German subject position anticipates Eric Santner's cogent statement on the postwar task of nationalist mourning when he writes that "Germans had to mourn as Germans for those whom they had excluded and exterminated in their mad efforts to produce their 'Germanness.'"[20] Perhaps the most symptomatic sign of Plath's postwar Germanness is her taking on the identity of victim, which, as the psychoanalytic theorist Martin S. Bergmann has observed, is the most characteristic feature of what Alexander and Margarete Mitscherlich describe as a German "inability to mourn" the Holocaust.[21] In "Daddy" Plath occupies both German and Jewish subject positions so as to confuse, reverse, and ultimately collapse the binary logic that would identify the former through its difference from the latter.

As early as 1958 in a synopsis for her story "The Shadow," Plath had explored the "SINGLE THEME . . . of a complicated guilt system whereby Germans in a Jewish and Catholic community are made to feel, in a scapegoat fashion, the pain, psychically, the Jews are made to feel in Germany by the Germans without religion. The child can't understand the wider framework. How does her father," Plath goes on to speculate, "come into this."[22] Four years later, her purpose—as she lays it out in her well-known BBC comment on the poem "Daddy"—would insinuate the enigma of Jewish difference precisely within the claim to a German self-possession of identity. "Here is a poem," Plath has said of "Daddy," "spoken by a girl with an Electra complex. Her father died while she thought he was God. Her case is complicated by the fact that her father was also a Nazi and her mother very possibly part Jewish. In the daughter the two strains marry and paralyze each other—she has to act out the awful little allegory once over before she is free of it."[23] If Plath claims a German identity, she performs it as a provisional speech act: one that disavows the universalizing tendency in her critical reception to interpellate her as an American poet.

But more provocatively, Plath complicates her German ethnicity by dramatizing its oppositional dependence on the Jew as other. Jacqueline Rose has analyzed the poem's complex shuttling among metaphor, fantasy, and nationalist identification. "Jewishness," for the speaker in the poem, Rose contends, "is the position of the one without history or roots" (HSP, 228). What is at stake in the poem, Rose contends, is Plath's relation to language, where the figure of the Jew as diasporic exile is read—as it is in poststructuralists such as Maurice Blanchot, Jean-François Lyotard, Julia Kristeva, Philippe Lacoue-LaBarthe, Jean-Luc Nancy, and Jacques Derrida—as a sign of alterity, strangeness, and otherness.[24] The issue, however, of what it means in terms of Holocaust representation for Plath to act out the murder of the father from the position of Jew has gone unremarked in her critical reception. The tendency here has been to divide the personal off from the public—to attribute this murder to Plath's personal mourning of the loss of her actual father. Following Freud's insight that giving in to loss involves a process of ambivalent grief work—including "disparaging the object, denigrating it, even . . . slaying it"—Plath's murderous affect is further read as a symptom of rage that responds to the failure of her marriage in the fall of 1962 to Ted Hughes: the poem's other daddy.[25] Nowhere, however, has criticism joined this personal narrative to the poem's other historic patricide—that of killing the father as a "bag full of God" from the subject position of the Jew.

In this vein, some three decades before writing *Moses and Monotheism,* Freud in 1908 told the following joke to Theodor Reik, "The Boy Itzig is asked in grammar school: 'Who was Moses?' and answers, 'Moses was the son of an Egyptian princess.' 'That's not true,' says the teacher, 'Moses was the son of a Hebrew mother. The Egyptian princess found the baby in a casket.' But Itzig answers, 'Says She!'"[26] Briefly, in Freud's account of the "new enigma" of the Egyptian Moses, Judaism originates with the worship of the Egyptian god Aton. Moses introduces Aton to the Semite tribes, who—in a repetition of the slaying of the Primal Father—later rebel against and murder the lawgiver. The memory of that murder is then re-pressed and displaced in the worship of the volcano God Yahweh with Mosaic monotheism returning in the period of the prophets. Thus, Judaic monotheism, for Freud, is doubly marked by a heightened obligation to the Other whose ethical de-mand is also fraught with the traumatic affect of patricide. The return of that re-pressed narrative is further repeated in Pauline Christianity that, unlike in Judaism, marks an atonement and shedding of guilt for the primal scene of the father's mur-der. As Freud speculates, that psychic departure from Judaism also serves to differ-entiate the two traditions. Ventriloquizing Christianity's implied attitude toward the Jews, Freud concludes, "In full, this reproach would run as follows: 'They will not accept it as true that they murdered God, whereas we admit it and have been cleansed of that guilt.'"[27]

Writing in 1939 in the wake of his exile from Vienna to London, it is not surpris-ing that Freud signifies on the trope of ethnic cleansing and further reflects on the "new enigma" of Moses as it is played out in the history of Jewish oppression: "In a certain sense," he writes, "they have taken a tragic load of guilt on themselves; they have been made to pay a heavy penance for it."[28] Not unlike the "penance" that Freud attributes to the Jews, Plath too has been made to pay in her critical reception for repeating patricide in "Daddy." Indeed, "there is a charge," as she claimed in "Lady Lazarus," in acting out that trauma, and Plath certainly occupies a con-tentious and highly cathected place in the archive of Holocaust studies. "The dis-tortion of a text," as Freud has it, "resembles a murder,"[29] and if there is patricide forgotten within Judaic monotheism, then it is doubly encrypted as it returns in the deferred action of Plath and her critics. In repeating the historic narrative of what Jean-François Lyotard calls the "Jewish Oedipus," Plath demonstrates that trauma's "foreign body" is complexly at work in the archive of Holocaust memory.[30] The pe-culiarly charged appropriation of the Holocaust at stake in Plath's confessional po-etics provokes the urgent question not just of whether she has a right to claim em-pathic identification with the Jews but, equally important, of whether the Holocaust can rightly serve as a paradigm for coming to terms with other, comparative scenes of social extremity. The long-standing debate over the uniqueness of the Holocaust runs the gamut from Elie Wiesel's credo that it remains "the ultimate event, the ultimate mystery, never to be comprehended or transmitted" to Peter Novick's counterclaim that "talk of uniqueness and incomparability surrounding the Holo-caust . . . promotes evasion of moral and historical responsibility."[31]

Negotiating this impasse, Geoffrey Hartman has cogently framed the key issue at stake in contemporary Holocaust studies: "Is there a way," he asks, "of bringing this disaster into the framework of comparative genocide?"[32] In chapter 1, "History's 'Black Page': Genocide and Modern American Verse," I engage Hartman's question precisely through the register of traumatic memory. To begin with, I read the literary representation of the Holocaust against that of its closest historical precedent on the continuum of twentieth-century mass murder: the Armenian Genocide of 1915. Scholars of comparative genocide link the Armenian Genocide to the Holocaust in terms of the "functionalist" and "intentionalist" similarities they share. Both events take place in the context of modern "total" war and they both conform to the United Nations 1949 definition of "genocide in whole."[33] Both were specifically modern events facilitated by centralized state planning, bureaucratic administration, modern technologies of rapid information exchange and propaganda, rail deportation, concentrated killing centers, and so on. The intentionalist ideology of the Nazis— bent as it was on exterminating every last Jew on the planet—is held to be unique to that event. Although not as thoroughgoing as the Nazis, the Young Turk Committee of Unity and Progress—headed by the triumvirate of Talaat Bey, Enver Bey, and Jemal Bey—similarly targeted the whole Armenian community for planned, state-administered extermination.[34] Indeed, as eminent Holocaust scholar Yehuda Bauer points out, "[T]he differences between the Holocaust and the Armenian massacres are less important than the similarities. . . . This is the closest parallel to the Holocaust. . . . On the continuum, the two events stand next to each other."[35]

Although comparative genocide scholarship has drawn attention to the well-known functionalist and intentionalist parallels between the Holocaust and the Armenian Genocide, very little attention has been paid to the ways in which the two events share a common paradigm of traumatic memory. In this vein, my second chapter, "The Holocaust at Home," employs the psychoanalytic insights of Nicolas Abraham and Maria Torok to read the traces of extremity inscribed at the level of literary form in the poetic cryptonyms underwriting the representation of genocide. Poetry, I argue, provides a formal medium for giving testimony to trauma across the generations otherwise separating primary and secondary witnesses. Cross-generational trauma is amply documented in such psychological studies of the Holocaust as Martin S. Bergmann and Milton E. Jucovy's *Generations of the Holocaust*, John J. Sigal and Morton Weinfeld's *Trauma and Rebirth*, Robert Prince's *The Legacy of the Holocaust*, and Dina Wardi's *Memorial Candles*, among others.[36] Similarly, the phenomenon of what Freud defined as deferred action (*nachträglichkeit*) in traumatic memory has been theorized as a general condition pertaining to what Terrence Des Pres, Lawrence Langer, and Geoffrey Hartman have characterized as "secondary" or "intellectual" witnessing in the post-Holocaust era.[37] Coming after the event, the secondary witness assumes not just an historical but, more importantly, an empathic stance toward traumatic memory. For it is precisely what escapes cognitive mastery in the event that resists the foreclosure of factual, historical understanding. Here, the sublime, inchoate excess of trauma touches upon the mind precisely as that which eludes consciousness— where, as T. S. Eliot puts it in "The Dry Salvages," "We had the experience but missed the meaning."[38] Similarly in Jean-François Lyotard's blunt formulation, traumatic memory "indicates the *quod* but not the *quid*." Following Freud, Lyotard defines "the essence of the event: that *there is* 'comes before' *what* there is."[39] Falling before and outside of consciousness, the essence of trauma—its quiddity— remains radically unknowable.

The return of trauma's enigma further ruptures the historical sense of time as such by intruding upon the normative continuities of linear temporality underwriting conventional narration. "The event," as Gilles Deleuze has written, ". . . is always already in the past and yet to come."[40] Insofar as secondary witnessing is defined by an encounter with extremity's unfinished business, it has to deal with a temporality marked by the future anterior of trauma's "after-effects" of time "out of joint." Thus, as Derrida has it, "memory is not just the opposite of forgetting . . . to think memory or to think anamnesis, here, is to think things as paradoxical as the memory of a past that has not been present, the memory of the future—the movement of memory as tied to the future and not only to the past, memory turned toward the promise, toward what is coming, what is arriving, what is happening tomorrow."[41] Beyond an encounter with radical loss, the unique temporal structure of trauma encompasses not just the period of latency between the event and its present return in memory but, equally important, the promise of an anticipated futurity of difference.

The special vantage point of the future anterior—conceiving a future in terms of what will have been—offers a salutary departure from history as a totalizing regime of the same. Moreover, the expanded temporal frame of traumatic latency opens important avenues for redefining the relationship between literary modernism and postmodernism in the makeup of their traditional disciplinary formations. The revisionary temporal understanding provided by trauma theory allows for a crucial rethinking of modernist periodicity. Instead of foreclosing modernity, say, at the end of the Second World War in 1945, the temporal rhythms that I explore throughout this book afford a much more dynamic view of literary periodicity. Specifically, I discern the "edge" of modernism's definitive scenes of extremity in terms of their punctuation of the present and their future returns. Thus, across several comparative contexts of traumatic historicity, I examine modernism's unfinished business as its edge cuts through the literary representations, themes, and formal techniques of contemporary poetics. Not insignificantly, this close attention to traumatic temporality opens up utopian possibilities for imagining transformative cultural identity, political agency and social change.

The shock of the traumatic past, paradoxically enough, calls for new modes of being in the world and new models of community. "What is new, newness itself," writes Judith Butler, "is founded upon the loss of original place, and so it is a newness that has within it a sense of belatedness, of coming after, and of being thus fundamentally determined by a past that continues to inform it. . . . Loss becomes condition and necessity for a certain sense of community, where community does not overcome the loss, where community *cannot* overcome the loss without losing the very sense of itself as community."[42] This new ethics of community, lodged precisely in resistance to reparative denials of traumatic loss, offers a salutary difference from what Fredric Jameson has described as the "triviality of daily life in late capitalism," where "the uniqueness and the irrevocability of private destinies and of individuality itself seem to have evaporated."[43] Thus, if there is a melancholic dimension to such secondary witnessing in literature, it is not necessarily reducible to the kind of paralysis we associate with the traumatized bystander to historical extremity. Jean Baudrillard, for example, offers a singularly pessimistic take on the melancholic politics of traumatic memory by framing genocide commemoration as itself a symptom of postmodernism's loss of civic society to the regime of simulation. "It is really," he writes, "only because we have disappeared politically and historically today (and therein lies our problem) that we seek to prove that we died between 1940 and 1945, at Auschwitz or in Hiroshima—which at least makes for a strong history. We are like the Armenians, who wear themselves out trying to prove they were massacred in 1917—a proof that is unattainable, useless, yet in some sense vital."[44]

In pursuing this latter "vitality"—alluded to somewhat enigmatically in Baudrillard's otherwise cynical take on genocide denial—the project I engage in *The Edge of Modernism* would glean the shock of difference that trauma insinuates into the otherwise foreclosed reproduction of postmodern historicity. Throughout this book, I demonstrate the ways in which the formal resources of the poet's craft—its figurative language, its reliance on catachresis (mixed and contradictory metaphors), aposiopesis (or invoked interruptions of absence and silence, often through ellipsis), anacoluthon (non sequiturs and shifting patterns of syntax), its grammatological techniques and the spatial arrangement on the page—together forge a salutary medium for staging traumatic histories in ways that resist the banal spectacle of the image world otherwise governing contemporary consumer society.

Beyond examining the poetics of memory in the context of modern genocide, my third chapter—"Harlem Dancers and the Middle Passage"—considers the traumatic legacy of slavery as it haunts contemporary African-American performance culture and its dialogue with the rich aesthetic heritage of the Harlem Renaissance. As a place of memory (what Pierre Nora defines as a *lieu de mémoire*),[45] Harlem has had a shaping influence on postwar black vernacular culture. Contemporary aesthetic debate between, say, Coco Fusco and bell hooks is anticipated by the key terms and core issues of disagreement at stake between earlier figures such as Langston Hughes and Countée Cullen. Moreover, as I demonstrate, modern and postmodern African-American aesthetics share a deeper historicity of trauma reaching back to the Black Atlantic. In discerning the trace and address of trauma in African-American expressive culture, I explore the tropes of dancing and the performance of black skin in the poetry of figures such as Countée Cullen, Gwendolyn Bennett, and Claude McKay coupled with the dance aesthetics of the celebrated jazz artist Josephine Baker. In reading the figure of the "Harlem dancer" as a forerunner of contemporary black performance art, I also trace it back through such urban sites as New York's Five Points, Congo Square in New Orleans, the Plantation Buck and Wing competitions at the Big House and, ultimately, to the trauma of dancing aboard the slave ships of the Black Atlantic. The contradictory impulses of this black dance tradition—staging as it does utopian and traumatic visions of African-American heritage—are most memorably performed in Josephine Baker's primitivist *danse sauvage* in *La Revue Nègre* of 1925. Signifying on the colonial codes of primitivist fantasy, Baker also invokes phantoms of traumatic memory in ways that remain salutary for later, postmodern generations of African-American performance artists.

In chapter 4—"Specters of Commitment in Modern American Literary Studies"—I pursue further the question, as Ross Chambers puts it of "what it means for a culture to be haunted by a collective memory."[46] Specifically, I explore the traces of such cultural hauntings by revisiting the traumatic specters of modernist political commitment on both the right and the left that have been otherwise repressed from the public mind of the postwar period. In particular, I recover the latter half of the Depression decade of the 1930s as a defining moment in the subsequent makeup of English studies in the United States. Revisiting the clash between the Southern Agrarians and the New York Popular Front, I demonstrate the crucial link between, on the one hand, the cultural wars of the Depression era—that culminate in the broader, internationalist political and military conflicts at stake in the Spanish Civil War—and, on the other hand, the formation of postwar American literary studies under the conservative agenda of the American New Critics. Major American writers such as Ernest Hemingway, Langston Hughes, Muriel Rukeyser, and countless others experienced the Spanish Civil War as a defining moment in the struggle for international social justice in the modern period. Yet, the defeat of the Spanish Republic remained a possessing political trauma for a generation of artists whose aesthetic legacy was then repressed by American New Criticism's decisive triumph over the American left in the postwar decades. Although American New Criticism purported to be an apolitical school of close, formalist reading practices, its Agrarian proponents had a far-from-disinterested stance toward modern culture. Just as New Criticism expunged historicist and socialist modes of literary reading, it also repressed its own radically right-wing roots in the Southern Agrarian cause. In today's contemporary culture wars, the trace of that reactionary political agenda continues to haunt the social rhetoric of the New Right. Similarly, the aesthetic legacy of the Old Left—blacklisted throughout the Cold War—possesses American literature in the specters of silenced voices like those of the poet Edwin Rolfe, whose poetic corpus has only recently been revived in contemporary critical discussions of American poetry.

Moving from the traumatic social antagonisms at the heart of modern American literary culture, I turn in the final chapter, "The Enigma of Witness: Domestic Trauma on and off the Couch," to examine the long-standing debate within psychoanalysis over the recovered memory of domestic trauma. From the beginning, modern psychoanalysis has been split on the question of whether the recovered memory of child abuse stems from actual seduction or reflects infantile sexual fantasy. This foundational controversy reaches back to Freud's own reversal of his early "seduction theory" first presented in his 1896 paper "The Aetiology of Hysteria" and later abandoned beginning in 1900 with *The Interpretation of Dreams* in favor of his new understandings of Oedipal sexual fantasy represented in *Three Essays on the Theory of Sexuality* (1905). Following Jeffrey Masson's provocative revisiting of Freud's paradigm shift, clinical psychoanalysis witnessed a popular return of that unsettled historicity.[47] Throughout the 1990s, the controversy between proponents of "recovered" memory and skeptics who decried the former as promoters of a "false memory syndrome" had wide-ranging theoretical, clinical, and legal ramifications for the practice of psychoanalysis.[48]

Rather than advocating either side of this interpretive clash, I consider instead the dialogic tensions it mobilizes for reading the complex, literary presentation of memory in the experimental modernism of Djuna Barnes and the "confessionalism" of Anne Sexton. Both authors revisit disturbing recollections of childhood trauma, but Sexton, more than Barnes, offers a considered vacillation on the status of such recovered memories. Barnes's experimental modernism encrypts the recovered memory of incest in the stunning stylistic innovations of *Ryder* (1928),

Nightwood (1936), and *The Antiphon* (1958). Unlike Barnes, Sexton never decided in her own mind whether her recovered memory of incest was based in fact or fantasy. Leaving open rather than foreclosing this question of desire, Sexton looks forward to Jane Gallop's controversial position that the daughter's incestuous fantasy is, paradoxically enough, produced by the "seductive function" of patriarchy's prohibitive law against incest.[49] In this vein, I examine the productive beginnings of Sexton's confessionalism as it emerges not just from the individual genius of the poet but, more to the point, from the disciplinary intersections of psychoanalysis and literature in the 1950s. Crossing literature and psychoanalysis, I study the collaborative settings of the analytic session and creative writing workshop that gave direction and shape to Sexton's performative stagings of domestic trauma both on and off the couch. Over the past three decades since her suicide in 1974, Sexton's critical reception, I argue, has not paid sufficient attention to the sophisticated, formal strategies through which her poetry inscribes a certain tension between seduction and fantasy in representing traumatic memory.

Ending with close readings of Sexton's confessionalism, *The Edge of Modernism* thus completes a trajectory that moves from the early modernist period to the latter half of the twentieth century, from the shock of total war to the memory of domestic abuse, and from unique historical events to the trauma of everyday life. While the scope of this book is broad-ranging and representative of the major topoi within the emerging field of trauma studies, it does not claim to exhaust, by any means, the work on trauma that still remains to be undertaken in such fields as Asian-American and Pacific Rim studies, Native American studies, queer theory, trans-Atlantic studies, Southern studies, and so on. These and other new horizons of scholarly work will, no doubt, constitute the challenge of further critical inquiry. For the moment, I will be satisfied if the historical events, poetic careers, theoretical questions, and methodological approaches that I have explored here will prove to be usable starting points for a next generation of American modernists.

CHAPTER ONE

History's "Black Page"

Genocide and Modern American Verse

Seldom in the theories of social, cultural, and aesthetic modernisms has the trauma of genocide featured prominently in what defines the modern condition. Benchmarks in the formation and reception of modernism would include Nietzsche's proclamation of the death of God in *The Gay Science;* the epistemological revolution of Darwinism, Marxism, and Freudian psychoanalysis; the Fordist transformation of industrial society with its proliferation of the latest consumer goods, reified services, and attendant information flows; the fragmentation of representation as seen, say, in the formal techniques of the impressionist, Cubist, Futurist, and Constructivist aesthetic movements, along with analogous tendencies in experimental poetics and prose, avant-garde music, dance, and performance art; the new discourses of, on the one hand, an agonized racial double-consciousness and, on the other, a celebration of the "renaissance" of race (albeit complicated by the colonial fetish of "primitivism"); progressive figures of class antagonism, experimental gender roles, "queer" sexual identities, and so on. Yet genocide is curiously elided in the critical reception of modernism.

Amidst the wears and tears of postmodernism, the reigning discourses of the state, the media, and the academy have served arguably to repress, deny, and normalize the extreme experiences of total war and industrial mass murder.[1] Not a phenomenon, however, that belongs to the distant past, genocide first happens within the turbulent forces of social modernism with its emerging systems of technology and rapid information exchange. Accompanying these sophisticated advances, genocide—it should be underscored—is not only a distinctively modern problem but one that persists as the underside to the progress of modernity otherwise witnessed in the twentieth century. Repressed for the most part in the modern public sphere, the legacy of genocide troubles the closure of modernist periodization with the repetition of its event. Returning in Cambodia, Rwanda, Bosnia, Guatemala, and Kosovo, the genocidal edge of modernism cuts through the social fabric of postmodernism. But equally important, the unfinished business of genocide's revisionist historicism and political denial bleeds into our own moment. Thus, in discerning literary modernism anew, we might begin with asking, what was the uniquely traumatic force of genocide in dissociating the modernist sensibility?

Although the high moderns were not unmindful of "[o]ld civilizations put to the sword," their psychic tendency was to affirm—as Yeats has it in "Lapis Lazuli"—a Nietzschean "gaiety transfiguring all that dread."[2] Similarly, T. S. Eliot's definitive work of modernist mourning *The Waste Land* (1922) also faces the Eastern European apocalypse of "hooded hordes swarming / Over endless plains, stumbling in cracked earth."[3] Yet *The Waste Land* turns toward the consoling metaphysics of "What the Thunder Said," which prefigure Eliot's later investments in the troubling conjuncture of Anglo-Catholicism and anti-Semitism.[4] It is, of course, a critical commonplace that Eliot's modern verse epic reflects the trauma of the First World War. Nowhere, however, has criticism observed that *The Waste Land* was conceived in the wake of the twentieth century's first case of "total" state-administered genocide, undertaken in 1915 by the Young Turk government against the Armenian people.

Canonical modernists such as, say, Ezra Pound, Ernest Hemingway, John Dos Passos, and Virginia Woolf were fully aware of the novum of human extermination as a modern portent of things to come. Pound, for example, foregrounded the ethicopolitical stakes of the Armenian Genocide in his political journalism while a contributor to A. R. Orage's weekly *New Age* in the 1910s. Just six months after the outbreak of mass murder in the Ottoman Empire, Pound cited the massacres as an unacceptable, international atrocity in order to press for U.S. entry into the First World War. Beyond the nationalist interests of its own domestic security, America in 1915, Pound argued, was being challenged by the broader "interest of humanity, concerning which Mr. Wilson has occasionally spoken." Such ethicopolitical concern, he maintained, went to the heart of the "humanitarian aspirations" of the American enterprise both in its Enlightenment foundations and its subsequent civil war over the abolition of slavery. Extending this humanitarian argument beyond America's national borders and into the new global arrangements of international modernism, Pound sought to extend such state resistance to "tyranny" into the transnational public sphere. Pound drew an analogy between American resistance to the tyranny of slavery in the Civil War and the present tyranny of the Ottoman Empire. Moreover, he criticized what he called America's "superneutrality," observing that "[i]f tyranny is visible in our modern world, it is visible in the militarism of Germany, in the rule of Ferdinand of Bulgaria and in the Armenian massacres."[5]

It was no accident, of course, that Pound should invoke the Armenian case as part of his political journalism in the mid-1910s for, right from the beginning, it was the era's most riveting human rights story. Not just an unprecedented modern horror, the Armenian Genocide was also an inaugural media event. The spectacle of concentration-camp internment, death marches, and mass murder—centrally administered throughout the Ottoman Empire under the watchful eye of the German and Austro-Hungarian alliance—was widely reported in the United States and among the other Entente nations of Britain, France, and Russia. In America alone, such newspapers and journals as the *New York Times, New York Herald Tribune, Boston Herald, Chicago Tribune, Atlantic Monthly, Nation, Outlook,* and *Literary Digest* covered the story. By October 1915, a Committee on Armenian Atrocities published a front-page *New York Times* article condemning Turkey's "Policy of Extermination" signed by, among others, Oscar Straus, former ambassador to Turkey and former secretary of commerce and labor; Cleveland Dodge; Rabbi Stephen S. Wise; the Right Reverend David H. Greer, Protestant Episcopal bishop of New York; George Plimpton; the Reverend James Barton, secretary of the American Board of Commissioners for Foreign Missions; and John R. Mott of the International Committee of the YMCA.[6]

Within diplomatic circles, Viscount Bryce in 1916 submitted a massive government blue paper to the British Secretary of State for Foreign Affairs. Edited by Arnold J. Toynbee, *The Treatment of Armenians in the Ottoman Empire, 1915–16* archived eyewitness accounts of torture, rape, and mass murder reported by missionaries, Red Cross volunteers, consular officials, German health workers, and Armenian survivors.[7] The previous year, Toynbee had published *Armenian Atrocities: The Murder of a Nation,* which included Bryce's address to the House of Lords appealing for British intervention in the Turkish massacres. Quoting from a 1915 *New York Tribune* editorial, Toynbee underscored German complicity with the Young Turk genocide: "What Germany has done," according to the *Tribune,* "is to bring us all back in the Twentieth Century to the condition of the dark ages."[8] German witnesses who dissented from Germany's denial of the massacres included Dr. Johannes Lepsius, head of the Deutsche Orient-Mision. His *Der Todesgang des armenischen Volkes* (death march of the Armenian people) had a 1919 print run of 20,000 copies, which were distributed, in part, to the Orient Mission and German Reichstag. Similarly, Dr. Armin T. Wegner of the German-Ottoman Health Mission Conference published an "Open Letter" to President Wilson for the Paris Peace Conference of 1919 based on two unpublished books documenting the Armenian Genocide.[9]

What did it mean in the mid-1910s to pick up, for the first time, any major daily paper around the world and read such headlines as "Armenians Are Sent to Perish in Desert: Turks Accused of Plan to Exterminate Whole Population," "Turks Depopulate Towns of Armenia," and "1,500,000 Armenians Starve"?[10] Just how shocking this new edge of modernism appeared for the expatriate generation can be gleaned from the traumatized persona of Ernest Hemingway's short story "On the Quai at Smyrna." As a foreign correspondent for the *Toronto Star,* Ernest Hemingway was familiar with the Armenian Genocide and accepted the assignment of covering the burning of Smyrna and the massacre of its Christian community by the Turks in the early 1920s. Hemingway arrived in Smyrna about three weeks after the ancient city was razed by the Turks during mid-September 1922.[11] The story takes the form of a bystander testimonial given by a British naval officer who has just witnessed the refugee Christian Greek and Armenian community driven to the quays of the harbor in flight from the atrocities of rape, torture, and mass murder perpetrated by the Turks. Foregrounded in the story's opening lines, is the arresting trace of genocide's uncanny presence in the modern scene:

> The strange thing was, he said, how they screamed every night at midnight. I do not know why they screamed at that time. We were in the harbor and they were all on the pier and at midnight they started screaming. . . . The worst, he said, were the women with dead babies. You couldn't get the women to give up their dead babies. They'd have babies dead for six days. Wouldn't give them up. Nothing you could do about it. Had to take them away finally.[12]

Presenting the shock of the bystander witness to "strange," "unimaginable," and "extraordinary," events, Hemingway registers his character's trauma in the patterns of verbal repetition that are symptomatic of his brush with extremity.[13]

Similarly, John Dos Passos's autobiographical account of the Armenian Genocide's aftermath, portrayed in *Orient Express* (1927), deflects the full emotive impact of mass murder in the numbed monotones and understated ironies of a deadpan narrative voice. An aspiring foreign correspondent, Dos Passos received commissions to report on the Middle East from the *Tribune* and *Metropolitan* magazine and he undertook them in the search after the kind of exoticism that would satisfy his "craving for new sights."[14] Through the assistance of Paxton Hibben, who was serving in Paris as secretary of a Near East Relief mission, Dos Passos booked passage on the Orient Express out of Constantinople. Arriving in the Armenian heartland in Erivan near Mount Ararat, he comes upon the evidence of the recent deportations:

> [A] dead wagon goes round every day to pick up the people who die in the streets. People tell horrible stories of new graves plundered and bodies carved up for food in the villages. . . . Opposite the station a crumbling brown wall. In the shade of it lie men, children, a woman, bundles of rags that writhe feverishly. We ask someone what's the matter with them.—Nothing, they are dying. A boy almost naked, his filthy skin livid green, staggers out of the station, a bit of bread in his hand, and lurches dizzily towards the wall. There he sinks down, too weak to raise it to his mouth. An old man with a stick in his hand hobbles slowly towards the boy. He has blood-filled eyes that look out through an indescribable mat of hair and beard. He stands over the boy a minute and then, propping himself up with his stick, grabs the bread, and scuttles off round the corner of the station. The boy makes a curious whining noise, but lies back silently without moving, his head resting on a stone. Above the wall, against the violet sky of afternoon, Ararat stands up white and cool and smooth like the vision of another world.[15]

Not unlike Hemingway's portrait of the British Officer at Smyrna, Dos Passos's autobiographical persona is afflicted with the trauma of the bystander witness assailed by the intrusive memory whose strangeness befalls the modern as if from "another world." Some four decades later in his 1966 memoir *The Best Times*, Dos Passos writing now after Auschwitz recalls the Armenian landscape whose uncanny scenes look forward to the Holocaust's world of "cinders," where "corpses were stacked like cordwood" (BT, 95). Like Hemingway's fictional persona, however, Dos Passos presents a numbed response to the edge of traumatic modernism.

Beyond such journalistic accounts of the unspeakable, what consequences, we may well ask, did genocide entail for the traditional paradigm of Western humanism? Such questionings of social modernism are seldom posed in literary criticism, in part, because the ethicopolitical issue of genocidal witnessing in the 1920s was struck from cultural memory along with its encrypted event. Three years after *The Waste Land*'s publication, Virginia Woolf's ironic portrait of *Mrs. Dalloway* (1925) marks the psychic limits of imagining this, by then, unconscious horror beneath the banality of everyday life. Clarissa Dalloway, writes Woolf,

> cared much more for her roses than for Armenians. Hunted out of existence, maimed, frozen, the victims of cruelty and injustice (she had heard Richard say over and over again)—no, she could feel nothing for the Albanians, or was it the Armenians? But she loved her roses (didn't that help the Armenians?)[16]

In discerning the modern subject, Woolf assigns Clarissa's lapse of conscience, her insensitivity to social justice, not so much to a shallow colonial naiveté: for Clarissa has a thoroughgoing, historicizing grasp of how the Armenians were "hunted out of existence." "No," Woolf observes, Mrs. Dalloway's symptom is that "she could feel nothing" about these disturbing facts of the case. Beyond simply recording the state-administered extermination of a people, Woolf witnesses to an event whose force breaches conventional representation. In the blocked psychic experience of her central character, Woolf gives testimony to how the trauma of genocide haunts modernism as a cognitive gap that necessarily eludes conscious registration in the public mind.

Like Yeats and Eliot, Woolf places the advent of modern genocide under erasure: at once acknowledging and denying its dread historicity. In the later writings of his career, Freud in *Civilization and Its Discontents* (1930) would similarly mark the limits of our empathy "to feel our way into such people" as the "Jew awaiting a pogrom" and other victims of traumatic oppression who suffer from what Robert Jay Lifton has theorized as "acute and chronic forms of psychic numbing."[17] Modernism's failure to mount a sustained cultural response to the genocidal emergency of its own moment may itself be symptomatic of what Lifton and others have studied in the survivors of the Holocaust, Hiroshima, and other human and natural disasters as the latency, or structure of temporal delay, that seems inherent in traumatic experience. Part of modernity's numbed silence may be assignable to such a post-traumatic lag—what Freud characterized as the "incubation period"—intervening between the extreme violence of the event and its later return as a felt stressor.[18]

Across the period of latency between the wars, such signs of cultural numbing and lapsed witnessing had devastating social consequences. One outcome of repressing—rather than commemorating—this genocidal moment was its repetition some three decades later in the Holocaust. In 1939, Adolf Hitler's diabolical quip—"Who after all, speaks today of the annihilation of the Armenians? . . . The world believes in success alone."—authorized, in his own mind, not just the invasion of Poland but the Final Solution as such.[19] Few spoke of the extermination of the Armenians due, in part, to the temporal latency of its traumatic event. But there were other, geopolitical interests that had a hand in its active censorship throughout the 1920s. Although the Armenian atrocities riveted world attention during the course of the war, America's diplomatic agenda of securing Turkey as a Mideast client state backgrounded the continuing plight of Armenians in the postwar period. But more to the point, the political silencing of the Armenocide, from the 1920s onward, even now raises crucial ethical questions concerning America's state complicity with genocide denial.

Following the World War I victory of the Allied powers, compelling evidence of state-sponsored crimes against humanity was presented at military tribunals held in Constantinople. These proceedings led the new Turkish state, created under Sultan Mustafa Kemal, to render the death sentence in absentia against the Young Turk triumvirate of Talaat Bey, Enver Bey, and Jemal Bey.[20] In 1921 Talaat was assassinated in Berlin by Soghomon Tehlirian, an Armenian survivor, who was subsequently acquitted of the murder charge, owing to Talaat Bey's crimes against humanity. Nevertheless, it would not be long before a resurgence of Turkish nationalism, coupled with the Allies' failure to lend material support to the creation of an Armenian state, would result in additional Turkish aggressions against the nominal Armenian republic created under the Treaty of Sèvres in 1920. Three years later, the Allies conciliated Mustafa Kemal by ceding Turkish Armenia back to the Republic of Turkey and by dropping the Armenian question from the language of the Lausanne Treaty of 1923.

The reconsolidation of Turkish nationalism during the early 1920s was supported, in part, by American foreign policy. The plan called for alliance with Turkey, whose strategic location would serve as both a hedge against the Soviet Union and a platform for Middle East oil interests. During the Harding administration, former Standard Oil official and Secretary of State Charles Evans, in league with Allen Dulles, U.S. Commissioner in Constantinople, and Near East High Commissioner Admiral Mark L. Bristol, undermined congressional resolutions of support for the Armenian cause. Bristol, in particular, belied a disturbing racism that coincided with the ethnic biases exploited by the Young Turk triumvirate. "The Armenians," Bristol wrote in his 1920 correspondence to Admiral W. S. Sims, "are a race like the Jews—they have little or no national spirit and poor moral character."[21] The same prejudicial logic betrayed in Bristol's ethnic notions had earlier shaped the racial essentialism underwriting the nationalist ideology of Pan-Turkism promulgated by Yusuf Akchura of the Young Turk Committee of Union and Progress. In "The Three Political Systems" (1904), Akchura had defined "political nationality" in terms of "a race, a language, a tradition" that was essentially Turkish and thus exclusive of the long-standing ethnic diversity of the Ottoman Empire—divided as it was into Turkish, Armenian, Jewish, Coptic, Kurd, and Greek *millets* or enclaves of civil and religious administration.[22]

The conjuncture of American ethnocentrism and what Allen Dulles defined as its perceived "commercial interests" created a national climate favorable to Turkish revisionism and genocide denial that persists to this day.[23] By the end of the 1920s, the American press, the Near East Relief agency, and Congress succumbed to the State Department's silencing of the century's first genocide. By 1929, the reversal of popular perceptions of Turkey's role in the Armenocide was a *fait accompli* as witnessed in the Institute of Politics summer session held at Williams College that year. There, Turkish representative Halidé Edib had, according to a *New York Times* report, "won the hearts and minds of 200 experts." The agenda, as Edib promoted it, was to popularize the revisionist position that Armenian nationalist aggression within the context of civil and world war justified Turkish deportations and internment of its ethnic minorities.[24]

Between the world wars, the Republic of Turkey set out to recode popular perceptions of the Armenocide. Its most visible intervention came in 1934 when Metro-Goldwyn-Mayer planned to produce a Hollywood film version of Franz Werfel's widely read novel *The Forty Days of the Musa Dagh*. Werfel's book chronicled Armenian resistance near Antioch, culminating in the dramatic rescue of four thousand Armenian freedom fighters by the Allied navy. Vigorously lobbied by the Turkish Embassy, the State Department brought pressure to bear on the studio to stop production of the Werfel movie and, following a year of fruitless negotiations, MGM canceled the project. By the fiftieth anniversary of the atrocities in 1965, with the passing away of many of the original survivors, the story of the Armenian diaspora received little world attention despite second-generation protests, demonstrations, and commemorations held that year in both the United States and Soviet Armenia. In the 1970s, a wave of largely third-generation acts of political reprisals and assassinations of Turkish diplomats again focused attention on the troubled legacy of survivor families of the Turkish massacres. Despite the media attention such acts garnered for the Armenocide, Turkey prevailed in dropping reference to it as "the first case of genocide in the twentieth century" from a 1978 report by the United Nations Subcommission on the Prevention of Discrimination and Protection of Minorities.[25]

During the 1980s, Turkey successfully lobbied against American congressional attempts to commemorate the Armenian Genocide in 1985 (the seventieth anniversary of the Armenocide), in 1987, and in 1990.[26] Trading on its continuing strategic value to the United States as a NATO "listening post" and military base against the former Soviet Union, Turkey was represented in congressional testimony and debate by, among others, Secretary of State George Shultz and Secretary of Defense Caspar Weinberger. As the issue played out in the House chamber, the appeal to geopolitical expediency clashed with the ethical question, posed by New York Congressman Thomas J. Downey. What "peculiar calculus," he asked, "will [we] use to weigh the loss of our moral stature if we give in to this veiled threat?"[27] By the time of the 1990 Senate resolution, the controversy had shifted onto the rhetorical terrain of denial. Against the evidence of some 1,500,000 Armenian victims of Turkish massacres, West Virginia Senator Robert Byrd laid down the caveat that "I do not know whether what happened to the Armenians constitutes a genocide. . . . [T]here have been injustices perpetrated against Turks. . . . [P]ractically every group has had an injustice done to it."[28] Similarly, Nebraska Senator J. James Exon's performative uncertainty—"I do not know whether a genocide occurred"—countered appeals to the facts of genocide as Illinois Senator Paul Simon reviewed them. "At a minimum," Simon argued, "hundreds of thousands of people were slain simply because they were Armenians. That is reality. Many will put the number higher. . . . But the evidence is just overwhelming that genocide occurred."[29] In the end, however, such appeals to historical fact did not carry the day then and they never have since.

The rhetorical strategies producing such state denials of genocide were grounded in a revisionist movement of academic scholarship that Turkey had nurtured from the 1970s onward in an effort to reshape the record of its nationalist past. Such figures as William L. Langer, Stanford and Ezel Kural Shaw, and Bernard Lewis, among others[30] questioned the semantic appropriateness of the term *genocide* for what they regarded as a civil dispute occasioned by the rise of Armenian revolutionary nationalism. Advancing what Robert Melson has characterized as the "provocation thesis," these historians sought to recast Armenian self-defense against the rising incidents of *fin de siècle* pogroms and massacres.[31] In their revisionist accounts, Armenian resistance to Turkish oppression was recoded as militant, domestic terrorism that escalated the threat of Russian adventurism on Turkey's eastern borders and of European imperialism on its western front. In addition, Turkish Studies discounted the estimated number of deaths attributable to the Armenocide from 1,500,000 to 200,000, which, it was further argued, constituted a small fraction of the 2,000,000 Muslim war casualties of the First World War.[32] Finally, documentary evidence proving that the Young Turk government centrally administered the Armenocide was questioned.

In the most troubling cases of historical revisionism, such as Erich Feigl's *A Myth of Terror* (1988), denial was couched in tropes that belied symptoms of racism and ethnic stereotyping. In his most telling passages, Feigl acted out a certain neofascism, vilifying Armenians and Jews as degenerate and racially impure peoples. In describing the ethnic subcultures of the Ottoman Empire, Feigl linked the Armenians to the obscure and "bastard" origins of Iberian Jews and gypsy tribes. Such slurs had a common denominator that repeated the scapegoating of ethnic difference underwriting the Armenocide and the Holocaust: "The Orthodox or Gregorian Armenians are, as a community, ignorant, superstitious, and poverty-stricken, but count more adherents than either of the later sects. The small Jewish community being mostly blonde and speaking a bastard Spanish, are evidently of Iberian origin;

while the origin of the few gypsy tribes who come and go is as great a mystery in Anatolia as in Europe."[33] To legitimate this kind of racism, Feigl relied on the standard arguments of denial employed in revisionist academic defenses of the Young Turk government.

Such strategies of denial have followed the same tactics that Deborah Lipstadt has cogently critiqued in postwar efforts to discredit the Holocaust as a documented event. Rhetorical moves that are common to denials of the Holocaust and Armenocide include blaming the victims for bringing genocide upon themselves, accusing the Allied powers of imperialism against Germany and the Ottoman Empire, discounting the actual number of deaths from genocide, rejecting perpetrators' postwar trial confessions as coerced testimony, questioning the evidence that concentration camps were in fact death camps, denying personal guilt, and so on.[34] Employing eight decades of evidence and scholarship on the Armenocide, Ronald Suny has refuted such denial arguments and posed key questions of what is at stake in the revisionist project. "Are we to suppose," Suny asks, "that the national interest of one people justifies the physical extermination of another? Are dual claims to a single territory to be settled by deportation or massacre? Should we not find the moral authority to condemn unequivocally killing so deliberately aimed at political advantage?"[35]

In the 1990s, controversy over Turkish support of revisionist historicism reached into the most prestigious institutions of higher education in the dispute sparked by Heath Lowry's 1994 appointment to the Ataturk Chair of Ottoman and Near Eastern Studies at Princeton University. To begin with, the Ataturk Professorship is a $1.5 million endowed chair that was established at Princeton through a $750,000 matching grant from the Republic of Turkey. Such Turkish funding has supported similar endowments at Georgetown University, Harvard University, and the University of Chicago. Many in the academic community questioned Lowry's appointment based on his previous position as executive director of the Institute of Turkish Studies, a nonprofit "educational" organization funded through the Republic of Turkey and grants from major defense contractors. Lowry's publication record had been sparse and, other than the institute appointment, he had held no academic teaching post since his stint as a lecturer at Bosporous University in Istanbul from 1973 to 1980.[36] What added urgency to the issue of Lowry's appointment, however, was the 1995 disclosure that he had a history of collaboration with the Turkish Embassy in efforts to undermine scholarship on the Armenian Genocide.

Specifically, as executive director of the Institute of Turkish Studies, Lowry drafted a memo advising the Turkish ambassador in Washington on tactics for discrediting Robert Jay Lifton's accounts of the Armenian Genocide in his 1986 study *The Nazi Doctors: Medical Killing and the Psychology of Genocide.* In addition, Lowry ghost-authored an embassy letter reprimanding Lifton. As it happened, the Turkish Embassy accidentally forwarded Lowry's memo with the letter to Lifton, who made it the object of sustained critique in "Professional Ethics and the Denial of the Armenian Genocide," a 1995 *Holocaust and Genocide Studies* essay he coauthored with Roger W. Smith and Eric Markusen.[37] "We feel strongly," Lifton later remarked of the affair in a *Chronicle of Higher Education* follow-up interview, "that there's been a violation of academic standards."[38] The following year, this tangible evidence of academic manipulation became the catalyst for a Concerned Scholars and Writers statement—signed by more than a hundred distinguished professors, scholars, writers, and clergy—condemning such state-orchestrated denials of the Armenian holocaust.[39] Not surprisingly, U.S. State Department officials defended Turkish gifts totaling $3 million in endowment grants to major American universities. Symptomatically, such state support repeated the same arguments of geopolitical expediency that reached back to the Harding administration in the 1920s. "Turkey," a State Department official remarked in 1995, "is very, very much in the forefront of US interests if you look at the vast oil reserves of the Caucasus and Central Asia and everything else going on in that area of the world. We can only smile on the growth of interest in Turkish studies."[40]

The impasse dividing, on the one hand, the moral imperatives and professional ethics of the scholarly community from, on the other, the politics of big oil and defense-industry interests in Turkey has an eighty-year record that is by now irresolvable. While the struggle to remember the Armenocide continues, its historical referent will remain in dispute. In our postmodern moment, where the truth of reference cannot be wholly divorced from discourse and its clashing *regimes du savoir,* contemporary accounts of modern genocide are met by counterrhetorics of revision and denial that challenge any fixed claims to knowledge. "Truth," as the late Terrence Des Pres remarked, "bends to that which is consistent with the program of empire, and what we see, when we observe the Turkish denial of the Armenian tragedy, is a small but vigorous example of the program in action."[41] In reading the historical text of modern genocide, the interpretative war over who victimized whom, how many perished and under what circumstances, where responsibility lies, whether one genocide is unique or comparable to others, and so on, will surely never end in disinterested consensus. Because it is the politics of cultural memory that is at stake in these debates, one cannot hope to achieve any lasting settlement over historical meaning. On the contrary, narrative representations of the event must be waged rather than assumed.[42]

Within that discursive war of position, however, the traumatic force of genocide presences another historicity: one that cuts against the grain of official state memory. Here, the truth of extreme experience lives on, possessing signified reference precisely within, and not prior to, the linguistic registers of the signifier. In the writing and testimony of genocide's generational survivors, the referential power of its event speaks through textual revenants encountered in the gaps, catachreses, and fissures that trauma opens in our conscious narratives of personal and cultural memory.[43] Not only does the shock of genocide unsettle linguistic representation as such, but it may well leave an impression—in our responses as witnessing readers—of the kind of traumatic side effects of latency, dissociation, and repression that Jean-Martin Charcot, Pierre Janet, and Freud theorized on the wards of Salpêtrière in the 1880s. Noting the subliminal communication of unconscious contents in his 1915 essay "The Unconscious," Freud allowed that "[i]t is a very remarkable thing that the *Unconscious* of one human being can react upon that of another, without passing through the *Conscious.*"[44] In taking note of Freud's observation in their own clinical practice, Nicolas Abraham and Maria Torok theorized the figure of the "phantom" as a psychic content that, however it may haunt the unconscious of the analysand, belongs finally to another at a second- or even third-generational remove.[45] For the inheritors of generational trauma, such revenants transmit what Maria Torok has characterized as "a *story of fear*" that is wholly subliminal.[46]

In theorizing the phantom's cross-generational return in literature, I would propose a new consideration of how the agency of the letter in poetic discourse testifies to the truth of traumatic reference in ways that make special claims on us in excess of our normal roles as authors and readers. Although literature's fictive grounding in the figurative use of language would hardly seem fitted to disclosures of referential truth, I would argue that the poetry of generational witness—precisely as a linguistic event—manifests its force in revolutionary ways.[47] What is properly an unspeakable or "buried" trauma in the ancestor, no matter how distant, appears like a ghost haunting the symptomatic actions, phobias, "puppet emotions," hallucinations, and—most tellingly—the "staged words" or *cryptonyms* of the descendant.[48] Not unlike the phenomenon of repetition compulsion, the performative, or "staged" symptom within the register of the poetic signifier does not just express the personal fantasy life of the survivor but serves to vent social trauma into a wider public sphere.[49] It's that repetition of the "unknown" that verse uniquely inscribes in the historical archive of genocide.[50]

In the poetry of witness we encounter the phantom as the emanation of an impossible mourning where the traumatic loss of others cannot be assimilated or worked through in sanctioned rites of social commemoration. Blocked over the course of three generations, the unmourned trauma of the 1915 Armenocide makes a special claim to historical reference through the phantom voices possessing contemporary Armenian-American survival literature. Troubling the foreclosure of modernist periodization, this particular body of literature revisits and renegotiates the edge of modernism's repressed historicity. The uncanny psychic effects of genocide have been the focus of Diana Der-Hovanessian's work in over ten books of poetry and translations. A winner of prizes awarded by the Poetry Society of America, the Columbia / P.E.N. Translation Center, and Massachusetts Arts Council, Der-Hovanessian is also the president of the New England Poetry Club. In her verse, the eighty-year silencing of the Armenocide is thematized as an agonizing, generational repetition:

My father, listening
to the broadcast news,
my mother said,
was exactly the same
as her father,
intent on every word
as if perhaps
he could lose
something added
since the last was heard.
The Monitor,
The New York Times consumed,
every hour on the hour
hushing the room,
they leaned toward news
that never came.[51]

Reproduced here in "Exiles" is the serial narrative of what "my mother said" and what Der-Hovanessian repeats to us. Figured in the poem's subtle pattern of enjambment, the insistent "listening" in this cross-generational tableau takes its passionate intensity from an event that, however repressed, returns "every hour on the hour" as a relentless public silence. Denied social acknowledgment, this communicative gap presences an absence "hushing the room," in the "news / that never came."

Elsewhere in Der-Hovanessian's verse, genocide's spectral claim to reference assumes a phantom voice: a haunting call that, in "The Dream," possesses the poet's identity through the formal anaphora of direct address:

"Children of massacre,
children of destruction,
children of dispersion,
oh, my diaspora . . ."
someone was calling
in my dream. (SP, 9)

Hailed in this way by the haunting "someone" of dream, the poet finds her place, paradoxically, in a modern genealogy of massacre, destruction, and dispersion. But what does it mean to be named in this ghostly fashion? What consequences do such revenants have for the poet's postgenocidal identity? What, moreover, does it mean to accept the call of the diaspora?

On the one hand, as a generational survivor of genocide, Der-Hovanessian experiences herself as a perpetual exile and tourist. Like a ghost, she is forever displaced from any homeland, always already estranged from any fixed selfhood: forever herself a revenant haunting someone else's celebration. "I am the stranger / in my father's land" she admits in "Diaspora":

I am the tourist
from far away
where I left the tables of plenty
thirsty and unfed. (SP, 11)

While a history of deportation and starvation banished Der-Hovanessian from her mother country, she nevertheless learns from the several truisms of relatives and fellow writers what it means to choose and affirm a reconstructed identity. In her poem "How to Become an Armenian," she quotes William Saroyan on ethnic self-fashioning: "'Being Armenian means merely / saying you are one'" (SP, 26). Supplementing the essential descent lines of one's given race by birth, such performative speech acts have ethicopolitical consequences for one's social becoming, as she learns here as well:

"To be Armenian is bad luck
and to choose to remain
is a trial and obligation,"
Avedik Issahakian claims.

.   .   .   .

"To be born Armenian," says my father,

"is to inherit a cause and a case;

to remain Armenian means using

pen, plough, and sword." (SP, 26)

Being an Armenian, as she finds out, exceeds any essential identity, dispersed as it is here through a dialogic process of social becoming. Remaining an Armenian is an experience in cultural difference because the nation of Armenia—located at the crossroads of Eastern Europe and Asia—has been made up since ancient times of several imagined communities divided by racial and ethnic origin, religion, region, class, and political commitment.[52]

On the other hand, if Der-Hovanessian chooses diasporic identity as a born-again Armenian, she is also chosen—in excess of any conscious intent—by the modern event of genocide.[53] Traditionally in the Ottoman Empire, Armenians—like the Jews—were considered to be a "chosen people of the book."[54] As a post-genocidal subject, however, Der-Hovanessian is chosen somewhat differently. Across the latency of three generations, she is claimed now and then by the event of trauma, whose questioning phantoms spirit her away to violent scenes of psychic dissociation. Her poem "In My Dream," for example, dwells on the paradox that what is "found" in the genocidal revenant is in every sense a fundamental loss:

I found the bloodied arm on the ground

before me. "You didn't need it," said the voice.

I saw a sea of dismembered limbs tossed,

strewn to the horizon and beyond.

"You didn't really need these bones."

They covered land that stretched, pressed past.

"You didn't need these provinces, did you?

What would you do with all these stones?"

A mountain of broken bodies rose.

"You didn't need Mt. Ararat, did you?"

I tried to speak. No tongue. My breath froze.

"You didn't need that language, did you?"

I woke, washed, and looked in the glass.

Only another American dressed in fine clothes. (SP, 43)

Betrayed in the mirror of assimilation, the poet is radically split between the fashionable mask of her American identity and an Armenian persona: the unconscious self who has suffered the trauma of psychic dissociation, cultural dispossession, and literal dismemberment. Here the phantom's tag questions are merely rhetorical as they deny the poet any connection to the past. Ironically, the force of historical reference is felt as an ontological negation, presencing a lost world that is everything the poet "didn't need" in order to become "another American."

Chosen, nevertheless, by that trauma, Der-Hovanessian is also given to her poetic vocation as she voices the phantom sisterhood of ancestresses who did not survive the crime of genocide. "But oh, my sisters," she writes,

> now that 75 years
> have passed and
> no one has spoken for you,
> I spit out words
> you swallowed unsaid. (SP, 40)

Repressed trauma that is here "swallowed unsaid" or—in Abraham and Torok's idiom—*incorporated* awaits the poet's act of verbal *introjection:* the linguistic work of mourning. For Abraham and Torok, mourning's oral moment is analogous to, and has its origin in, the infant's first utterances that attempt to fill the empty mouth: introjecting or "swallowing" words to supplement the loss of the (m)other, or primary caregiver.[55] Losses, and lost ones, that lack symbolic expression and figural substitution in language frequent the psychic crypts of their survivors as revenants of what has properly become unspeakable. Unlike the failed mourning of the melancholic, however, Der-Hovanessian's revisitings of the Armenocide express phantom representations of trauma that befell others.[56]

What is arresting in Der-Hovanessian's verse is the uncanny return of not her own unconscious contents but the unspoken tragedy of others at a third-generational remove. Haunting the silences and cryptic gaps of poetic discourse, the phantom signs of that earlier, and largely secreted, trauma possess their own agency— coming and going as they please—as in "For the Unsaid":

> Letterless, tongueless, and unpronounced
> the words sleep under their own heaviness.
> Do not disturb them.
>
> Their silence is not golden,
> is not assent, is not guilty.
> Their silence is not the handmaiden
> of death. They will wake
> in their own time.

They are in that silent place,
the eye of the storm,
the edge of the heart,

the day before it knows
it is struck down. Let words
wake themselves. (SP, 68)

Against the "empty" discourse of official state denial, poetry witnesses through its aesthetic medium to the "full" speech of cross-generational truths.[57] Encrypted in the silence that Der-Hovanessian figures here as the "eye of the storm, / the edge of the heart," the "unsaid words" of the phantom are signs of a subtextual agency that eludes even as it possesses our conscious speaking. Neither "golden" nor "guilty"— inhabiting the in-between of the living and the dead—this awakening into another tongue (hitherto "tongueless"), this presencing of a signifier (formerly "letterless"), takes place in its "own time" of linguistic parapraxis: at once outside and within the official discourse of state and academic history.

Marking the similarities between the Armenocide and the Holocaust, Pierre Vidal-Naquet has also theorized the generational pattern that characterizes the chosen people of diasporic survival:

> One could be tempted summarily to categorize the generations. The first, that which survived the great massacre, led a hard struggle toward adaptation. Today it has largely passed away. The second benefited from the efforts and money accumulated by the first and has provided large numbers of the assimilated. The third is a classic generation, in quest of its roots precisely because in fact it has lost them.[58]

If, as Vidal-Naquet observes, the third generation searches for a past that is "lost" to assimilation, there is also a way in which history makes a special claim on the descendants across the latency of the second generation. In this third moment, first-generation trauma returns in the haunting disjuncture between two incommensurate worlds. It is this postgenocidal breach that poet Peter Balakian explores as a third-generation Armenian-American writer.

Similar to the psychic splitting that Der-Hovanessian negotiates, Balakian's poetry shuttles between the banality of postwar suburbia and the trauma of the 1915 death march that his grandmother Nafina Hagop Chilinguirian survived from Diarbekir, Turkey, to Aleppo, Syria. Crossing these antithetical moments creates surreal effects in "The History of Armenia." History, in this poem, does not belong solely to the past; rather, the force of its referent lives on—haunting the present in the figure of

Nafina's revenant. The grandmother's ghost appears in a dreamscape split between, on the one hand, a "backdrop of steam hammers / and bulldozers" recollected from the poet's childhood memory of construction along New Jersey's Oraton Parkway and, on the other hand, memory traces that revisit the primal scene of genocide:

> I was running
> toward her
> in a drizzle
> with the morning paper.
> When I told her
> I was hungry, she said,
> in the grocery store
> a man is standing
> to his ankles in blood,
> the babies in East Orange
> have disappeared
> maybe eaten by
> the machinery
> on this long road.[59]

Bearing the sign of the "starving Armenians," the poet here is also "hungry" for Nafina's untold story that—as we have seen in Der-Hovanessian's verse—he will never find in the "morning paper." Yet in voicing his symptom, Balakian enters the historical dialogism of another kind of news. However unreported, the event of what "she said" as a revenant speaks beyond a lifetime otherwise consumed by silence. As a discourse of phantoms, poetry nevertheless offers a redemptive supplement to the dead letter of historical narrative. "Where is the angel," the poet asks, "with the news that the river / is coming back, / the angel with the word" (SDL, 5). The angel of history who bears witness to the word of history's countermemory returns, for Balakian, in the questioning that poetry poses to the received past.

However denied by Turkey today, the brutality of modernism's first genocide was, nevertheless, amply documented as it occurred. For his part, Commissioner G. Gorrini, the Italian Consul-General at Trebizond, testified to the "unheard-of cruelties" and "execrable crimes" against humanity that was the "work of the Central Government and the 'Committee of Union and Progress.'" Recorded in Gorrini's firsthand account is the shock of genocidal reference, whose "black page," as a rhetorical catachresis, marks a *mise en abyme* in the historical narrative of Western civilization: "It was a real extermination and slaughter of the innocents, an unheard-of thing, a black page stained with the flagrant violation of the most sacred rights of humanity, of Christianity, of nationality."[60] However unreadable, trauma's black page leaves its collective impression in the modern repetition of subsequent genocides in the Holocaust, Cambodia, Bosnia, Rwanda, and Kosovo. However shocking, the systematic cruelty and scope of the first modern genocide—reported in the 684 pages and 150 exhibits of Bryce's blue book—should "never again" lapse from cultural memory. The eyewitness narratives collected by Viscount Bryce and Arnold Toynbee confirm American Ambassador to Turkey Henry Morgenthau's judgment that "the whole history of the human race contains no such horrible episode as this . . . destruction of a race."[61]

In Harpout and Mezré the people have had to endure terrible torture. They have had their eye-brows plucked out, their breasts cut off, their nails torn off; their torturers hew off their feet or else hammer nails into them just as they do in shoeing horses. . . . The shortest method for disposing of the women and children concentrated in the various camps was to burn them. Fire was set to large wooden sheds in Alidjan, Megrakom, Khaskegh, and other Armenian villages, and these absolutely helpless women and children were roasted to death. Many went mad and threw their children away; some knelt down and prayed amid the flames in which their bodies were burning; others shrieked and cried for help which came from nowhere. And the executioners, who seem to have been unmoved by this unparalleled savagery, grasped infants by one leg and hurled them into the fire, calling out to the burning mothers: "Here are your lions."[62]

According to eyewitness testimony, the Turkish method of genocide began with the nominal "arrest" of a community's Armenian men anywhere between the ages of fifteen to seventy, marching them to a remote site where they were tied in pairs or larger groups and then hacked, strangled, or shot to death, as in the following account from Angora:

In the valley of Beyhan Goghazi, six or seven hours' distance from the town, they [the Armenian men] were attacked by a wild horde of Turkish peasants and, in pursuance of the order, were all massacred with clubs, hammers, axes, scythes, spades, saws—in a word, with every implement that causes a slow and painful death. Some shore off their heads, ears, noses, hands, feet with scythes; others put out their eyes. Thus was exterminated the whole male Armenian population of Angora. . . . The bodies of the victims were left in pieces in the valley, to be devoured by the wild beasts. The gendarmes boast about the part they played in these exploits.[63]

Following such mass executions, the female survivors with children and the elderly were then forcibly paraded—or "deported"—by Turkish gendarmes into the remote deserts, hills, and back country of the Ottoman Empire. Here, over the course of days, weeks, and months, they were continually robbed, assaulted, raped, and harassed by bands of Kurds, Circassians, Bedouins, and Turkish peasants. Amidst such dire straits, hundreds of thousands of Armenians lost their lives through exposure to the elements, starvation, thirst, murder, or the suicide at times of whole families, who, joining hands, would drown themselves in the Euphrates River.[64]

The sheer scale of the massacres can be gleaned in such apocalyptic accounts as Dr. Martin Niepage's reportage, *The Horrors of Aleppo*. Relating the Mosul German consul's eyewitness narrative, Niepage writes that "in many places on the road from Mosul to Aleppo, he had seen children's hands lying hacked off in such numbers that one could have paved the road with them."[65] Similarly, in his "Open Letter to the President of the United States of North America," Dr. Armin T. Wegner provides a gripping eyewitness account of the ways in which the death marches robbed Armenians of their basic humanity:

> Children cried themselves to death, men threw themselves to their death on rocks while women threw their own children into wells and pregnant mothers leapt singing into the Euphrates. They died all the deaths of the world, the deaths of all the centuries. I saw men gone mad, feeding on their own excrement, women cooking their newborn children, young girls cutting open the still warm corpses of their mothers to search their guts for the gold they had swallowed out of fear of the thieving gendarmes.[66]

Ultimately what is at stake in such abject scenes of suicide, cannibalism, and corporeal violation is the radical dissociation of the human image as such. Moreover, the century's first world-historical crime against humanity faced survivors with the kind of "choiceless choices" that Lawrence Langer would later define in the context of the Holocaust.[67] For example, in interviews conducted by Donald E. Miller and Lorna Touryan Miller, survivors gave testimony to how exhausted mothers during the deportations would be forced to choose which child to leave by the side of the road,[68] of groups of mothers who, en route to certain death, collectively abandoned their children under trees and bushes,[69] of parents having to decide which son or daughter to sell into bondage for a loaf of bread.

Similarly, Armenians were not only denied their status as human beings through the death marches but were reduced to so much rolling stock, transported as they were in cattle cars along the Ottoman railways to Aleppo for final deportation into the desert.[70] Not just an efficient means of exterminating the Armenian population, such death trains and deportation caravans—as spectacles of dehumanization—served the nationalist agenda of the Young Turk regime by staging a cultural logic of ethnic subordination. Once Armenians were demonized as infidels (*gâvur*), that nominal status could be acted out in rituals of public scapegoating as seen in the accounts of American evangelists at the time: "They [Armenian women, children, and elderly] were brought into Aleppo the last miles in third-class railway carriages, herded together like so many animals. When the doors of the carriages were opened, they were jeered at by the populace for their nakedness."[71] Such collective scenes of degradation and scapegoating were symptomatic of larger, nationalist crises at the time. Ottoman anxieties about the integrity of its imperial borders in 1915 were projected, arguably, in the spectacle of genocide, publicly acted out through the ritualized torture of Armenian bodies.[72] Moreover, Turkish nationalism—similar to the Aryan ideal of the Nazi period—was constituted only in opposition to a demonized other. In this case, the ethnic difference between Turk and Armenian was recoded through a human/nonhuman binarism inscribed in the performative opposition between the jeering "populace" and naked "herd."

The public venting of such widespread cruelty had its roots, arguably, in the shifting social foundations that accompanied modernization in the Ottoman Empire at the time. The influx of European capital and Western industry—coupled with the spread of Enlightenment thinking and missionary efforts during the so-called Tanzimat, or reformist, period of the previous century (1838–76)—not only gave new political power to the non-Muslim ethnic constituencies but undermined the traditional religious and civic authority of the Ottoman sultans. Educated and financed by American missionary societies, the Christian Armenian community was the agent of such modernization. Before the genocide, according to Dr. Johannes Lepsius, Armenians accounted for 60 percent of imports, 40 percent of exports, and 80 percent of the commerce in the Ottoman Empire. Armenians largely made up the ranks of the Empire's professional classes, industrialists, and skilled artisans.[73] Not surprisingly, the Armenians' access to European markets bred class resentment in the provinces where such sayings as "[t]wo Greeks equal an Armenian, and an Armenian equals two devils" or "one Greek cons two Jews, and one Armenian cons two Greeks" demonized Armenians for their entrepreneurial savvy in much the same way that Jews were stereotyped in Germany and throughout Europe generally.[74] The Young Turk government fueled anti-Armenian attitudes as part of a strategy to redefine the Empire's traditional ethnic diversity in favor of the more homogeneous myth of a racially unified Pan-Turkish nationalism.

The recoded figure of the Armenian as infidel was needed as a demonized other against which the imagined community of Turkish nationalism could then be constituted. In what Elaine Scarry has described as the "hidden pedagogy" of scapegoating,[75] the fiction of Pan-Turkism received material transubstantiation through an archaic logic of sacrifice, inscribed on the disfigured Armenian body. In this precursor of contemporary "ethnic cleansing," anxieties over a fragmented Ottoman Empire were projected onto the dismembered, castrated, or beheaded bodies of Armenians. Through the semiotic labor of torture, horseshoes nailed into the soles of Armenian feet became signs of a readable, subhuman status. Similarly, red-hot crowns applied to the heads of the "infidels," crosses branded into their flesh, stigmata pierced into their hands, feet, and vital organs, and literal crucifixion all signified religious difference on the bodies of Armenians who refused Muslim conversion.

For the descendants of genocide survivors, the psychic work of revisiting such extremely traumatic episodes is fraught with difficulty. According to Nadine Fresco, genocide experiences, because they are encounters with mortality as such, are by their very nature ontologically "forbidden" to consciousness. Based on her interviews with children of Holocaust survivors, Fresco has described the generational repression of genocide as a gap in the family narrative of what can be remembered: as a metaphoric "black hole of the unmentionable years in which an impossible 'family romance' had been swallowed up. . . . The forbidden memory of death manifested itself only in the form of incomprehensible attacks of pain."[76] As is the case in Der-Hovanessian's verse, knowledge of the "swallowed" or *incorporated* event is not accessible by any direct cognition but can only be registered through the agency of its affect and its symptom. Building on the early clinical work of Pierre Janet, neurologists Bessel A. van der Kolk and Onno van der Hart have contrasted the ways in which the "speechless terror" of trauma may be "engraved" differently from normal memory encoding in the central nervous system.[77] As a nonlinguistic event, the radical violence of traumatic reference exceeds narrative memory to surface in the form of "somatic sensations, behavioral reenactments, nightmares, and flashbacks."[78] In these hypnoid, dissociated, and hysterical registers, patients reenact the moment of earlier trauma but without conscious awareness of its event.

Such a moment where "state-dependent memory" becomes "action" (IP, 175) happens in the symptomatic return of trauma dramatized in Peter Balakian's poem "First Nervous Breakdown, Newark 1941." As told to Balakian by his maternal Aunt Gladys, the incident narrated in the poem is based on the experience of his grandmother Nafina Hagop Chilinguirian, who survived a 1915 death march from Diarbekir, Turkey, to Aleppo, Syria:

In the street, she said,
you were walking
past a laundry

muttering to the shirts
hanging without heads
in the window
and when you walked
into the store
you kicked the empty
pants and asked for legs.

Outside the butcher's
those were cows' eyes
and moon-fat black balls
you took and gathered
to your chest
as if to say without
a word, they were alive
and beckoning for care.

And hanging ribs
fresh and red
with the bright white
bone like a scythe
running through—
she said you hit it
with your cane
until it screamed. (SDL, 17)

Across the latency of twenty-six years, the traumatic memory of Nafina's survival—triggered by the reported bombing of Pearl Harbor—recalls the burning of the grandmother's house, the violent deaths of several family members including her husband, and the unspeakable conditions of her own deportation. Memory becomes action in this work both as it is revisited in the hypnoid behavior of an earlier, dissociated self, and as it signifies within the linguistic registers of poetic discourse. Here, the force of traumatic reference surfaces in the catachresis, or verbal "breakdown," that mistakes the figurative expression "pant leg" for a literal limb. The grandmother's demand as she "kicked the empty / pants" acts out what Abraham and Torok have described as a certain "demetaphorization" or disruptive repression of the sign.[79] In this case, kicking a pair of pants performs the repressed signifier of the missing "leg" that, incorporated as a phantom limb, haunts the poem's psychic topography as a loss denied conscious acknowledgment. Similarly, in the butcher shop, the grandmother, "without / a word," acts out a symbolic incorporation of other unspeakable signs of dismemberment in the "cows' eyes" and "moon-fat black balls" that are "gathered / to [her] chest." But unlike the castration anxieties that belong to the Oedipal domain of repressed infantile sexuality, the repetition of castration here reenacts an event that has a historical, not fantasized, referent.

Signs of psychic dissociation mount in the fourth stanza's surrealist image, which projects the scream of the torture victim into a bloody carcass. The poem's final foregrounding of the "fresh and red" fact of a butchered body alludes, perhaps, to the Turkish practice of bastinadoing: beating human limbs into pulp with sticks (acted out here in the grandmother's cane). Yet "First Nervous Breakdown, Newark 1941" does not conclude with some grave and memorable pronouncement about torture. More radically, the poem stages it in the distortion of an unreadable thing: a raw torso that is further defamiliarized in the grandmother's symptomatic beating. Nevertheless, as a dramatic disfiguring of the bodily imago, the literal hunk of "hanging ribs" performs what Elaine Scarry has theorized as the intended effect of torture, which is to reduce the victim's world, persona, and voice to the body in pain. "World, self, and voice," Scarry writes, "are lost, or nearly lost, through the intense pain of torture . . . a destruction experienced spatially as either the contraction of the universe down to the immediate vicinity of the body or as the body swelling to fill the entire universe."[80] Beneath the popular cliché of "having a nervous breakdown," Balakian's poem explores the complex psychosocial phenomenon of trauma and its possessing claim to reference persisting beyond the latency of its event.

Ultimately, it is the authenticity of such revisited trauma that empowers Nafina Hagop Chilinguirian's legal suit for damages against Turkey in "The Claim." Within the American tradition of encyclopedic poetics—as you find it, say, in William Carlos Williams's *Paterson,* Charles Olson's *The Maximus Poems,* or Muriel Rukeyser's *The Book of the Dead*—Balakian's long poem employs his grandmother's 1919 Department of State "Claims Against Foreign Governments" so as to cut and mix historical documentation with lyric utterance. Part of the poem's pathos stems from the anacoluthon of translating human loss into monetary damages, in the $4,000 or so claimed for each of ten family members listed on the government form. By crosscutting italicized sections of traumatic testimony with the language of government reparations, Balakian's poetic strategy subverts the legal fiction of administrative justice:

> The blood value for a person
> was ordered to be 350 Ltq.
> by decree of the Sultan

I feel the jackal
in my pants.

at my sister's house Hadji Anna . . .
captured by Turk named Hadji Bakkar

take nothing   house
burning   horse-flame

C) My father Hagop Shekerlemedjian, 75 years old,
        killed by Turks
My mother Lucia Shekerlemedjian, 50 years old
        killed by Turks   350
My brother Dikran Shekerlemedjian, 35 years old
        killed by Turks   350
His son Karnig Shekerlemedjian, 7 years old,
        killed by Turks   350 (SDL, 39)

Such crimes against the humanity of one's murdered family members can never be compensated either by money or, for that matter, by poetry. Nevertheless, Balakian's verse, as an act of mourning, would testify to his grandmother's claim to justice. The "full" utterance of her appeal breaches the "empty" discourse of the legal affidavit and its "documentary evidence" in the signifying absences, gaps, and ellipses of traumatic truth:

I am a human being. . . . it was impossible to
have by me the documentary evidence concerning my
losses but my co-deportees saved from death
witness that
        I am
I am human   herewith affidavit. (SDL, 43)

Nafina's 1919 legal claim was a necessary, yet impossible, attempt to redress the loss not only of loved ones but also of her own psychic self-possession. For, despite the latency of two decades, the genocidal event returns, as Balakian depicts it, in "First Nervous Breakdown, Newark 1941." The previous year, as the poet relates it in his memoir, his grandmother had given a lucid, public address on her exile for the twenty-fifth anniversary of the Armenocide. But the following year with the stressor of the Japanese attack on Pearl Harbor, a certain splitting befalls the self who has a narrative mastery of the event versus the internalized persona who unknowingly acts it out. Haunting the crypt of traumatic memory, that earlier, dissociated self complicates any straightforward identity both for the grandmother and for the poet in his attempts to remember her through the palimpsest of historical naming: "Nafina Hagop Chilinguirian, born Shekerlemedjian, remarried in the United States, in New Jersey, Aroosian."[81]

The difficulty of negotiating those several selves is evident in the poignant 1941 story of how, in a fit of paranoia, Nafina locked her daughter (Balakian's mother) out of the house. In its subtle pattern of enjambment and ambiguous syntax, Balakian's poem "World War II" captures the ambivalence of that mother-daughter relationship: "My grandmother feared / my mother would disappear / into the brick buildings / of the college catalog."[82] Given the biographical subtext of his grandmother's breakdown at the time, it is undecidable whether Nafina fears her daughter *tout court* or her potential assimilation into American society. For their part, Nafina's daughters sought to cure their mother by submitting her to electroshock therapy. "World War II" marks the ironic disjuncture between the first and second generation survivors by splicing the daughter's wartime job in a defense factory with the psychic trauma of Nafina's ECT sessions. "My mother," Balakian writes, "boxed khaki / and flint, and a hand / placed electrodes on / my grandmother's head" (DT, 30). Completing the "white genocide" of assimilation, ECT becomes the final solution to Nafina's split subjectivity. Once exiled from her mother country, the survivor self is now burned from memory as such through the psychic numbing of electroshock. In the concluding lines of "World War II" the aftermath of ECT is complexly inflected through the daughter's ambiguous status as both an agent of her mother's repression and her cure:

> On cool sheets in the evening
> when the poplar shadow
> disappeared, my grandmother rested
>
> and my mother returned
> from work, when the sun
> on the oil drums of the Pike
> was pure acetyline
>
> like a road out of Armenia,
> out of Turkey, out of Treblinka
> out of New Jersey. (DT, 30)

Returning as she does with the evening sun's "pure acetyline," the daughter—however assimilated—revisits the engraved memory of deportation that she shares with the mother and with all diasporic survivors.

Although the "convulsive seizure" of ECT expunged any symptoms of the traumatic event, it did not exorcise Nafina's genocidal phantom. Instead, the event of trauma crosses the generational divide of her daughters' American assimilation to reemerge as the grandson's revenant. In early poems such as, say, "Road to Aleppo, 1915," Balakian revisits the historical experience of the grandmother's deportation, himself possessed by the event of desert survival whose trauma is world-dissolving:

> There must have
> been a flame
> like a leaf
> eaten in the sun,
> that followed you—
> a white light
> that rose higher
> than the mountain
> and singed the corner
> of your eye
> when you turned
> to find the screaming
> trees dissolving
> to the plain. (SDL, 8)

Employing the formal resources of an effaced line length, Balakian registers a certain humility in the face of the other's unspeakable suffering. "Dissolving" into the opaque, unreadable space of the page, such truncated utterances suggest traumatic experience that, in its perceptual intensity, exceeds conventional representation. Indeed, a readable report of genocide, no matter how faithful to the facts of history, would simply mask the properly nonlinguistic event of trauma's "speechless terror."

In *Dyer's Thistle*, Balakian wrestles with this difficult paradox of finding a discourse that will represent the unrepresentable. If trauma is marked—as Cathy Caruth has theorized—by an "inherent latency," then Balakian mines precisely the referential force of its "blankness," its "space of unconsciousness" as a poetic resource.[83] From the opening lines of *Dyer's Thistle*, Balakian reckons with opaque, unreadable signs of phantom events that underwrite the cognitive gaps and numbed absences of consciousness:

> That's how I woke
> to a window of chalk sky

like indifference, like the sheet wrapped
around two people,
and the radio sounded like fuzz
on a boom mike
the rhetoric needling in about the dead in Croatia
.   .   .   .
I looked out to the Fisher-Price toys
blue and yellow in fog,

silver light, gouache on the spruces,
and the words Pol Pot
the geese chromatic, then gone.

Phnom Penh static like snow the day may bring
like a monsoon sweeping over a menorah

like the falling barn seeming to rise in white air. (DT, 11)

White air, fog, "silver light, gouache," a sky "like a numb pillow of radar" (DT, 12): such images—spliced with references to genocidal regimes in Croatia, Cambodia, Nazi Germany, and Turkey—punctuate the visible landscape with lacunae and cognitive ellipses. In this volume, truncated thoughts trail off into the aposiopesis of lines that fall silent and bleed eerily into the white space of the page. Awareness comes through non sequitur and association; thought wanders through the errancy of anacoluthon:

I was thinking like

the cows by the paddock in a peel of sun

when they cut a wide arrow
their feathers oily with tundra,
the gabbling like field-holler. (DT, 11)

For Balakian, the poetry of witness negotiates between, on the one hand, commemorations of histories that must never be forgotten and, on the other hand, a poetics of traumatic transmission whose inherent latency always already eludes conscious memory. "After the Survivors Are Gone" adopts the first strategy of conscious testimony to twentieth-century genocide:

I tried to imagine the Vilna ghetto,
to see a persimmon tree after the flash at Nagasaki.
Because my own tree had been hacked,
I tried to kiss the lips of Armenia.

At the table and the altar
we said some words written ages ago.
Have we settled for just the wine and bread,
for candles lit and snuffed?

Let us remember how the law has failed us.
Let us remember the child naked,
waiting to be shot on a bright day
with tulips blooming around the ditch.

We shall not forget the earth,
the artifact, the particular song,
the dirt of an idiom—
things that stick in the ear. (DT, 74)

In these moments, Balakian pledges himself to an activism whose politics is lodged against forgetting. He makes the conscious commitment to remember the particular incidents of atrocity, to witness against injustice, to empathize with history's victims, to preserve the cultural nuances and particular historicities that have been otherwise lost to extermination. Suggested in his formal use of anaphora, the responsibility of remembrance is interminable. Its covenant must be asserted continually against the forces of denial and revisionism that would complete genocide's unfinished business. Moreover as poet, Balakian challenges us to rededicate ourselves to that struggle again and again. Yet, that politics of testimony also assumes that we possess, rather than are possessed by, the agency of genocidal witness. Presupposed in the poem's title "After the Survivors Are Gone" is the assurance that they have departed once and for all. Even as it would remember, the poem forgets that the surviving remnant of those earlier generations can never clearly differentiate themselves from the phantom transmission of their revenants.

Unlike such conscious commemoration, the trace of the traumatic moment comes in its own time and presences its reference in excess of what we would choose to recall or repress. This is the other, and less consoling, lesson of Balakian's poetics of memory. Across the latency of the genocidal event, the "child naked, / waiting to be shot on a bright day / with tulips blooming around the ditch" will come again and in unguarded and uncanny moments as Balakian witnesses them in, say, "My Son Stares Into a Tulip":

He was nuzzling
in the grass I had just cut.
Crushed bluebells on his palms.

He nudged a few inches
like a caterpillar or something amphibious
and then caught by accident

his hand on the ha-ha
and so braced his pale, slightly bowed legs,
to bring himself upright

for the first time, I think,
in his life,

and found himself face to face
with a tulip, which was falling

apart from a week of sun
and a recent harsh shower,

and so its black stain
was like sticky dye.

I watched him stare into it.
In the house his mother's
breasts were drying up
like the crabapples of September.

If words could fill the
gap in his life
each petal would become a tongue,

each black anther
a stalk of light.

I hope his upright grasp
of the green stem holds him
when he's fallen back to ground.

I hope a breeze descends
on him from the blue. (DT, 62–63)

Not unlike the vegetal otherness that Theodore Roethke depicts in his greenhouse poems, Balakian's backyard flora, where the child "found himself face to face / with a tulip," stages a scene of uncanny encounter. On the one hand, this nostalgic tableau celebrates what any parent would never want to forget: a child's first attempts to stand, here braced by a flower. Yet moving beyond the poem's otherwise sentimental and somewhat banal suburban setting, replete here with the freshly mowed lawn, is the revenant of the tulip.

The flower itself is "falling / apart" and, whether intended or not on the poet's part, it bears within itself—as a linguistic parapraxis—the *two lip* phantom of a wound, whose "black stain" bleeds "like sticky dye." We have already seen rows of "blinding" tulips "like a smear / of poppies" (SDL, 40) in Balakian's long poem, "The Claim." The same floral trope in "The Field of Poppies"—a poem Balakian dedicates to his mother—are figured in the death of her father, that is in turn associated with the murder of Nafina's first husband Hagop Chilinguirian along the deportation route from Diarbekir to Aleppo. Here, Balakian visualizes traumatic violence as a "stain" bleeding from the genocidal scene of physical dismemberment: "foot, knee, stomach, face / disappearing in the stain of this field, / in the light wind that sang / in the red flowers" (SDL, 57). The encounter with the tulip, then, as Balakian recollects it in the great-grandson's experience, functions as a kind of "screen memory" insofar as it both stages and masks the transmission of a traumatic phantom. As a figure of psychic compromise it negotiates between memory and repression. The poet's child finds himself in the same frame as the great-grandfather complete with the earlier "light wind" (SDL, 57)—here the "breeze" that "descends / on him from the blue" (DT, 63). Through the linguistic work of poetry, however, what is a potentially disabling revenant of trauma becomes a redemptive resource. Here the figure of the two / lip is not just a wound but also a mouth and, "If words could fill the / gap in his life / each petal would become a tongue" (DT, 62).

Through the poem's subtle association of inner flower with the "house" where the "mother's / breasts were drying up / like the crabapples of September," the complex figure of the wound and mouth are also imbricated with the feminine labia of the tulip. Elsewhere, Balakian inflects floral imagery through erotic desire as in his sexual communion with the imagined flowers of "The Oriental Rug":

> Wrapped this tight
> I suck my way into the nectaries;
> feel a hummingbird's tongue
> and the chalky wing of a moth.
>
> That wet, I wash
> to the cool leaflets,
> rim their toothed edges,
> then back-rub

the remains of sepals
which kept the rose alive
in blighted April
when Adana and Van were lopped
off the map.

I come apart in the thorn—
(the spiky side that kept the jackal out)
and disperse whatever is left
of me to the downward pull
of cells sobbing in the earth. (DT, 36)

In his memoir, Balakian relates the biographical context that makes "The Oriental Rug" a crucial link in his family's exodus out of the Armenian Genocide. After her deportation, his grandmother by sheer chance happened upon her family's oriental rug that had been confiscated at the time of her deportation and sold to a Turkish household in Aleppo, Syria. After winning a civil suit to regain the rug, Nafina sold it and used the proceeds to book passage from Beirut to Marseilles and on to America. Thus, the Kashan rug's highly wrought ensemble of color, texture, and design not only connects the poet to the recollected fantasies of his childhood but, further back in time, to the transmitted scenes of his "grandparents' world: eastern Turkey, once Armenia" (DT, 32).

The sensuously conceived landscape of "The Oriental Rug" comes from the metamorphosis of the Kashan floral designs, heightened through the poet's sensuous imagination. On the rug, sexuality happens as a fantasy of polymorphous becoming that is charged at the moment of climax with the improbable subtext of dismemberment, castration, and torture that belongs to the Armenian Genocide. References to the 1909 massacre of some 20,000 Armenians at Adana and the April 1915 siege of the city of Van, where an estimated 55,000 Armenians were killed by Turks—as "lopped" historicities—lend curiously, a sexual urgency to the poet's imagined pollination that, as a kind of sensual gravity, ends in the "downward pull / of cells sobbing in the earth." Balakian borrows this pictorial inmixing of trauma and sexuality, arguably, from the painterly art of Armenian émigré Arshile Gorky, transcoding the estranged eroticism of his nonrepresentational modernism into a verse idiom. Oddly enough, Gorky's visual design in works such as *Xhorkom* explores, according to Balakian, "the ambiguous relationship between eros and dismemberment. The feminine / Mother appears simultaneously as a dance of images in the earth and a dispersed body—a genocidal emblem. Mother: an image of resurrection as she rises out of the earth in her son's imagination."[84]

Following the Armenian Genocide, in 1919 Gorky's mother—Shushan Adoian, neé Der Marderosian—died of starvation in the artist's arms, and her traumatic revenant is most powerfully mourned in Gorky's family portrait, *The Artist and His Mother*. For sixteen years, from 1926 through 1942, Gorky labored on two versions of this work, the first now part of the permanent collection of the Whitney Museum of American Art and the second housed at the National Gallery of Art. Both portraits dwell on a sole surviving photograph taken of Gorky and his mother in 1912 while they were living in Van City, Turkey. Gorky's painting of this image owes as much to the Egyptian Fayum mummy portraits as to the Christian symbolism of the Virgin and Child, depicted enthroned on the south façade of the Church of the Holy Cross on Akhtamar Island. The artist's significations on the death and resurrection motifs of Egyptian and Christian iconography produce an uncanny visual canvas. Gorky invokes the trauma of his mother's loss through the force of her gaze that addresses neither her son nor the viewer but rather seems to collapse inward into the black, fully dilated pupils of her haunting regard. The National Gallery version links mother and son where they lean into each other before the camera with their sleeves touching. The Whitney composition, however, insinuates an ominous gray gap between mother and son that more fatefully severs them irretrievably from each other. While the artist holds the floral symbol of his art in his right hand, his left arm seems withered as if to suggest his attenuated relationship to his mother's memory. Perhaps most poignantly, the surface textures of both canvases bear the traces of endless painterly reworking as Gorky turned again and again to his art as the only medium where he might recapture a fleeting connection to Shushan. "It is," writes Hayden Herrera, "as if painting, scraping, repainting these canvases was Gorky's way of holding his mother in his memory and coming to terms with her loss."[85] Indeed, both for Gorky as painter and for Balakian as poet, the maternal archetype inflected by genocide is at once a source of bereavement, a symbol of cultural exile, and a lost love object. In this last role, as Maria Torok observes of the libidinal forces released in the mourning process, the dead mother is powerfully cathected by desire.[86] Resurrection, rebirth, and the libidinally charged forces that attend them everywhere inscribe the at once traumatic and erotic surrealism of what Balakian calls "the Gorkey green world" in his poem "Flat Sky of Summer." But without an understanding of the traumatic historicities that underwrite these painterly and poetic oeuvres, they would be otherwise unreadable.

As the definitive precedent of what the United Nations would later define in 1949 as "genocide-in-whole," the history of the Armenocide lodges a somewhat different claim on our social witnessing than that of the Holocaust.[87] Unlike the Nazi extermination of the Jews, the Turkish massacre of the Armenians has no recognized place in the modern archive of commemoration and mourning. Differing from the Holocaust, the genocide of the Armenian people, continues, arguably, in the extremely proactive agenda of the Republic of Turkey and its representatives. In this highly politicized context, writing the history of genocide always already happens as an intervention fraught with risk. For what is at stake here is a special case of genocidal memory that must be continually defended against the state-sponsored distortion and repression that are acted out, even now, at the highest levels of government, the media, and the academy. Denied, contested, and largely forgotten, the Armenocide persists nevertheless *sous rature*—presenced in contemporary Armenian-American poetics as an absence: as a phantom event haunting today's public sphere. Negotiating these complex psychic and political registers, this special body of verse also troubles the received closure of modernist periodization, calling for a new history of literary and cultural modernism. In this vein, reading the spectral revenants of genocide transmitted across the generations of the Armenian diaspora is especially pertinent for discerning the traumatic legacy of the Holocaust in postwar American verse. Poetry's power to bear witness to the novum of this unique event is the subject of chapter 2.

CHAPTER TWO

The Holocaust at Home

"The Holocaust is above all unique," Claude Lanzmann has remarked, "in that it erects a ring of fire around itself."[1] Whether after Auschwitz any space for witnessing can be discerned "inside" its "ring of fire"—*inside* the event—is the pressing, ethicopolitical question at stake in representing its extremity. In writing the Holocaust, Irving Greenberg has cautioned, "no statement, theological or otherwise, should be made that would not be credible in the presence of the burning children."[2] Yet precisely there inside the ring of fire—there, where Jean Améry marks "the mind's limits"[3]—what kind of knowledge and what manner of speaking could possibly satisfy such an extreme criterion of truth? For survivor witnesses such as Elie Wiesel, witnessing to the Holocaust entails a double return not only of conscious memory but, equally important, of something more: a certain excess that breaches one's intentional testimony with the force of the "unknown."[4]

Not insignificantly, in Wiesel's deposition of survival at the killing center of Auschwitz-Birkenau—given during the Klaus Barbie trial—such psychic breaching happens as a trauma to visual representation as such:

> What I saw is enough for me. In a small wood somewhere in Birkenau I saw children being thrown into the flames alive by the S. S. Sometimes I curse my ability to see. It should have left me without ever returning. I should have remained with those little charred bodies.[5]

The Holocaust experience, for Wiesel, marks a crisis in visuality as such. Before Auschwitz, the metaphoric power of light underwrites the truth claims of Western metaphysics reaching back to the pre-Socratics. The Platonic allegory of the cave is inscribed by the trope of illumination. Gnostic, Stoic, and Neoplatonic traditions of inner radiance predate the medieval synthesis of Jewish, Arabic, and Hellenistic traditions of *lux veritas*. Experimental forms of *lux naturalis* in Galileo, Bacon, and Descartes culminate in the Enlightenment proper.[6] Illuminated space, as Emmanuel Levinas argues, comes to be regarded as equiprimordial with thought, subjectivity, and the representation of knowable objects.[7] With the Holocaust, however, light as a guarantor of truth suffers a profound trauma. In place of the *lichtung*—the forest clearing where beings, according to Martin Heidegger, are disclosed in an illuminating unhiddenness (*aletheia*)—we encounter Wiesel's "small wood in Birkenau" and its ghastly backlighting from the burning children. This latter blaze cannot be fixed as an imaginary figure for *theoria* or *contemplatio*. Rather, its fire befalls the symbolic order of things, incinerating the everyday world of knowing subjects and representable objects.

Conventional visuality in its Heideggerean mode of *ge-stell*—its ocular power of fixing, enframing, and dominating the world for subjectivity (what Heidegger describes as the "conquest of the world as picture")—is itself lit, in Wiesel's account, by modernity's radically infernal gaze.[8] The force of this other backlighting traverses the beholding witness with a violence that leaves him strangely beside himself, split in his mode of testimonial utterance: "What I saw," Wiesel attests, "is enough for me." Here the shock of the event is registered symptomatically in the temporal rift that divides the "eye" witness to mass murder, the *sujet d'énoncé* (subject of the statement), from the testimonial I, the *sujet d'énonciation* (the subject of the enunciation). Wiesel's statement—"What I saw is enough for me"—is itself an indeterminate performative. What is "enough" cuts both ways: evidencing a sufficient truth claim and marking a certain terminus of selfhood as such, as if to say, "enough already." Witnessing takes place under the double sign of sworn testimony that breaks down in the catachresis of what one both avows and curses in the visible. Although registered in the subjunctive, Wiesel's repudiation of vision—"It should have left me without ever returning. I should have remained with those little charred bodies"—testifies to the disturbing truth that the Holocaustal event— as a missed encounter with the Real[9]—offers no return to a familiar universe, that the survivor inhabits a world of ash: that, as Charlotte Delbo declared, "Je suis morte à Auschwitz et personne ne le voit" (I died in Auschwitz and no one sees it).[10]

Wiesel's survival at Auschwitz-Birkenau, as he depicts it both in the Barbie Trial and some thirty years earlier in *Night*, cannot be entirely resolved by a therapeutic "working through" (*Durcharbeiten*) of memory. Indeed, the interminable testimony of Wiesel's postwar career might be characterized, as a witnessing to what was "humanly impossible" inside Auschwitz.[11] Symptomatic in Wiesel's verbal repetition

is the fateful encounter with an event whose source in the Real opens a more profound, ontological trauma than mourning can ever console:

> Never shall I forget that night, the first night in camp, which has turned my life into
> one long night, seven times cursed and seven times sealed. Never shall I forget that
> smoke. Never shall I forget the little faces of the children, whose bodies I saw turned
> into wreaths of smoke beneath a silent blue sky.
>
> Never shall I forget those flames which consumed my faith forever.
>
> Never shall I forget that nocturnal silence which deprived me, for all eternity, of
> the desire to live. Never shall I forget those moments which murdered my God and
> my soul and turned my dreams to dust. Never shall I forget these things, even if I am
> condemned to live as long as God Himself. Never.[12]

The vigilance of survivor memory, as Wiesel renders it here, is radically incon-
solable. Beyond the rhetoric of either pledge or catalogue, this celebrated passage
from *Night* intones the unmaking—the "murder"—of the poet's "faith" and more,
his very "desire to live." The particularly vivid traces of recollected detail—repeated
here in the catalogue of demonstrative pronouns (that night, that smoke, those
flames, that nocturnal silence, those moments, these things)—stand out in their
signifying presence as markers, paradoxically, of irretrievable loss. Not unlike the
summoning refrain of Poe's "The Raven," Wiesel's anaphoric negations are possessed by a traumatic encounter. In the terminal present after Auschwitz, where
"eternity" has become retrospective, who is to say that acting out, rather than
working through, is the less authentic discursive form for the survivor witness?

What is at stake in this difference is a key issue for Dominick LaCapra and others
who interrogate the ethics of Holocaust representation.[13] The difference between
particular social losses, which may be mourned, versus absence as such is underwritten in LaCapra's project by Freud's well-known distinction between the symptoms of acting out and processes of working through (*Durcharbeiten*) in psychoanalysis. On the one hand, LaCapra points to the loss of critical objectivity that
happens when historical narrative succumbs to a certain melancholic obsession
with its objects of study: a melancholy that acts out and thereby repeats a traumatic
referent. LaCapra also cautions, on the other hand, against the symptoms of numbing and foreclosure through "facts" that characterize much of historical "objectification." For LaCapra, such "numbing (objectification and splitting of object from
subject, including self-as-subject from self-as-object) may function for the historian
as a protective shield or preservative against unproblematic identification with the
experience of others and the possibility of being traumatized by it" (WHWT, 40).
Moreover, the specific historicity of the Holocaust hazards a kind of psychic

implosion of *Durcharbeiten:* a radical escalation of the paradoxical recognition that "working through is itself a process that may never entirely transcend acting out and that, even in the best of circumstances, is never achieved once and for all" (WHWT, 148–49). The Holocaust, then, challenges historical witness with the force of a singularly traumatizing event.

Taken to an extreme, however, tropes of singularity in Holocaust representation present its "uniqueness" as a break with historical knowledge. Positing such a rupture, as Geoffrey Hartman suggests, can become an "isolating maneuver."[14] But equally, it risks setting certain limits on the agency of ethical response by acting out, rather than working through, the stock metaphors of "impossibility." Encoded through the figures of novum, tremendum, caesura, rupture, crack, and cleavage (to borrow the lexicon of theorists as diverse as Emil Fackenheim, Arthur Cohen, and Jean-François Lyotard, among others),[15] the representation of the Holocaust as an unprecedented event sacrifices cognition as such. Repeatedly in the text of its critical discussion, the Holocaustal referent is deferred through the rhetorical figure of aposiopesis, an invoked silence before an unnamable and unknowable abyss. However apt in capturing the special horror of the event, the metaphor of the abyss risks a certain reification in critical usage that naturalizes history and historical responsibility.

Theological discussion of the Holocaust as, for example, in Arthur Cohen's formulation of the tremendum relies on the figure of the abyss to mark an ontological difference between the Holocaust and human understanding. "As abyss," Cohen writes, "the tremendum transforms everything that went before into distance and remoteness, as though an earthquake had overturned the center of a world, obliterating mountains that had once been near at hand and that we had formerly dreamt of scaling."[16] However compelling as metaphor, the abyss here also tends to deflect social accountability from what is, after all, a man-made rather than natural disaster. A similar naturalization marks Hannah Arendt's depiction of 1933— the infamous year that Hitler becomes Reich Chancellor, legalizes the Nazi Party, opens Dachau, creates the Gestapo, and presides over public book-burnings. In responding to this fateful moment of German history, Arendt subsumes concrete political events under the somewhat mystifying bent of an abyssal trope: "This," Arendt reflects, "was really something quite different. This is really as if the abyss opened up before us because we had imagined that all the rest could be sorted out in some way or other, as can always happen in politics. But not this time."[17] Again, while respecting the unprecedented event of the Holocaust, Arendt's invocation of the abyss also tends to dehistoricize the Holocaust by removing it from political analysis in the public sphere.

The figure of the abyss as a symptomatic tendency in Holocaust writing also sets a limit to witnessing through imposing an absolute silence. Marking the implosion of all thought, knowledge, language, agency, memory, and existence as such, its "fearful symmetry," like Blake's "Tyger," can be interrogated but never fully understood. Thus in *The Writing of the Disaster*, a certain repetition of mixed metaphors and rhetorical questions act out Maurice Blanchot's attempts to name what eludes any assignable meaning. In approaching the event horizon of the Holocaust, the very language in which one presences its truth is "alien to naming": disfigured by the catachresis of history's "utter-burn" that is, in turn, "swallowed up" in a "gift" further personified in the "keeper of the Holocaust" and "guardian thought":

> The unknown name, alien to naming: The Holocaust, the absolute event of history—which is a date in history—that utter-burn where all history took fire, where the movement of Meaning was swallowed up, where the gift which knows nothing of forgiving or of content, shattered without giving place to anything that can be affirmed, that can be denied—gift of very passivity, gift of what cannot be given. How can it be preserved, even by thought? How can thought be made the keeper of the Holocaust where all was lost, including guardian thought?[18]

The only credible answer, perhaps, to these impossible questions is an analytic silence that, as a "letting be," would witness to the phenomenological disclosure of the disaster in the parapraxis of forgetting that inhabits survivor testimony. "Let the disaster speak in you," Blanchot advises, "even if it be by your forgetfulness or silence" (WD, 4). Such silence pays respect to the extralinguistic force of Auschwitz that, according to George Steiner, "lies outside speech as it lies outside reason."[19]

While this reverential silence denotes a certain hermeneutics of faith, silence also has another history belonging under the sign of suspicion. André Neher, for example, observes how during the Holocaust a continuum of silence had extended from the banal complicity of the bystander witness through the passive response of the Allied powers, reaching all the way to the absent "silence of God." The net political effect of silence, for Neher, was to withdraw public attention from everyday life in the killing centers: "At Auschwitz," Neher writes, "everything unfolded, was fulfilled and accomplished for weeks, months, and years on end in absolute silence, away from and out of the mainstream of history."[20] The persistence of such silence in the cross-generational repression of the Holocaust is the special feature of postwar perpetrator culture examined by Dan Bar-On, Barbara Heimannsberg, and Christoph J. Schmidt, among others. Here the etymological agency in the Latin *silere* (to keep quiet) and the German *schweigen* (whose imperative *Schweig* translates into the English slang "shut up") denotes a more active prohibition on speaking that censors historical accounts of past crimes.[21]

In the psychic economy of postwar Germany, fear of reprisals after Allied occupation, coupled with perpetrator guilt and mass feelings of defeat, worthlessness, shame, and humiliation together have acted as powerful blocks to the mourning process. In their classic cultural study of the Federal Republic of Germany, *The Inability to Mourn* (1975), Alexander and Margarete Mitscherlich have offered a sophisticated analysis of the psychosocial barriers that silenced the tremendous losses both to the Germans themselves and to their Jewish victims following World War II.[22] Where ordinary Germans were complicit with singularly horrific crimes—committed in the name of a wholly idealized nationalism—memory proved too traumatic to "master" through public rituals of mourning. In the domestic context of family storytelling, in the civic mania to reconstruct a ruined economy, in the careful encoding of public monuments, German repression silenced Nazism's perpetrator role in destroying European Jewry.

As Theodor Adorno observed in the 1970s, "coming to terms" with the Holocaust in postwar Germany has meant not so much a "serious working through of the past, the breaking of its spell through an act of clear consciousness"; rather, it belies the wish "to turn the page and, if possible, wiping it from memory."[23] This burial job of history was quite literally performed in the Bitburg controversy of the mid-1980s. In laying commemorative wreaths at Bitburg cemetery, where forty-eight members of the SS were buried, the late President Ronald Reagan unwittingly acted out Germany's "inability to mourn." Not surprisingly, his "Remarks at Bitburg Air Base" adopted the intentionalist narrative line on the Holocaust, attributing it to "one man's totalitarian dictatorship." In a commemorative gesture actually lodged against mourning, Reagan absolved Germany of its responsibility to its victims by recoding the status of German war dead from being perpetrators of genocide to victimized "human beings, crushed by a vicious ideology."[24] The symbolic alliance Reagan struck between the "American and German people" (B, 258) had its subtext, arguably, in Germany's strategic position as NATO ally and hedge against the former Soviet Union.

Moreover, it was within this geopolitical context that the *Historikerstreit* emerged the following summer of 1986 sparking a celebrated debate—among such historians as Ernst Nolte (former student of Martin Heidegger), Jürgen Habermas, and Andreas Hillgruber—over cultural memory and the postwar identity of the Federal Republic of Germany. In *Zweierlei Untergang. Die Zerschlagung des Deutschen Reiches und das Ende des europäischen Judentums* (two kinds of destruction: the shattering of the German Reich and the end of European Jewry), Hillgruber split "the end of

European Jewry" from the "shattering of the German Reich." This revisionist strategy contained the former by assigning responsibility for genocide to Hitler and valorized the latter by commending Germany's heroic defense of its eastern border
against the Russian advance. Choosing a different strategy of revisionist historicism,
Nolte did not so much divide German militarism from SS war crimes but reversed
Germany's perpetrator status to one of victim. In a perverse twisting of Nazi in-
tentionality, Nolte argued that "Auschwitz is not primarily the result of traditional
anti-Semitism. It was in its core not only a 'genocide,' but was above all a reaction
born out of the anxiety of the annihilating occurrences of the Russian revolution."[25]
This concession to the historical fact of genocide ultimately works to reverse and
thereby silence national responsibility through what Deborah Lipstadt has critiqued
as the "yes, but" strategy of denial. Yes, Jews were the subject of genocide, but in the
total context of Bolshevik terror, the Nazis were compelled to commit an "Asiatic
deed" in defense against the same.[26]

On the one hand, acknowledging the significance of the Holocaust begins with
a certain humility, even reverence, for the silence of its singularity. Unprecedented
in the archive of human experience, the Holocaust is presenced, paradoxically, in
the silence of an event horizon that lies beyond the range of historical understanding. On the other hand, fetishizing uniqueness for its own sake, according to Emil
Fackenheim, risks "taking the event out of history and thus mystifying it."[27] The response of witnessing, therefore, as an historical task, demands a second moment:
one that sacrifices silence in favor of testimony. In the case of the Holocaust, the
imperative to bear witness is driven by the engraved memory of unspeakable acts:
crimes against humanity, mass violence, cruelty, personal trauma, loss, and so on.
The testimonial moment is thus occasioned by a radical negation: a violent breaching of the everyday world and its normative conventions of communicative ratio-
nality. Such a linguistic silence or gap possesses discourse, as a "negative phrase"
that, for Jean-François Lyotard, "nevertheless calls upon phrases which are in principle possible." In The Differend, the "unstable state and instant of language" is the
subject of Lyotard's ethicopolitical concern: "what is at stake," he writes, "in a literature, in a philosophy, in a politics perhaps, is to bear witness to differends by finding idioms for them."[28]

Recent psychoanalytic writing on the Holocaust is one such discourse where the
"negative phrase" of the differend has found an idiom whose repetition, however
acted out, nevertheless makes a difference in working through the event. Dori
Laub and Shoshana Felman invoke the Holocaust in the silence of an abyssal
metaphor, but in their texts the extreme event is considered through the more
complex understanding of time and memory afforded by trauma theory. In his

controversial essay "Truth and Testimony: The Process and the Struggle," Laub
takes up the position of the "listener" who attends to the victim's "silence": the
"gaping, vertiginous 'black hole' of the experience of trauma."[29] Laub extends this
astrophysical metaphor by presenting the Holocaustal event as analogous to the
implosion of light into the gravitational singularity at the heart of a black hole. Just
as any illumination fails to escape the event horizon of a black hole, so the Holocaust, as "event produced no witnesses" (TT, 65). The figure of the black hole, however, neither denies history nor acts out trauma for its own sake as some have
charged.[30] Inside the Holocaustal moment, Laub argues, disinterested witnessing
was compromised by the immediate proximity of extreme trauma. No insider
could remain outside the "trapping roles, and the consequent identities, either
of victim or of the executioner." Indeed, in Laub's model there is no "outside" un-
tainted by the violence of this world-historical catastrophe. From the mundane
complicity of the bystander up through the absence of God, as the Holocaust pro-
ceeded "most actual or potential witnesses failed one-by-one to occupy their position as a witness, and at a certain point it seemed as if there was no one left to witness what was taking place" (TT, 66). Felman and Laub would deny neither the
possibility of survivor resistance discussed, say, by Terrence Des Pres, nor the fact
that attempts at archival documentation were undertaken in the ghetto, labor
camp, and death factory.[31] Rather, they would argue against the notion that political resistance or even survivor witnessing as such fully escaped the global legacy of
the Holocaust.

For the Holocaust survivor—as for the accident victim or war veteran—trauma,
by definition, effects a violent breaching of what Freud described as the psyche's
protective shield—the *Reizschutz* regulating the boundary between self and worldly
stimuli.[32] As both a collective and individual trauma, the Holocaust, poses a limit
to psychological witnessing inside its unfolding disaster, however much its event
persists symptomatically as dream, flashback, or engraved memory. If trauma
breaches the subject position of the witness inside Auschwitz, then testimony from
its interior can only be received, "belatedly" through a second moment, that of the
psychoanalytic dialogue. For the survivor analysand, it is the temporal structure of
latency that—as in post-traumatic stress disorder (PTSD)—mediates the survival of
the event and its subsequent repetition as symptom. Through the narrative contract of analysis, the extremity that possesses the survivor witness as dream, flashback, anxiety, dissociation, and so on, is at once reenacted and negotiated in working through traumatic memory. Yet as Felman cautions, entering into the dialogue
from without, insofar as it succeeds in revisiting the interior scene of the event,

risks the implosion of yet another, repeated traumatization. In recalling the event, Felman poses key questions of testimonial practice that probe a self-reflexivity gleaned precisely in repetition: "How to *transmit* at once the pathos and the dis-connection, the abyssal lostness of the inside, without being either crushed by the abyss or overwhelmed by the pathos, *without losing the outside?* How to be, thus, at the same time inside and outside? And how to guide the audience into an inside which nonetheless can keep in touch with the outside?"[33] Secondary witnessing thus involves a kind of phenomenological attention that negotiates the event's structure of temporal latency made up as it is of highly conflicted, affective forces.

Just as revisiting the event poses special conditions of witnessing in psychoanalysis, it similarly presents unique challenges for literary representation. One symptom of the difficulties in writing the Holocaust is the very paucity of contemporary verse devoted to the event. In the American postwar context, fewer poems have been written on genocide than, say, the historical struggles over race, gender, sexuality, the environment, native ethnicities, and so on. "We never discussed the Second World War much when I was growing up," Charles Bernstein has acknowledged. Moreover, he admits, "I don't feel much like discussing it now." Reflecting the la-tency of a global trauma, Bernstein notes that it is only some five decades after the Holocaust that "we are just beginning to come out of the shock enough to try to make sense of the experience."[34] Peculiar to the temporal structure of extremity, the encounter with death, missed through survival, gathers traumatic force only through the passage of time. Echoing an observation made by Terrence Des Pres, among others, Bernstein notes that for him "each year, the Extermination Process seems nearer, more recent."[35]

It would be normal to expect repression to follow upon a death encounter. As an unprecedented trauma, however, the Holocaust changes the ontological status of death as such. "Planet Auschwitz," as Yechiel Dinur called it, marks a radical negation of life that thereby introduces a new anxiety into human existence.[36] For his part, Adorno concludes that "the administrative murder of millions made of death a thing one had never yet to fear in just this fashion."[37] Similarly, the shock effect of "Not one death but many," as Charles Olson has it in "The Kingfishers," poses new challenges in representation for postwar poetics.[38] Given the novum of industrial mass murder, the psychic impulse would be either simply to repress it through the kind of psychic numbing theorized by Robert Jay Lifton or to displace its horror: screening out its force through more familiar, human-scale tropes of experience.[39]

As a symptomatic response to such world-historical loss, this latter poetic tendency is fully patent in W. D. Snodgrass's long verse cycle *The Fuehrer Bunker* (1995). Snodgrass attained early notoriety in American poetics by winning the Pulitzer Prize for his first book of verse, *Heart's Needle* in 1960. He is also credited with being "responsible for the emergence of American confession poetry,"[40] certainly a dominant movement in postwar verse. Composed over the course of some twenty-five years, *The Fuehrer Bunker*—if not the poet's magnum opus—is no doubt intended to rival his early achievement. Indeed, the volume was nominated for the National Book Critics Circle Award for Poetry and adapted for the American Place Theatre by Wynn Handman. Such a major investment of the poet's psychic energy, public identity, and creative labor deserves considered analysis both in terms of the kind of aesthetic task Snodgrass undertakes in the book and the cultural work it performs. To begin with, *The Fuehrer Bunker* revisits the final days of the Third Reich from the imagined vantage point of Adolph Hitler and his inner circle of advisors, ensconced as they were during April–May 1945 below the Reich Chancellery in a fortified air raid shelter.

The choice of this fateful moment inflects the poet's earlier concern with subjective, confessional values through a broader engagement with public history.[41] In fact, *The Fuehrer Bunker* takes on the proportions of epic. Its formal range of poetic technique moves in more ambitious directions beyond personal lyricism. For example, Snodgrass's reliance on the theatrical conventions of the dramatic monologue and chorus serves to mediate the monumental scope of epic through a more situated witnessing to what T. S. Eliot, following Mallarmé, called "the dialect of the tribe."[42] The eclecticism of Snodgrass's project in *The Fuehrer Bunker* not only mixes the genres of epic and drama but features lyric utterance in the plainspoken registers of slang and obscenity. The volume's colloquial idiom, in turn, is stylized visually through concrete typography. Moreover, its vernacular utterances are given ritualized elevation in the formalism of rhymed couplets and such fixed forms as the villanelle. Not unlike the aesthetic wager, say, of James Merrill's *The Changing Light at Sandover*, Snodgrass's American long poem would similarly lay claim to an authoritative cultural statement by means of its technical virtuosity in poetic performance.

Not content to reflect history, this cycle of eighty-seven poems would take its place in the modern verse epic tradition, which according to Roy Harvey Pearce, forwards "a new ordering" of the world: one that aims to "make rather than recall the history" of chronicled events.[43] In supplementing, rather than displacing, his earlier stake in confessional poetics, Snodgrass would give us an *intimate* history. He would locate the book's point of address inside the binary divide marking Fel-

man's and Laub's abyssal representation of the Holocaustal event. But more controversial, by staging dramatic monologues of the Nazi High Command—Hitler,
Martin Bormann, Joseph Goebbels, Heinrich Himmler, Hermann Goering, Albert
Speer, and the rest—Snodgrass risks identification not with the Jewish victims of
genocide but with its German perpetrators, themselves cast as tragically victimized. More provocative still is his positioning of the reader as bystander to a trauma
that invites identification with the psychic life of Nazi war criminals. The two
epigraphs taken from Joseph Goebbels and Mother Teresa invest the volume with
a double framing of the inside:

> Even if we lose this war, we still win, for our spirit will have penetrated our enemies'
> hearts.   —*Joseph Goebbels*

> Mother Teresa, asked when it was she started her work for abandoned children,
> replied, "on the Day I discovered I had Hitler inside me."

From Goebbels's standpoint as perpetrator, the loss encrypted inside *The Fuehrer
Bunker*—despite the historical passing of Nazism—will achieve victory nevertheless
in the "spirit" or phantom whose return will haunt the world war's nominal victors
with a radical negation. After Auschwitz, as Mother Teresa attests, Hitler—the cultural signifier—lives on as an internalized sign marking the site of a universal bystander guilt. So far-reaching, for Snodgrass, is the force of this legacy that it positions every secondary witness as a complicit bystander to an ultimate moral crime.
Thus as Snodgrass implies, the trace of Auschwitz's interior extremity is inscribed
ever after as an ontological given: not so much a specific historic crime against humanity as an inhuman universal. As we shall see, this broadening of the perpetrator crime as an all-encompassing psychic potential that everyone shares entails a
troubling politics: one that lends a certain pathos and even absolution to actual war
criminals.

Not unlike the interior of Auschwitz, what is inside the bunker, by virtue of its
own horror, resists comprehension in its own moment. Consequently, its primal
scene of despair, insanity, infanticide, murder, and suicide returns in the deferral or
latency peculiar to the temporal structure of trauma.[44] However displaced in time,
poetry affords passage, for Snodgrass, inside the heart of the Holocaust. Chancing
the inside, nevertheless, hazards—as Felman and Laub attest—being "crushed" and
overwhelmed by its singularity. Such psychic disaster, as Blanchot theorizes, escalates the stakes of Nietzsche's question, "Have you suffered for knowledge's sake?"
In rereading Nietzsche, Blanchot underscores the negativity of such "suffering" as
the *"pas* ['not'] of the utterly passive" before what is not simply "knowledge of the

disaster" but "knowledge as disaster."[45] The latter befalls the subject precisely as an epistemological limit in the impasse to conscious understanding. Disaster not only undermines one's cognitive mastery of the "impossible" referent but denies *prima facie* any knowledge at all.

Signs of trauma, which stem from inside the bunker, show up in Snodgrass's presentation in the formal repetition of verbal motifs that act out more than they work through the possessing force of the Holocaustal *differend*. The nonsense rhymes that make up Snodgrass's chorus in "Old Lady Barkeep" provide an ironic point of departure to and return from the impossible forces of the inside. The poet's choral satires on Frau Wirtin—a Renaissance figure Berliners revived in parody of the Reich—plumb the moral depths of Nazism through the conscious repetition of cultural critique staged here as black humor. Obscenity is the operative idiom of these World War II limericks, and Snodgrass quite forcefully maps military rhetoric onto the discourse of pornographic sexuality:

> "If they bite back, the bloody cunts,
> We'll bang them on two fronts at once;
>> You can't resist a God!"
> Like ladykillers at a dance,
> His troops advanced in goosestep prance
> Through Austria, Czechoslovakia, France,
> Then found they'd shot their wad.[46]

Snodgrass darkly alludes here to the Nazi *Einsatzgruppen,* who became literal "lady-killers" in acts of genocide against the European Jews. Although Snodgrass would master that legacy through the serial forms of his choral passages, its force breaches the poet's intended strategies of verbal containment. Pornography in the conceits of gender that pit masculine soldiers against a feminized enemy does not so much parody as screen out the horrors of Nazism.

Repetition acts out far more trauma inside *The Fuehrer Bunker* than the poet can work through. Verbal obscenity, sadomasochism, pornography are so pervasive in Snodgrass's book that its staging is less critical than symptomatic. Whether Snodgrass succumbs to or critiques the sexual lure of what Susan Sontag defines as "fascinating fascism" is not an easy call to make.[47] Certainly, Snodgrass offers a thoroughgoing portrait of the kind of sexual masochism attributed to Hitler by Walter C. Langer, Robert G. L. Waite, and others. To his credit, Snodgrass artfully cross-cuts passages depicting the adoration of the Fuehrer's admirers on "Hitler's Birthday" with the flipside analysis of his alleged scatological sex play with his niece Geli Raubal.[48] Working through Hitler's aberrant sexuality in dramatic monologue,

Snodgrass explores the pathology that has a well-known role in Hitler's masochistic self-doubts and, in turn, his sadistic anti-Semitism:

My pills; Morrell's injections.
My cake, chairs, rugs—without them,
Bare concrete. Same as any
Jew degenerate at Auschwitz. (FB, 104)

Hitler's escalating regimen of medication, coupled here with various fetishized signs of domestic sentimentality, as Snodgrass implies, only partially assuages the deep-seated anxieties that plagued the Nazi dictator about his own racial identity, owing to the specter of Hitler's rumored Jewish grandfather.[49]

The dread of death as such leads in the final poems of the book to "Old Lady Barkeep's Bacchanal," where the poet writes, "Beasts' brawl and orgy proved that all / Who find they face a flank stone wall / Can still make one last stand / Against themselves" (FB, 161). Inside the bunker, Snodgrass's dramatic revelation of character acts out a certain excess of sexual bawdiness that in his portrait of Joseph Goebbels is meant to underscore the erotics of power and political domination:

Here's Runty Joe, the cunt collector
Who grew to greatness, first erector
Of Myths and missions, fibs and fables,
Who pulled the wool then turned the tables
He piped the tunes and called the dance
Where shirtless countries lost their pants. (FB, 114)

The sexual allure of mass persuasion is something Snodgrass had foregrounded through Goebbels's role as minister of propaganda referring to Goebbels's famous "Total War" address of February 18, 1943, in the Berlin Sportpalast hall where he "diddled thousands to one vast / Insane, delirious orgasm" (FB, 99). Certainly, the cultural phenomenon of mass desire that Nazism mobilized through oratory, spectacle, and kitsch ritual reflects an erotic demand for power that was widespread throughout German society at the time. "It is easy to see" in Nazism, according to Michel Foucault, "the procedures that transmit and reinforce this eroticization. But for the eroticization to take hold, those who are attached to power and have accepted it must already be erotic." Snodgrass's reduction of power's libidinal techniques to Goebbels's seductive oratory tends to mystify the otherwise complex social practices of desire bonding ordinary Germans to one another in the public sphere of the Third Reich. Nevertheless, his focus on Goebbels as the personification of power's charismatic allure as it declines into the kitsch obscenity of fascism proper is not without contemporary resonance. Today, as Foucault observed, the resurgent fascination with sadomasochistic sex-role play along with "the shoddiest aspects of the erotic imagination are now put under the sign of Nazism."[50] Similarly, in theorizing the current popularity of Nazism as a sexual metaphor in contemporary literature, film, and the material culture of everyday life, Susan Sontag finds a compelling eroticism imbricated with the stylized self-presentation of the Nazi leaders:

> In the sex shops, the baths, the leather bars, the brothels, people are dragging out their gear. But why? Why has Nazi Germany, which was a sexually repressive society, become erotic? How could a regime which persecuted homosexuals become a gay turn-on?
>
> A clue lies in the predilections of the fascist leaders themselves for sexual metaphors. Like Nietzsche and Wagner, Hitler regarded leadership as sexual mastery of the "feminine" masses, as rape. (The expression of the crowds in *Triumph of the Will* is one of ecstasy; the leader makes the crowd come.) (FF, 102)

For his part, Snodgrass reenacts the pleasure Goebbels no doubt took in massaging his audience. In this way, the poet exposes the erotic politics of desire that held ordinary Germans in sway to Nazism. Yet, Snodgrass's presentation tends to exceed the critique of working through, reproducing instead a certain vicarious investment in fascism as such. Repeatedly staging these sex roles in various dramatic monologues, Snodgrass seems enthralled with perverse sexuality for its own sake. His acting out of the obscene, precisely in its insistent verbal repetition, differs from the more therapeutic modes of what Sontag describes as a "sophisticated playing with cultural horror."[51] Thus, Snodgrass writes in character as Goebbels:

> Stone cold, my mind controlled each spasm,
> Teased them so high, so hot and mad
> That they'd take everything I had
> To give them. They could only roar
> "Ja!" and "Ja!" and "Ja!" once more,
> Begging me: let them have it—total war.
>
> We pant for, but we're scorned of,
> What we can screw. If we want love,
> We lie. In politics, in bed. (FB, 99)

Repetition becomes compulsive here and throughout the volume in the linguistic character of Snodgrass's verse. Here the poet's alliterated verbal textures and anaphora act out a manic redundancy of signification in excess of the author's crit-

ical intent. Characteristically in Snodgrass's book, the poet's performative investment in fascist aesthetics lapses into a celebration, rather than a critique, of domination taken to orgiastic lengths.

Snodgrass's obsession with the obscene, the scatological, the pornographic succumbs, arguably, to the inside of his book's extreme subject matter. His project becomes so enthralled by Nazism's inner circle that he repeats the perpetrator's own
symptomatic fascination with fascist erotics. Snodgrass's compulsive eroticism is itself a sign, no doubt, of the Holocaust's traumatic history, which culminates in the
horrific suicides of Hitler, Eva Braun, and Joseph and Magda Goebbels and the poi-
soning of the six Goebbels children. The poet's imaginative proximity to that "disaster" is symptomatic not just at the level of poetic form but, more troublingly, in
the "disastrous" political investments that echo the revisionist debate over the Nazi
legacy. To begin with, Snodgrass's portraits of Hitler and the High Command tend
to contain perpetrator responsibility to this inner ring of leaders thus absolving "ordinary" Germans from moral accountability for the Holocaust. In limiting himself
to the intentional pathology of the Nazi elite, Snodgrass backgrounds the social
complicity that Daniel Jonah Goldhagen and Christopher R. Browning assign to "ordinary Germans" in the broader functioning of what Goldhagen defines as "elimi-
nationist anti-semitism."[52] In his interviews, Snodgrass not only explicitly denies
Germany's national responsibility for the Holocaust but tends as well to normalize
its event through the kind of comparativist apology found in revisionist historicism
of the German *Historikerstreit:*

> Well, it [the Holocaust] wasn't entirely with the consent and approval of the nation.
> And that isn't so unique as it's often presented to be. Look at the attitudes toward the
> American Indians a few years ago. "The only good Indian is a dead Indian." Every one
> of the nations involved against the Nazis has things in its past that take away its
> privilege to feel too superior to the Nazis. . . . Look at the history of the British em-
> pire, look at the history of the French in North Africa, look at the history of the Jews
> against the Arabs. (PR, 187)

Snodgrass not only echoes comparativist rhetoric of German revisionists like
Ernst Nolte, but, equally disturbing, his representations inscribe the same cultural
logic of such revisionist historians as Andreas Hillgruber. In particular, Snodgrass's
poetry splits the Nazi genocide from a certain valorization of the Nazi military effort. His portraits of German military leaders such as Lt. Gen. Helmuth Weidling,
commander of the 56th Panzer Corps and Col. Gen. Gotthard Heinrici, commander of the Army Group Vistula present them as hard-nosed and heroic in their fi-
delity to military discipline in the face of Hitler's final pathology. Unlike the High

Command, Weidling boasts that "I don't screw my friends' wives. I don't rob / Cripples or lead 14-year-old soldiers." Rather, he affirms, "I fight. / I trained for war, get paid, gained my rank / In battle" (FB, 59).

Part of Snodgrass's problem in converting Hitler's bunker into the setting for high tragedy is that playwriting—however closeted—demands plot, dramatic action, and conflict between antagonists and protagonists. Against extreme portraits of psychopathic evil, Snodgrass tends to split his dramatis personae into equally one-dimensional caricatures of heroism. For example, Snodgrass valorizes Albert Speer's military role in saving Germany's industrial base in the last days of the war. But the same dramatic logic that positions Speer as protagonist against the Fuehrer as antagonist necessarily elides the history of Speer's otherwise spirited fortification of the industrial Ruhr heartland, which prolonged Hitler's ability to wage total war. Moreover, Snodgrass takes Speer at his word when he claims not to have known anything about the Final Solution.[53] As architect, he once again shores up Germany's diminished state, this time building on the "good" lie so as to countermand Hitler's "scorched-earth" policy. "I swear I still have faith," Speer pledges, "which"

> Means I'll destroy anything he orders.
> Then I tell his generals, gauleiters, our
> Factory managers to ignore his direct command
> For total destruction, a charred, barren land. Lord,
> Lord, who ever said you can't build on lies? (FB, 32)

Speer emerges in *The Fuehrer Bunker* not as the Nazi bureaucrat who administered war production through forced slave labor and was later convicted at Nuremberg for crimes against humanity. Presented as the book's protagonist, Speer the war criminal recedes from view.

I have dwelt on *The Fuehrer Bunker* not just to call attention to the problematic political stances that Snodgrass both partly intends and unknowingly acts out. But equally important, I have stressed the book's difficulties because they are symptomatic of a certain overidentification with the inside of extremity that characterizes much of postwar Holocaust poetry.[54] Such overidentification mistakes an imaginary representation of the event—mediated as it is by the intellectual and linguistic distance of the secondary witness—for the immediate experience of the primary witness as such. As a discourse of the imaginary, this kind of Holocaust poetry—no matter how graphic in its depiction of horror—returns the radical otherness of genocide to the regime of the familiar. Such imaginary representations actually serve to screen out the inside by deflecting the force of what is otherwise unimaginable. Instead of defamiliarizing poetry's representational limits, the impossible heart of the Holocaustal event is translated into discursive conventions that render it all too readable.

Recycling the familiar icons and scripts of documentary film, much of Holocaust poetry lapses into the stock images and stereotypical scenes that belong to the representable text of the event. For example, Alicia Ostriker's "The Eighth and Thirteenth" would shock the reader with the known facts of the Babii Yar massacre, but in fact, the poem preserves a certain representational remove from the real force of its truth. Ostriker's project in this poem would transcode into verse the nonverbal witnessing to atrocity heard in Dmitri Shostakovich's symphonic evocations of the Eighth Symphony, his 1943 memorial to the siege of Leningrad, and the 1962 Thirteenth Symphony based on the massacre at Babii Yar, the ravine outside of Kiev where in just two days the Nazi *Einsatzgruppen* killed some 33,000 Soviet Jews. The very extremity of Ostriker's subject, however, leads her to screen out—through verbal abstraction and figurative language—the otherwise unspeakable primal scene of mass murder. By her own account, Ostriker is well outside the event as she sips wine listening to Shostakovich's Eighth "played on public radio."[55] Just as her witnessing is secondary as a consumer of the contemporary culture industry, so her rhetorical situation as poet is further mediated by the linguistic subtext for Shostakovich's Thirteenth Symphony: Yevgeny Yevtushenko's poem "Babii Yar." That chain of aesthetic and cultural mediations makes up the discursive exterior to what takes place inside the real event.

Unlike Ostriker, Yevtushenko avoids the pitfall of any realistic representation of what transpired in the actual ravine of Babii Yar. Through a subtle use of oxymoron his verse invokes the traces of what genocide has rendered present, paradoxically, as a palpable absence:

The wild grasses rustle over Babii Yar.
The trees look ominous,
                    like judges.
Here all things scream silently,
                    and, baring my head,
slowly I feel myself
                    turning grey.
And I myself
                    am one massive, soundless scream
above the thousand thousand buried here.[56]

As a witnessing to the impossible, Yevtushenko's "soundless scream" haunts a landscape of secondary affect that evokes—but does not describe with any verisimilitude—the horror of mass murder. He is careful not to violate the truth of the inside by presuming to represent its imaginary scene from without. Figurative language supplements what has no representable referent. The simile of the trees that stand in judgment and the personification of absence in the oxymoron "soundless scream" testify to the inhuman legacy of Nazi atrocities.

In contrast to Yevtushenko, Ostriker's poetic strategy is to revisit the event in "realistic" detail, which she nevertheless imagines as she listens to her car stereo cassette player:

> For the thirteenth—
> I slip its cassette into my car
> Radio—they made Kiev's Jews undress
> After a march to the suburb,
> Shot the hesitant quickly,
> Battered some of the lame,
> And screamed at everyone.
> Valises were taken, would
> Not be needed, packed
> So abruptly, tied with such
> Frayed rope. Soldiers next
> Killed a few more. The living ones,
> Penises of the men like string,
> Breasts of the women bobbling
> As at athletics, were told to run
> Through a copse, to where
> Wet with saliva
> The ravine opened her mouth.
> Marksmen shot the remainder
> then, there, by the tens of thousands,
> Cleverly, so that bodies toppled
> In without lugging. An officer
> Strode upon the dead,
> Shot what stirred. (CIE, 30)

In restaging Babii Yar in poetry, Ostriker's imagery is actually less realistic than opaque in its verbal character. Jewish victims are rendered, for example, in a wholly abstract idiom as "the hesitant," the "lame," "everyone," "the living ones," "the remainder," "the dead," "what stirred," and so on. Whereas "art," for Shostakovitch, "destroys silence" (CIE, 31), Ostriker's anonymous diction—as a kind of screen idiom buffering the real trauma of actual, historical persons—tends to maintain it. Equally problematic, her personification of the ravine as a devouring female "mouth" reproduces the very conventions of naturalized gender representation that feminists have criticized from as early as Simone de Beauvoir's 1952 analysis in *The Second Sex*. One wonders here whether Ostriker's troping of the earth, death, and horror as feminine is meant to parody the sexist equation of woman and demonic nature (as well as, for that matter, castration) or if she tries to exploit such feminized personification for its "deep" psychic shock value. Either way, however, Ostriker's figurative phrasing in "[t]he ravine opened her mouth," as a secondary, "exterior" representation of a primary event, remains an uncanny mapping of gender onto Babii Yar's interior. Ostriker's coda, which attempts to encapsulate and thereby master what is heard in Shostakovitch's symphony, succumbs to a somewhat kitschy verbal play on what is, by now, an all-too-familiar Holocaust cliché:

> The words *never again*
> Clashing against the words
> *Again and again*
> —That music. (CIE, 31)

Rewriting the phrase "never again" as "again and again," Ostriker would foreground the pathology of genocidal repetition as well as the struggle against it. Yet, such a clever performative rephrasing of what is by now a stock Holocaust slogan itself repeats, arguably, the poem's symptomatic foreclosures of extremity.

"Such an event as an external trauma," Freud theorized in *Beyond the Pleasure Principle*, "is bound to provoke a disturbance on a large scale in the functioning of the organism's energy and to set in motion every possible defense measure."[57] Similarly, the psychic difficulty of dealing with what Nadine Fresco characterizes as the "unknown" memory of the Holocaust is not only an issue in primary testimony but a challenge to the literary representations of secondary witnessing to the event.[58] Much of postwar Holocaust poetry does not so much reflect its historicity as screen out the traumatic force of its genocidal event. As we have seen, Snodgrass's somewhat compulsive eroticization of Nazism and Ostriker's screen representations of mass murder can be read as psychic defenses against what Fresco has characterized as "the blindspot of some primal scene."[59] Not only poets but literary critics of Holocaust verse are likewise susceptible to symptoms of trauma stemming from the event insofar as they disavow critical judgment in the name of empathic identification with the Holocaust's victims. Thus, Susan Gubar in *Poetry after Auschwitz* admits that "[s]ome readers may take issue with my refusal . . . to fault poets for overidentifying, misusing, or sensationalizing the materials they adopted, but I have withheld judgment so as to learn as much as I could from the poets' daring invocations."[60] What would it mean, however, to "take issue" precisely with such acts of "withheld judgment" suspended as they are in the name of an empathic ethics of critical reading? Might criticism, operating in this traumatized field of inquiry, all the more insist precisely on the imperative to discern exactly where "daring invocation" treads on "misuse"? Here perhaps more than ever, criticism may be ethically bound to ask the tough questions of value that, however difficult to pose of Holocaust poetry, may better adjudicate art's formal negotiations of extremity.

In this vein, how should we regard a work such as Sharon Olds's "That Year," whose comparative identifications the poet later discovers to be premature and thus trivializing. Published in her 1993 volume *Satan Says*, "That Year" marks the poet's coming of age, which intersects with her first encounter with the Holocaust as part of a school assignment. In the poem, Olds intends to juxtapose the comparative victimization of the child survivor of parental abuse and the Holocaust survivor. Yet as a psychic defense against the latter's unspeakable trauma, her depiction of the comparison as such serves to naturalize what otherwise exceeds conventional representation:

That was the year
I started to bleed,
crossing over that border in the night,

and in Social Studies, we came at last
to Auschwitz, I recognized it
like my father's face, the face of the guard
turning away—or worse yet
turning toward me.

The symmetrical piles of white bodies,
the round white breast-shapes of the heaps,
the smell of the smoke, the dogs the wires the
rope the hunger. It had happened to others.
There was a word for us. I was: a Jew.
It had happened to six million.
And there was another word that was not
for the six million, but was a word for me
and for many others. I was:
a survivor.[61]

It is one thing to theorize comparative methodologies as viable approaches to understanding trauma. Indeed, David Blumenthal in *Facing the Abusive God: A Theology of Protest* employs theories of child abuse to intervene in discussions of post-
Holocaust theology. And conversely, as Olds testifies, it is just as enabling for the
abused child to see in the Holocaust survivor a model for her own psychic endurance of domestic harassment. Yet, to conflate parental cruelty with genocide in
the images that Olds foregrounds in "That Year" reduces both to the kitsch stereotypes of adolescent melodrama.

   To begin with, Olds rehearses the stock formula of the father as Nazi that has
long been a controversial rendering in Sylvia Plath's "Daddy" poem.[62] Instead of
encountering the Holocaustal event in "That Year," Olds, more than Plath, falls
back on the kind of fetishized screen images of the death camps that both learned
from high school "Social Studies." Lacking the primary testimony of the Holocaust
survivor, as well as any convincing rendering of it, Olds's performative identification with the "six million" stages a certain overidentification. To claim as Olds does
the literal status of Jew and Holocaust victim from outside the event risks trivializing the destruction of actual persons inside Auschwitz. The most convincing proof
of this pitfall is, perhaps, the poet's own subsequent revisions to "That Year" in the
1995 reprint of *Satan Says* that qualify the insistent declarations of her earlier psychic
investment:

> The symmetrical piles of white bodies,
> the round, white breast-shapes of the heaps,
> the smell of the smoke, the dogs the wires the
> rope the hunger. This had happened to people,
> just a few years ago,
> in Germany, the guards were Protestants
> like my father and me, but in my dreams,
> every night, I was one of those
> about to be killed. It had happened to six million
> Jews, to Jesus's family
> I was not in—and not everyone
> had died, and there was a word for them
> I wanted, in my ignorance,
> to share some part of, the word survivor.63

Not insignificantly, Olds's revision of what "had happened to others" becomes,
more precisely, what "had happened to people / just a few years ago, / in Ger-

many." While Olds's use of the term "Jew" signifies a universal condition in the first version of "That Year," her revised emphasis on "people" suggests the plurality of experiences that belong to the Holocaustal event. No longer splitting herself as victim from the figure of the father as concentration-camp guard, she now identifies not just with the Jew as victim but also with the "Protestant" perpetrators. In hindsight, the earlier desire for unequivocal identification with the Holocaust is now less acted out than it is worked through. Olds's revision inflects secondary witnessing through the mediating registers of language—casting it now as a nominal pledge to the "word" *survivor*. The earlier version, while naive, is more striking in its dramatic utterance. The revision, while more "correct" politically, is so qualified in its poetic statement that it intones a banal confessionalism.

The poet's earlier, more performative investment in being rather than understanding the Holocaust survivor is attributed, in retrospect, to "ignorance." In appropriating the figure of the Jew as an analogue for the victim of domestic abuse, Olds does indeed belie a telling ignorance about the actual circumstances and psychic effects of Holocaust survival as such. In both versions of the poem, Jews are denied full subjectivity, reduced as they are to the familiar icons of Holocaust victimization. Seldom in her verse does the sacrificed humanity of the Jews penetrate through the linguistic screenings of metaphor. Lacking the actual testimony of human beings, what Olds presents are the remains of Auschwitz, stylized metaphorically in the poet's "round, white breast-shapes of the heaps."

A more considered portrait of Holocaust survivors would restore the full, complex humanity to those who are otherwise stereotyped in the popular imaginary either as innocent victims or as heroic survivors. The identity of the survivor, for poets William Heyen and Charles Reznikoff is less of a valorized condition than it is an ambivalent fate. Not infrequently, their poems explore the conditions and psychic consequences of guilt, shame, rage, despair, and emotional numbness stemming from the "choiceless choice" that survival demands in extremity.[64] Staying alive, in their poetry, is often fortuitous, morally ambiguous, and even futile in circumstances where life has already lost its value or where existential experience cannot be recalled from a state of death-in-life. Especially in the case of having lost most or all of one's community and family members, the survivor may indeed have a deeper identification with the victims who have not returned from inside extremity than with the world that persists outside it. For example, in "Mass Graves" from *Holocaust* (1975), Charles Reznikoff relates the story of the Jewish Sonderkommando whose job is to dig up and burn the corpses of thousands of mass-murdered Jews.

After discovering his loved ones among the dead, this survivor is condemned, despite his best efforts, to live:

> After the Jew who had recognized the man from his home town
> had been working in the woods for some time,
> other Jews from his own town were among the dead
> and among them—
> his wife and his two children!
> He lay down next to his wife and children and wanted the
>   Germans to shoot him;
> but one of the SS men said:
> "You still have enough strength to work,"
> and pushed him away.
> That evening he tried to hang himself
> but his friends in the cellar would not let him
> and said, "As long as your eyes are open,
> there is hope."
> The next day the man who had tried to die was on a truck.
> They were still in the woods
> and he asked one of the SS men for a cigarette.
> He himself did not smoke usually
> but he lit the cigarette and, when he was back where his
>   companions were sitting, said:
> "Look here! He gives out cigarettes.
> Why don't you all ask him for a cigarette?"
> They all got up—
> they were in the back of the truck—
> and went forwards
> and he was left behind.
> He had a little knife
> and made a slit in the tarpaulin at the side
> and jumped out;
> came down on his knees
> but got up and ran.
> By the time the SS men began shooting
> he was gone in the woods.[65]

In relating the mystery of survival, Reznikoff never tells us definitively whether the man who seemingly escapes ever really makes it out of the woods, where he has lost everything he values. The survivor's resolute act of lying down in the ditch with his dead family is an uncanny narrative of death-in-life that deranges the binary that otherwise marks a difference between the two. His escape seems gratuitous and ventured beyond any hope or redemption. It is impossible to tell whether he will take the advice of his friends against hanging himself. Having failed twice already at suicide, he receives, ironically, a kind of life sentence.

William Heyen's poem "Kotov" relates a similar brush with disaster in the story of Ivan Ivanovitch Kotov, a Russian Jew who escapes narrowly from a German *dushegubka*, or gas van:

Ivan Ivanovitch Kotov, short of speech,
clarity drifting away to mindlessness—
Kotov of stutter and suddenly empty eyes—
only Kotov, in all Russia, of all those locked inside,
survived the *dushegubka*,
the murder wagon, the gas van. Only Kotov,

pushed with his new bride
into the seatless seven-ton gray truck,
stood on that grated floor, and lived. Only Kotov,
pressed together with fifty others, would wake
in the ditch of dead, half buried, and crawl away.
He'd smelled gas, torn off one sleeve,
soaked it in his urine, covered nose and mouth,

lost consciousness, and lived, waking
in a pit of bodies somewhere outside of Krasnodar.
His wife?—he could not find her.
Except for the dead, he was alone. . . .
He stood up, staggered and groped through fields
back to the city, where he hid until the end.

Only Kotov, saved by his own brain and urine, woke
from that wedding in the death van,
in Russia, in the time of that German invention,
the windowless seven-ton gray *dushegubka*.[66]

Heyen's portrait of Kotov presents his status as survivor at "the end" of the Holocaust by way of what remains an ongoing trauma "locked inside" the event. As a split subject, Kotov is divided between his survivor self and the repressed persona who is bound by communal ties to "the dead"—consigned as they are to what Charlotte Delbo describes as the "deep" memory of the Holocaust.[67] In Kotov's "mindlessness," stuttered speech, and "empty eyes," Heyen notes the signs of psychic numbing and dissociation that are defining symptoms of his trauma. Intoned by the poem's refrain of "Only Kotov," Heyen underscores at the level of form the paradox of the survivor's luck as inseparable from the curse of his aloneness. Insofar as such verbal repetition marks a symptomatic return of trauma, the poem's dramatic action further suggests that it is the aftermath of one's survival as a missed encounter with death—not the actual moment of confronting it—that is the more traumatic awakening. Thus, the phrase "Only Kotov" acts out a retraumatization precisely as a failure to claim survival beyond the event. "Except for the dead," the poet writes, "he was alone. . . ." Employing aposiopesis, Heyen's line drifts into the eerie silence that is the only fit testimony to the death-in-life status of the survivor.[68]

To write poetry after Auschwitz is also to write outside Auschwitz. As we have seen, the belated representation of its event is fraught with cultural risks, political pitfalls, and the symptoms of retraumatization for the poet as secondary witness. Yet that more self-reflexive understanding is also possessed by the insight that what is left over from Auschwitz in the Holocaust's displaced and disjointed signs of death-in-life belong properly to neither the inside nor the outside of the binary. Circulating in excess of any imaginary mimesis, such linguistic traces of extremity take on a phantom agency as they possess the letter of one's unintended discourse in the verbal disclosures of parapraxis, catachresis, and aposiopesis. Encountered in the afterglow of Auschwitz, these arresting slips and accidents of signification clue us to the flash of a disclosed otherness as it befalls the "known" regime of the familiar.

In post-Holocaust philosophy, Jacques Derrida's phrase for that uncanny linguistic haunting, *il y a là cendres,* signifies the phantom disclosure of what is absent in genocide's discursive return. *Il y a là cendres,* as a performative paradox, repeats the verbal technique of Derrida's early neologism *différance.* Read but not heard, the silent *a* possesses *différance* as a "mysterious being" or a "hole with indeterminable borders." Its adventurous verbal agency acts as a constituting negation to defer and displace the closure of ontotheology: that is, any structuring order that would master, fix, or impose a totalizing regime of truth."[69] Similarly, what the phrase *il y a là cendres* presences as a signifying disclosure "there" (*là*) via its silent *accent grave* is effaced when heard as the feminine definite article *là* or "the." Like the "unheard-of nomination" of the *a* in *différance,* the speechless, signifying element of the *là* disseminates in excess of the binary difference between what is and is not, presence and absence, being and nonbeing. As a phenomenological disclosure, the phrase *il y a là cendres* presences what returns after Auschwitz under erasure as ash, cinder, charred leftover. Taking place as gift—as in Heidegger's *es gibt* ("it gives")—the cinder also designates the double movement of *ereignis,* which Derrida modifies from Heidegger as "inscription [that] occurs only by effacing itself."[70] The gift of fire and its light for Derrida, however, differs from Heidegger's somewhat idealizing metaphors for the disclosure of being as radiance, coming to light (*schein*), unconcealment (*aletheia*), a receiving of light (*erhellende Licht*) in the forest clearing (*lichtung*), and so on.[71]

After Auschwitz, however, fire and light no longer find their sources in the unconcealment of truth but in the demonic burning of the death-camp crematories. Heidegger's silence on the Holocaust, for Philippe Lacoue-Labarthe, is symptomatic of the latent spiritual essence of the West, whose pathology becomes fully manifest in the extermination of the Jews. "In the Auschwitz apocalypse," he writes, "it was nothing less than the West, in its essence, that revealed itself—and that continues, ever since to reveal itself. And it is thinking that event that Heidegger failed to do."[72] Derrida would supplement Heidegger's phenomenological witnessing to the shining of *aletheia* with the testimony of its monstrous other. Presenced in the cinder is the phantom trace of what has been rendered absent by industrial murder and its subsequent cultural repression. Beyond the foreclosure of historical facticity, the cinder signifies what haunts the archival limits of what we "know" about the Holocaust in what is "unknown." It speaks to the *differend* of silence that, for Lyotard, "surrounds the phrase, *Auschwitz was the extermination camp . . .* the sign that something remains to be phrased which is not, something which is not determined" (D, 57). Genocide's unfinished business calls for new discursive phrasings that address not only the dispute over historical revision but, equally important, the suffering of the traumatic past whose mourning is held in abeyance.[73] What Derrida's phrase discloses, then, is not the sign of illumination but the evidence of incineration:

> If a place is itself surrounded by fire (falls finally to ash, into a cinder tomb), it no longer is. Cinder remains, cinder there is, which we can translate: the cinder is not, is not what is. It remains *from* what is not, in order to recall at the delicate, charred bottom of itself only non-being or non-presence. Being without presence has not been and will no longer be there where there is cinder and where this other memory would speak.[74]

Ashes, insofar as they "recall" nonbeing/nonpresence, invoke an absence not unlike the affective silence of Lyotard's *differend,* whose "negative phrase . . . calls upon phrases which are in principle possible" (D, 13). Holocaust poetry of secondary witness after Auschwitz would undertake the task of writing that "other memory" effaced in the cinder whose nonpresence nevertheless returns with palpable force in language. Testimony to that charred world of nonbeing happens in the poetic recoding of key terms inflected back through the particular historicity of the extreme event.

Poetry's capacity to encrypt the phantom traces of genocide is staged in the formal returns of Anthony Hecht's masterful sestina "The Book of Yolek." A twelfth-century poetic form employed by the Provençal troubadours, the sestina is composed of thirty-six lines divided equally into six stanzas, followed by a three-line envoy. The formalism of Hecht's sestina—as a kind of poetic crypt—provides a complex, linguistic site for mourning the revenants of the Holocaust:

> "The Book of Yolek"
>
> *Wir Haben ein Gesetz,*
> *Und nach dem Gesetz soll er sterben.*
> (We Have a Law,
> And according to the Law, he must die.)
>
> The dowsed coals fume and hiss after your meal
> Of grilled brook trout, and you saunter off for a walk
> Down the fern trail. It doesn't matter where to,
> Just so you're weeks and words away from home,
> And among midsummer hills have set up camp
> In the deep bronze glories of declining day.
>
> You remember, peacefully, an earlier day
> In childhood, remember a quite specific meal:
> A corn roast and bonfire in summer camp.
> That summer you got lost on a Nature Walk;
> More than you dared admit, you thought of home:
> No one else knows where the mind wanders to.
>
> The fifth of August, 1942.
> It was the morning and very hot. It was the day
> They came at dawn with rifles to The Home
> For Jewish Children, cutting short the meal
> Of bread and soup, lining them up to walk
> In close formation off to a special camp.
>
> How often you have thought about that camp,
> As though in some strange way you were driven to,

And about the children, and how they were made to walk,
Yolek who had bad lungs, who wasn't a day
Over five years old, commanded to leave his meal
And shamble between armed guards to his long home.

We're approaching August again. It will drive home
The regulation torments of that camp
Yolek was sent to, his small, unfinished meal,
The electric fences, the numeral tattoo,
The quite extraordinary heat of the day
They all were forced to take that terrible walk.

Whether on a silent, solitary walk
Or among crowds, far off or safe at home,
You will remember, helplessly, that day,
And the smell of smoke, and the loudspeakers of the camp.
Wherever you are, Yolek will be there, too.
His unuttered name will interrupt your meal.

Prepare to receive him in your home some day.
Though they killed him in the camp they sent him to,
He will walk in as you're sitting down to a meal.[75]

As a soldier serving in World War II with the 386th Infantry of the 97th Division, Hecht helped liberate the Flossenberg Concentration Camp, where Pastor Dietrich Bonhoeffer, among many other political prisoners, had been executed. Nothing, even in Hecht's battle experience, had prepared the young soldier for the "inexpressibly horrible" scene he witnessed in the camp.[76] As poet, Hecht revisits the Holocaust belatedly to give testimony through the craft of his verse. The poem's ingenious strategy seizes on key words of everyday life—"meal," "walk," "home," "camp," "day"—to ground the present in a world that is normal, consoling, and familiar. The formal resources of the sestina allow Hecht to alter the normalizing connotations of the repeated end words, whose permutations give shape to the poem's six-line stanzas and final envoy. In the opening stanza, the conventional markers of the pastoral tradition frame these ordinary terms in a landscape whose "midsummer hills" are at a safe, bucolic distance from the disaster that is Hecht's real subject. The poem's narrative progress in the second and third stanzas subtly shifts registers from what Charlotte Delbo describes as common memory (*mémoire ordinaire*) to deep memory (*mémoire profonde*). Gradually, the poet's personal childhood memory of being lost at summer camp recalls a profound memory whose public context is based on the story of the well-known Jewish teacher Janusz Korczak, who refused to abandon the orphans under his care when they were to be deported from the Warsaw ghetto, choosing instead to accompany them to their death in the gas chambers of Treblinka. Thus, as the sestina unfolds, the present's midsummer day becomes haunted by the phantom signs of a day in 1942, whose walk for Jewish children would never return home.

Hecht's strategy in "The Book of Yolek" draws perhaps from Freud's insight in "The Uncanny"—that what is *unheimlich* (un-home-like) shares a common rootedness in its proximity to death with what is, paradoxically, most *heimlich* (home-like). Freud follows Schelling, who says of the uncanny that "everything is *unheimlich* that ought to have remained secret and hidden but has come to light."[77] "Thus," Freud concludes, "*heimlich* is a word the meaning of which develops in the direction of ambivalence, until it finally coincides with its opposite, *unheimlich*" (U, 226). Freud, of course, published "The Uncanny" in 1919—the year before *Beyond the Pleasure Principle*—where he would theorize the death instincts as underlying "repetition-compulsion." While he had not yet formulated the former in the fall of 1919, he nevertheless notes the compulsion to repeat and our awareness of our own repetitions as sources of uncanny dread and terror: "For it is possible to recognize," he writes, "the dominance in the unconscious mind of a 'compulsion to repeat' proceeding from the instinctual impulses and probably inherent in the very nature of the instincts—a compulsion powerful enough to overrule the pleasure principle, lending to certain aspects of the mind their daemonic character. . . . All these considerations prepare us for the discovery that whatever reminds us of this inner 'compulsion to repeat' is perceived as uncanny" (U, 238). Similarly, Hecht converts what were once humane signs of the good life—what we ordinarily depend on as *heimlich*—into uncanny cryptonyms of genocide. Not insignificantly, Hecht stages these genocidal hauntings precisely *in* language, whose archived linguistic traces make up the *Book* of Yolek. Thus, by operating on ordinary language precisely in the verbal repetitions constitutive of the sestina form, Hecht's midrash on genocide radically defamiliarizes everything we otherwise take for granted in everyday life. The pastoral lyricism that belongs to the poet's individual recollection dilates into the historical tragedy of a profound, social memory. After Auschwitz, Yolek's fate is imbricated in a communal trauma whose force breaches the present as a collective, involuntary memory. "You will remember, helplessly," the poet insists, "that day." Just as secondary witnessing will befall us "helplessly," so the cryptonym as a signifying gap—Yolek's "unuttered name"—will "interrupt" our daily rituals through the agency of the letter.

The phantom signs of the Holocaust possess an uncanny errancy that haunts the descendants of its victims and perpetrators alike. The poetry of William Heyen, for example, offers a sustained reflection on the legacy of the Shoah in the psychic life of his German-American family members. In the title-piece of his volume *The Swastika Poems,* Heyen remembers the Nazi graffiti defacing his house as phantom signs returning from the "unknown" night of genocide:

> They appeared, overnight,
> on our steps, like frost stars
> on our windows, their strict
> crooked arms pointing
>
> this way and that, scare—
> crows, skeletons, limbs
> akimbo. My father
> cursed in his other tongue
>
> and scraped them off,
> or painted them over.
> My mother bit her lips.
> This was all a wonder,
>
> and is: how that sign
> came to be a star flashing
> above our house when I dreamed,
> how the star's bone-white light
>
> first ordered me to follow,
> how the light began
> like the oak's leaves in autumn
> to yellow, how the star now
>
> sometimes softens the whole sky
> with its twelve sides,
> how the pen moves with it,
>
> how the heart beats with it,
> how the eyes remember.[78]

Heyen, who is of German-American descent, has reflected carefully on the dilemma of his divided allegiances both to ordinary Germans—many of whom were to varying degrees complicit with crimes against humanity—and to Jewish victims and survivors of the Holocaust. Reminiscent of Coleridge's "Frost at Midnight," Heyen's opening simile of the "frost stars" naturalizes the violent signs of vandalism that disfigure his family's steps each night. As phantom icons of the Third Reich, the swastikas take on the personified death-in-life status of "skeletons, limbs / akimbo." Dutifully "scraped" and "painted" over, this history is also encrypted in the "other tongue" of the father's German curses and the mother's speechless gesture of biting "her lips."

The family drama of repressing, rather than verbalizing, the past is symptomatic, according to Barbara Heimannsberg and Christoph J. Schmidt, of a breakdown of intergenerational communication that typifies postwar German culture. "A widespread symptomatic pattern today," they write, "is the silence within families. There is no longer any innocent tradition of storytelling between the generations."[79] Such silence also characterizes what Alexander and Margarete Mitscherlich characterize as a German "inability to mourn" the disavowed past.[80] But equally telling is the poem's narrative of German victimization, which itself, according to Eric Santner, is a common symptom of postwar German culture. After the collapse of the Third Reich, German identification with national victimization actually deflected the psychic task that ordinary Germans needed to undertake of mourning "*as Germans* for those whom they had excluded and exterminated in their mad efforts to produce their 'Germanness.'"[81] The more subtle screening out of the German shame and guilt over the Nazi genocide is the poet's identification with its victims signaled in the transcoding of the German swastika into the Jewish Star of David. Against the swastika's disturbing reminder of German atrocities, the metaphor of the "yellow" star offers a psychic consolation that "sometimes softens the whole sky / with its twelve sides." As "the pen moves with it," the star serves to dispel the unspeakable phantoms of genocidal trauma into the familiar registers of language. Poetic discourse promises to naturalize the unrepresentable into a visible, imaginary order that the "eyes remember."

Indeed, several of Heyen's poems that are meant to memorialize Jewish victims of the Holocaust actually foreclose the task of mourning through compensatory metaphors. To take one example, figurative language in "New Year's Eve: The Bridge" serves to screen out the unspeakable legacy of Auschwitz, which otherwise marks the death of God in post-Holocaust theology. "Lord," the poet charges, "Your desertion, Your clouded grace, / Your death camps still / hover over the seas, over / this slash of the new world's water, / and will."[82] Nevertheless, in the course of his prayer, Heyen welcomes the "new year" as a bridge between past and future, but only through reducing the destruction of the European Jews to a trivializing metaphor:

> Though six million
>
> stars rise in the black heavens
>
> (motes in Your myriad eye),
> I pray this still,
> and pray for earthly wisdom,
> that the new year can come. (MHS, 16)

Despite this kind of unfortunate troping—which here dehumanizes Nazi victims as "motes" in God's eye—Heyen, to his credit, has made it his lifework as poet to commemorate the Holocaust in anguished, historical detail.

As a German American, Heyen does not disclaim the psychological difficulties of his particular heritage "born of German forebears, some of whom were Nazis."[83] In "Stories," for example, he mourns the deaths of family members Wilhelm and Hermann "killed in Holland," and "over Russia . . . when Berlin / burned to the ground" (MHS, 14). His complex, familial investment in, and distance from, German national culture—with its postwar historicity of shame, guilt, loss, anger, and so on—is the subject of "Men in History." Repeating the same scenario of victimization portrayed in "The Swastika Poem," Heyen frames the annual celebration of the Volksfest on Long Island's Franklin Square with the stigma of his postwar German-American past: "Born in Brooklyn of German parents, / I remember lines scratched on our doors, / the crooked swastikas my father cursed / and painted over." Just as the swastika is "cursed / and painted over" as a motif of psychic repression, similarly, Heyen's poetry witnesses to the postwar encrypting of the name Hitler—as an effaced signifier of Nazism. The lived experience of displaced Germans takes on a rhythm of investment and disavowal of ethnic identity, recorded in Heyen's rich and sensual catalogue

> of dark bread, raffles, shooting galleries,
> beer halls, bowling alleys,
> boys in *lederhosen*
> flooded by an ocean of guttural German
> they never learned, or learned to disavow.
> I remember hourly parades under the lindens,
> the elders' white beards, the sad depths of their eyes.

I remember their talk of the North Sea,

the Rhine of Lorelei, Cologne's

twin towers, the Black Forest, the mountains,

the Hamlin piper who led everyone's children to nowhere.

But I, too, was a child: all those years

there was one word I never heard,

one name never mentioned. (FFH, 26)

Immersed in the culture and language that they "learned to disavow," Heyen's generation of German-American children are left, like the victims of the Hamlin piper, suspended "nowhere" in the diasporic space of immigrant America. Moreover, the "one name never mentioned," as a synecdoche for an entire historical epoch struck from cultural memory, marks a similar disjuncture. Denied in the German-American public sphere, such temporal deferrals and spatial displacements of communal mourning return in the phantom traces that haunt Heyen's secondary witnessing as poet of the Holocaust.

While the encrypted history of Nazism haunts Heyen's German-American identity, it is the Holocaustal revenant of Jewish victimization that possesses Adrienne Rich's divided self. In her autobiographical essay "Split at the Root: An Essay on Jewish Identity," Rich's family origins divide between, on the one hand, her mother's Southern-white-Anglo-Saxon Protestantism and, on the other, her father's Ashkenazic and Sephardic Judaism. But equally important, her testimony itself inscribes a formal doubling of narrative witness: one whose conscious story of clashing domestic investments is punctuated by the phantom of genocide's latent historicity. In the manifest narrative of her Southern past, reminders of Jewish victimization repeat themselves in the chance events of being cast as a child in school plays as Portia, Shylock's daughter in Shakespeare's *The Merchant of Venice,* and later as a character in *The School for Scandal,* which also expresses, according to Rich, "scorn for Jews and the disgust surrounding Jews and money."[84] Other than these literal occasions for acting out the stigmatized role of Jew, Rich was brought up as a Christian, owing to her father's atheism and her mother's Southern Episcopal roots. Denied in this way, any sign of Rich's Jewish identity was radically effaced in a world where "the norm was Christian . . . [and] anti-Semitism was so intrinsic as not to have a name" (SR, 106).

The splitting of her manifest, Christian self from a latent, Jewish identity was imbricated in a broader constellation of Southern cultural binaries. Jews, she explains, "were of the past, archaic, primitive, as older (and darker) cultures are supposed to be primitive; Christianity was lightness, fairness, peace on earth, and combined the feminine appeal of 'The meek shall inherit the earth' with the masculine stride of 'Onward, Christian Soldiers'" (SR, 107). Not insignificantly, it is to such earthbound and transgressive signs that Rich would later turn in fashioning a lesbian-feminist identity at midlife. As she notes in "Split at the Root," her quest for a lesbian alternative to patriarchy intersected with a return to her Jewish roots and finds embodiment in her first female lover. "The suppressed lover I had been carrying in me since adolescence," she writes, "began to stretch her limbs, and her first full-fledged act was to fall in love with a Jewish woman" (SR, 121). Rich's attachment to her Jewish lover can also be viewed as a transference that partly acts out and partly resists a key question: "what did it mean," Rich asks, "to feel myself, as I did, both anti-Semite and Jew?" (SR, 121).

That interior division is unconsciously staged early in the relationship through the key dream of a lovers' quarrel. In the dream, Rich's defensive argument with her lover reaches a telling impasse—a splitting—that befalls the couple in the revenant of the Holocaust: "Of course, I said to her in this dream, if you're going to bring up the Holocaust against me, there's nothing I can do" (SR, 121). Rich's dream of the divided self—cast in the dispute between lesbian lovers—also discloses the difficulties of mourning the Nazi genocide. Earlier in the essay Rich recollects viewing the first newsreels of the Allied liberation of the death camps as something that even now leaves her "overwhelmed by a memory of despair, a sense of inevitability more enveloping than any I had ever known" (SR, 106–7). Like the key repression of the "one name never mentioned" from William Heyen's childhood, the language that would allow Rich to mourn the past is psychically unavailable to her. The poet's overwhelming despair is symptomatic of a missed encounter not only with the dead but also with her own Jewish identification as such. The kernel of that at once public and personal trauma is doubly encrypted in the "taboo name" of Jew. "And I," she realizes, "who believed my life was intended to be so interesting and meaningful, was connected to those dead by something—not just mortality but a taboo name, a hated identity" (SR, 107).

In relating her journey back to her Jewish roots in her flirtation with ethnicity at college, in her marriage in Harvard's Hillel House to Alfred Conrad—a "real Jew" (SR, 115) with an Orthodox family background—in her mothering three sons within the Jewish culture of her husband's family, Rich also testifies to the failure not only to mourn the unknown event of the Holocaust, but to transmit its meaning for the next generation. Similar to the breakdown in generational communication typifying postwar German families, Rich's own silence represents an inability to mourn. "My sons," she admits:

> grew up knowing far more about the existence and concrete meaning of Jewish
> culture than I had. But I don't recall sitting down with them and telling them that

millions of people like themselves, many of them children, had been rounded up and murdered in Europe in their parents' lifetime. Nor was I able to tell them that they came in part out of the rich, thousand-year-old Ashkenazic culture of eastern Europe, which the Holocaust destroyed. . . . I could not tell them these things because these things were still too indistinct in my own mind. (SR, 118)

Rich's repeated insistence that she could not tell "these things" to her children presents what, precisely, she cannot knowingly tell us either.

Signs of the Holocaust punctuate the autobiographical narrative of "Split at the Root" as phantasmal non sequiturs. Disjointed and displaced, allusions to the Shoah break the manifest storyline with a latent subtext that is more often than not repressed as soon as it surfaces. For example, in the midst of musing on her identity as a woman, a lesbian, a white Southern woman, and social Christian, she writes, "According to Nazi logic, my two Jewish grandparents would have made me a *Mischling, first-degree*—nonexempt from the Final Solution" (SR, 103). This sudden and fateful identification, however, ends with a white space—a typographical gap—into which this entire line of thought disappears visually on the page. Neither does the next paragraph go on to unpack the Nazi allusion but returns to the Christian, social world of the poet's childhood. A similar repetition happens in the essay's final paragraph, where Rich again reclaims, however belatedly, the sign of the Holocaust victim by "saying, in 1982 Right Wing America, *I, too, will wear the yellow star*" (SR, 123). Other phantoms of the Holocaust return in the real survivor, who hails Rich as a fellow Jew, which the poet at age eighteen can only deny. This missed encounter with a Holocaust survivor then swerves away from any further exploration of its event to dwell on the silence of Jewish ethnic self-hatred. Elsewhere, Rich's reference to scholarship on the Holocaust similarly breaks the surface of Rich's comparative questioning of identity only to be effaced. Toward the end of the essay, the poet finds herself synthesizing African-American and Jewish scholarship, "trying in one week to read Angela Davis and Lucy Davidowicz; trying to hold throughout to a feminist, a lesbian, perspective—what does this mean?" (SR, 122). Indeed, this is the key question that goes repeatedly unanswered precisely because the poet does not possess, but rather is possessed by, the trauma of a missed encounter with the Holocaust.

More than the personal essay, poetry becomes the testimonial medium that allows Rich to witness to what returns from Auschwitz. In her sequence poem "Sources," the first section of *Your Native Land, Your Life,* Rich is careful not to screen the event through the all-too-familiar icons of Holocaust mimesis. Foregrounding instead her belated position of secondary witness, she would invoke the terminal moments where such imaginary figures of disaster—mediated as they are

by prior textual representation—reach their limit in the Real: where they are themselves consumed as cinders. "The Jews I've felt rooted among," she says, "are those
who were turned to smoke":

> Reading of the chimneys against the blear air
> I think I have seen them myself
>
> the fog of northern Europe licking its way
> along the railroad tracks
>
> to the place where all tracks end
> You told me not to look there.[85]

In such passages it is the vanishing point of the Real that is at stake in Rich's identification with the Jewish victims of the Holocaust. However naturalized here in the
personified fog "licking its way" to the site of industrial murder, those traces of disaster invoke a process of witness whose ongoing risk exceeds literary foreclosure.
The father's denial of the event's inside, his warning "not to look there"—however
internalized as resistance—is, nonetheless itself a testimony of sorts to the fact that
the impossible indeed exists and that it is "there" (*il y a là*)—it gives itself (*es gibt*)
"there"—to be witnessed. Such nonpresent nonbeing is not simply absent *there* in
the tracks where the poet's gaze reaches the end of the line. Rather, that degree
zero of the known is also the site of an address beyond the familiar: one that beck-
ons her toward the horizon of an ethical relation.

Throughout "Sources" the encrypted signifier denoting the absent "Jews"
haunts the poet with such insistent force that she must stage its address through the
figure of prosopopoeia.[86] That spectral linguistic agency calls the poet as secondary
witness into an ethical relationship with what exceeds the everyday world of the
same: "*From where?* the voice asks coldly":

> This is the voice in cold morning air
> that pierces dreams. From where does your strength come?
>
> Old things . . .
> > *From where does your strength come, you Southern Jew?*
> > *split at the root, raised in a castle of air?* (YNL, 5)

As a revenant emanating from the Holocaust, the voice personified here does not
simply interrogate the poet. More to the point, it hails her as a "Southern Jew." As
an interpellation, this query bestows a multiple and conflicted identity whose
sources are themselves "split at the root." The rhetorical question "from where?"
has no simple answer. Rather, as a speech act it asserts the otherness of an unknown

address. This verbal agency "that pierces dreams" also disorients the poet's location, deranging the frame that divides what belongs to the inside of extremity from
its outside. The implicit violence of this address lays siege to the poet's assimilated
self "raised in a castle of air" so as to unsettle any shelter she would take in the
security of her imaginary identity. This kind of psychic displacement—which is
requisite for ethical relation—begins, for Levinas in the "attestation of oneself"—
"a bearing witness to oneself": an epiphany that is "not a species of consciousness
whose ray emanates from the I; [rather] it puts the I in question. This putting in
question emanates from the other." If, as Levinas has it, "the epiphany of the face
is ethical," then it is in the face-to-face relation with the forgotten specters of the
Jews that Rich avows herself as belonging to their number.[87]

In sections 17 and 18 of "Sources," Rich attests to the ethical nexus of witness
joining her to her deceased husband, her departed father, and ultimately the
specters of the deported Ashkenazi community. The insistent repetition here of
Rich's enigmatic phrase "there is something more" conjures an ethical horizon of
secondary witness that is similarly disclosed in Derrida's enigmatic phrase *il y a là
cendres*. In mourning her husband's suicide, she also attests to herself in a face-to-
face relation to her father's ghost: "For so many years," she writes, "I had thought
you and he were in opposition. I needed your unlikeness then; now it's your likeness that stares me in the face. There is something more than food, humor, a turn
of phrase, a gesture of the hands: there is something more."

There is something more than self-hatred. That still outlives
these photos of the old Ashkenazi life:
we are gifted children at camp in the country
or orphaned children in kindergarten
we are hurrying along the rare book dealers' street
with the sunlight striking one side
we are walking the wards of the Jewish hospital
along diagonal squares young serious nurses
we are part of a family group
formally taken in 1936
with tables, armchairs, ferns
(behind us, in our lives, the muddy street
and the ragged shames
the street-musician, the weavers lined for strike)
we are part of a family wearing white head-bandages
we were beaten in a pogrom

The place where all tracks end
is the place where history was meant to stop
but does not stop where thinking
was meant to stop but does not stop
where the pattern was meant to give way at last

                                          but only

becomes a different pattern

                       terrible, threadbare

strained familiar on-going. (YNL, 20)

In this ethical face-off, Rich casts the voice of the specter in an indeterminate mode of address. Indeed, the voice inscribed here disrupts the visual frame of the photographic image—separating then and now, inside from outside, us from them.[88] Dispersed as it is here in the first-person plural "we," Rich's poetic address incorporates the relation of a nonpresence—the absence of the "orphans," and "gifted children"—with her own ethical presence as witnessing poet and, by extension, our participation as readers. Who "we" are "in our lives" is thus imbricated in the poem with those "gifted children," who at once bestow and are given to a spectral, death-in-life aura that backlights and "outlives" their documentary remains. They are not fixed "there" by the imaginary mimesis of the visible, and they will not stay put "there" "in 1936." What is "more" "there" *inside* Auschwitz "where all tracks end" is, as Rich attests, not just a terminus but a horizon of ethical relation where "we" enter into the at once familiar and terrible address of witness.

The return of the repressed—here, in the poetic intersection of personal Jewish identity and collective Jewish victimization—also gives shape to the serial poetics of Rachel Blau DuPlessis. Not unlike Rich, DuPlessis also witnesses to the phantom address of the Holocaust as it befalls the formal defiles of the letter. Her poem "Working Conditions" from her 2001 volume *Drafts 1–38, Toll* thematizes the aleatory, chance event where language as such is possessed by the "enormities" of what history has rendered precisely "unspeakable":

This kind of speaking
doubles the unspeakable.

With every word
ossuarial shadows.

Come, the gathering. But chancy.
Which randomness is shocking

and may thus motivate more
toward silence than toward speech.

For who can, not silent,
accept the vocation

to acknowledge, to describe,
or even to allow

the enormities

of which one must,
if speaking,
speak.[89]

More than a craft, the poet's job of work for DuPlessis assumes the ethical demands of a "vocation." Such a calling, moreover, borders on the priestly, speaking as it does here out of the "ossuarial shadows" that connote literally the crypt where the bones of the dead are interred. Not unlike Wallace Stevens's poet as "metaphysician in the dark,"[90] DuPlessis's authorial persona is committed to working conditions that demand a special form of attention to the *via negativa* wherein is revealed "[n]othing that is not there and the nothing that is."[91] But DuPlessis's ruminations on the Holocaust are more historically specific than modernism's existential ruminations on nonbeing, mortality, dread—everything that, say, Hemingway conjures through the incantation of "nada" in "A Clean Well-Lighted Place." What is at stake in the absence that DuPlessis addresses and that she is addressed by, increasingly in the evolution of her long poem *Drafts*, goes to the heart of the Holocaust and "the enormities" of its postwar legacy. Not merely a subject, theme, or content for her writing, the Holocaust actively shapes the formal presentation of DuPlessis's long poem in the rhetorical situation of speaking to and being spoken by its traumatic event.

Silenced for the most part in the critical reception of postwar verse, the Holocaust as an encrypted subtext has left its mark, nevertheless, on the formal evolution of American poetry. Yet the determining role of the Holocaust on the formal mode of DuPlessis's avant-garde poetics—her writing's spatial arrangement and temporal presentation on the page—is something that has eluded critical readers of her work. Despite the poet's own theoretical foregrounding of Jewish identity as a key issue in her writing, her critical reception has curiously avoided discussing it. For example, Lynn Keller's chapter on DuPlessis in *Forms of Expansion* places her in the formal continuum that joins Robert Duncan and George Oppen to *Language* poets such as Beverly Dahlen, who write in the American long poem tradition. Keller follows DuPlessis's own definition of her "serial poetry" as "an argument made of leaps," noting that "its flexible structure is generally disjunctive, so that meaning develops as much from the gaps between the constituent parts as from their suture."[92]

While offering a helpful description of DuPlessis's poetic method, Keller's reading of the nature and significance of serial form in *Drafts* is blocked by her strategy of affiliating DuPlessis to the literary tradition of the American long poem. In Keller's critical narrative, DuPlessis owes a fourfold debt to her precursor, Robert Duncan. Keller's framing of Duncan as a poet who is subtly mindful of his own literary genealogy follows from a line of generic criticism on the American long poem best exemplified in the work of Michael Bernstein.[93] In Keller's reading, Duncan becomes a crucial literary forerunner for DuPlessis in his turn from Pound's emphasis on the poetic line to the "unbounded field," in his investment in Freud, in the example of his social alienation, and in both poets' "shared response to linguistic belatedness, their being frankly and unembarrassedly 'derivative' writers."[94] While Keller's reading strategy would both legitimate the American long poem as a literary tradition and open it to the specific innovations of female talents, she misses the ways in which DuPlessis's poetic form in *Toll* is profoundly inflected by Continental theory as it intersects with the modern destruction of the European Jews. As a consequence of her critical agenda, Keller elides DuPlessis's crucial links to Walter Benjamin, Nicholas Abraham, Maria Torok, Charlotte Delbo, and Paul Celan. A more attentive reading of *Toll* would account for DuPlessis's sophisticated appropriations of Benjamin, post-Freudian psychoanalysis, and Holocaust testimony to compose a poetics of mourning: one that would "witness / after the eclipse of witness" (T, 119–20).

Such a post-Holocaust reading of DuPlessis would interpret the "belatedness" she struggles with in *Toll* as signifying not just the anxiety of a literary relation but the trauma of a world-historical condition:

> I'm after everything, and after nothing.
> A belatedness so strong
> I come,
> even after what is
> not there,
>
> after eradication
> Who inhabits one's own time

who can be witness
after the eclipse of witness

cannot speak. O poetry
—again and again no more poetry. (T, 119–20)

Clearly, the poet's belatedness describes not just her marginality to a past literary
tradition but, more profoundly, her loss of historical location. How else are we to
account for the key term "belatedness" linked as it is here to the ominous phrase
"after eradication"? A literal uprooting—*e* (out), *radix* (root)—eradication inflects
the poet's belatedness through the connotations of extermination and annihilation.
This belatedness expresses a breaching of time. Employing the white space of the
page, DuPlessis's pattern of poetic enjambment eloquently deranges the immediacy of the moment as it now presences "what is / not there": the absence that has
befallen temporality as "eradication."

The rhetorical consequences of the "after" entail the same complication of subject positioning—the same doubling of the personal lyric I and the collective witness—that Adrienne Rich negotiates in testifying to oneself mediated by the spectral address of the Other. Moreover, for Duplessis the task of bearing "witness /
after the eclipse of witness" poses the urgent, post-Auschwitz question of the ethics
of poetic form. What manner of poetics, that is, can testify to that which for the secondary witness is not only unknown but ever at risk, as Adorno reminds us, of barbarous cultural reification. For his part, Adorno insists that any contemporary
thinking that fails to reflect on its belatedness after Auschwitz is complicit with the
obscenity of the death camps. "If thought," he writes, "is not measured by the extremity that eludes the concept, it is from the outset in the nature of the musical
accompaniment with which the SS liked to drown out the screams of its victims."[95]
Adorno, of course, included affirmative poetics in the "superfluous trash" thrown
up by postwar culture, declaring in his famous slogan, "To write poetry after
Auschwitz is barbaric."[96] This judgment, however, has not stood as the final word
on contemporary verse; in fact, it has prompted a number of counterstatements, as
in the rejoinder, say, of Edmond Jabès: "Adorno once said that after Auschwitz we
can no longer write poetry. I say that after Auschwitz we *must* write poetry but
with wounded words."[97] It is precisely against this ethicopolitical dilemma that
DuPlessis marks poetry's, by now, impossible vocation. As poet, she invokes her
muse through a conflicted, double sign of apostrophe—one that inscribes both
faith in and suspicion of the poet's job of work: "O poetry / —again and again no
more poetry."

Contemporary criticism's framing of *Toll* within the canonical protocols of literary tradition, advanced as it is through a critical silence on DuPlessis's text of the Jews, not only misses the self-reflexive belatedness of her rhetorical situation but is itself symptomatic of the disciplinary forgetting that *Toll* otherwise resists. Read psychoanalytically, Keller's desire to affiliate DuPlessis to Duncan—to return *Toll* to the formal regime of likeness, resemblance, sameness—forgets precisely that which—by virtue of difference, heterogeneity, excess—escapes the totality of the One in what Lyotard nominates as "the jews." Lyotard's lowercase usage of "the jews," distinguished from the uppercase signifier for the historical Jews, signifies the irreducible difference of *ek-sistence* that is forgotten, expunged, repressed in any act of conceptual representation, political instantiation, or ideological narration. "The jews are the object," Lyotard explains, "of a dismissal with which Jews, in particular, are afflicted in reality."[98] What is definitive about DuPlessis's poetic achievement in *Toll,* particularly in its later "Drafts," does not derive from any conventional or normative representation of the Holocaust. More radically, her poetry inscribes a phantom textuality—one that presences "the jews" in the forgotten trace that returns after eradication of the historical Jews.

Belatedness happens for DuPlessis, as for Rich, not only in the missed encounter with the world-historical eradication of the Jews but also in her personal repression of Jewish identification. Similar to Rich's childhood, DuPlessis's upbringing replaced Judaism with the secular humanism of the Ethical Culture movement. In this milieu, she recalls, "the Holocaust was the great shadow"; its specter haunted her household in the "shadowy comments" that were further screened in her mother's Yiddish cryptonyms of *chaserei* and *tsuris* (filth and trouble), *gefeyrlach* (dangerous, terrible), and *mishigas* (madness, craziness).[99] The obscured legacy of both Judaism and the Holocaust inflects DuPlessis's Jewish identity through a phantom textuality. Speaking from the belatedness of world-historical trauma, the Jewish subject position, as she inscribes it, is a "posthumous site":

> I have a post-Holocaust identity as confronting (though one never can) an ineffable enormity that Happened (with many Agents) to many persons, some just like myself. Post-Holocaust writers—Paul Celan, Edmond Jabès, Primo Levi, George Oppen—I read as a significant core of my cultural and ontological identity. My current poetry makes many allusions to Jewish materials—Yiddish words, Old Testament narratives like Jacob and the Angel, midrashic form, self-commenting questions, as well as allusions to the concentration camps. I take it that the only apt cultural ambition is to speak from a posthumous site, to speak as if yours were the

only shard that would be rescued, to speak in the medium "anguage." This poetics clearly bears the marks of its origins. (C, 136)

Opening verse writing to the unique social pressures and psychic affects of Jewish historicity, for DuPlessis, calls for an avant-garde mode of poetic testimony—one that complicates her filiation to the American tradition. If DuPlessis composes a poetics of serial traces, then her method in *Toll* takes its "origin" as much from midrash as from American literary modernism. Serial technique in *Toll* is not merely a formal intervention in the modernist encyclopedic long poem. More to the point, DuPlessis's avant-garde procedures are imbricated in an ethicopolitical mode of poetic testimony: one that witnesses to the trauma of "the jews" as it has been visited on the Jews.[100]

DuPlessis's poetic witnessing has consequences for the visual arrangement and pacing of the verse line in relation to the opaque space of the page. While poetic phrasings are collaged in relation to each other as texts, they also emerge and recede in testimony's punctuated, temporal relation to the kind of affective silence that Lyotard identifies in the *differend*. "The differend," he writes,

> is the unstable state and instant of language wherein something which must be able to be put into phrases cannot yet be. This state includes silence, which is a negative phrase, but it also calls upon phrases which are in principle possible. This state is signaled by what one ordinarily calls a feeling: "One cannot find the words," etc. . . . What is at stake in a literature, in a philosophy, in a politics perhaps, is to bear witness to differends by finding idioms for them. (D, 13)

Linguistic collage, for DuPlessis, is shot through with psychic moments that befall language in the "gap," silence, or "negative phrase" where one is speechless before disaster. As poet, DuPlessis questions precisely "what illusion, what delusion, what disillusion / writes these gaps?" (T, 111). Poetic form for DuPlessis, then, involves not just the flat spatial arrangement of collaged citation on the page but also inflects this visuality through a temporal interplay between the spoken phrase and the negative phrase. This dynamic process of poetics is something she describes as "disfigured / form as experienced / struggle, over the mark. / And over the effacement" (T, 128–29). "Anguage" is the ludic neologism that captures DuPlessis's crossing of the anguish that belongs to Jewish historicity with poetic utterance:

> There have appeared, as the work goes along, a number of allusions to elements of Jewish tradition. It's a creolized mix: certain holidays and customs; certain compelling Hebrew scriptural stories such as Jacob and the angel; some words in Yiddish; a

pervasive and incurable nomadism and sense of the exilic; a number of humble shadows of the Holocaust. Can this be summarized? The poem is inflected with a peculiar (and of course resistant) "Jewishness" because it is about text and textuality? about debris? about "anguage"—a cross between language and anguish, and maybe anger?[101]

By her own account, DuPlessis grants a certain autonomy of expression to the "anguage" she witnesses in her verse. Not only does her repeated questioning of her writing's Jewishness imply its overdetermined textual status, but her passive phrasing in regard to composing her poetic midrash—"there have appeared"—signifies on the phantom haunting of the Jews in Derrida's phrase *il y a là cendres*. As a consequence of anguage, poetic form in *Toll* advances beyond the example of encyclopedic modernism by inflecting its collaged, visual surface through the phenomenological registers of the phantom trace. Thus, *Toll's* rhythms of incarnation and withdrawal, of remembrance and forgetting—the poem's temporal interplay of absence and presence, "gap" and "shard," "missing scrap" and ephemeral "thing"— are not merely to be read but "rescued" through secondary acts of witness.

What is at stake in "the shard that would be rescued" through poetic witnessing is the subject of "Draft 17: Unnamed." The trauma of this poem's primal scene is mediated by the found citation of a *Philadelphia Inquirer* headline, "Lithuanians haunted by Holocaust":

But what I meant is this.
> *She stood at the pit*
>> *where, this 50 years,*
155 Jews were shot.
> *There, near a field of rye,*
>> *she'd found dozens of notes and addresses*
tossed away
> *moments before their deaths.*
>> *To this day,*
she regrets
> *that, out of fear,*
>> *she did not pick them up.*
The poetics seems plain.
> Since then
>> there are many people spend their time
picking up the notes.
> But they are not there.
>> They are as gone as possible to be.

So the gathering
    is impossible.
        But still the shapes are bowed,
and search
    this otherwhere of here.
        Yet had they actually
been there
    that time
        being remembered,
it is equally possible
        they too would have left
            all of them where they lay.
What illusion, what delusion, what disillusion
      writes these gaps?
            tries these missing bits and scraps?
It is not elegy
    though elegy seems the nearest category of genre
        raising stars, strewing flowers. . . .
It's not that I have not
    done this, in life or wherever I
        needed to
or throwing out the curled tough leather
    of the dead
        the cracked insteps of unwalkable shoes,
but it is not the name or term
    for what is meant
        by this inexorable bending.
And it is not "the Jews"
    (though of course it's the Jews),
        but Jews as an iterated sign of this site.

Words with (to all intents and purposes)
no before and after
hanging in a void of loss
the slow and normal whirlwind
from which it roars
they had not ever meant to be so lost,
so little wordth. (T, 110–11)

Unlike Alicia Ostriker's representations on Babii Yar, DuPlessis does not attempt to revisit the literal scene of genocide in her poetry. Mass murder is mediated by the *Inquirer*'s readable report, but its actual referent remains—as the title has it— unnamed and unknowable. But more to the point, "Draft 17: Unnamed" is not so a much a poem about the Holocaust as it is about writing the Holocaust.[102] The story of the literal event is itself an allegory for the situation of poetry after Auschwitz.

To begin with, none of the "dozens of notes" survive the disaster from which they are addressed. Each becomes the lost sign of a missed encounter between writer and reader. Composed at the literal edge of the eradication, these last words no longer possess the humanist faith in communicable meaning. Rather, as dead letters they circulate in excess of any normative correspondence. "Tossed away" when there was no one to "pick them up," these "missing bits and scraps" of tex-tuality remain undelivered and unclaimed, "as gone as possible to be." "Hanging in a void of loss," such spectral signifiers befall the poet's discourse reducing lan-guage itself, in her ludic coinage, to "little wordth." Witnessed in "The Unnamed" are the dire consequences of the Holocaust on language's symbolic correspon-dence between words and things. The industrial murder of the Jews also marks a terminus in any romantic faith in the organic symbol that signifies, according to Walter Benjamin, the "unity of the material and transcendental object."[103] It is this severing of language's organic connection to a given world of transcendental sig-nified meaning to which DuPlessis alludes in her linguistic figure of the "Jews as an iterated sign of this site": the site, that is, where poetic language passes from sym-bol into allegory.

DuPlessis's poetics of the fragment, the shard, the trace is shaped by Benjamin's displacement of romantic symbolism in his allegorical reading of the baroque Ger-man "mourning play" (*Trauerspiel*). In *The Origin of German Tragic Drama*, Benjamin substitutes the image as fragment and ruin for the organic wholeness of the ro-mantic symbol. The aesthetics of catastrophe, destruction, ruin—which also create the possibility for historical redemption in time—derive in part from the Lurianic Kabbalah, which Gershom Scholem reads as a response to Jewish expulsion from Spain in 1492. Specifically, according to the doctrine of the "Breaking of the Ves-sels," as Susan Handelman summarizes it, "in the process of creation, the divine forces 'shattered' their containing 'vessels'; the fragments of those vessels 'fell' and became 'embedded' in the lowest material worlds. Humanity's task is to repair those vessels and so bring about redemption of the cosmos itself."[104] Writing in the ruins of twentieth-century anguage, DuPlessis composes a process poetics that mortifies the aura of the lyric voice even as it resists the narrative closure of epic. Punctuated by rupture, her verse valorizes such key terms as "errancy" (100), "disconnection" (106), "simulacra" (112), "fragments" (115), "incomplete leavings" (122), "effacement" (129), "diaspora" (131), "randomness" (132), "unfinished business" (136), "vagaries" (136), "labyrinth" (138), "accidents" (148), "fissures" (150), "diffusion" (155), "forgetting" (162), "corrosion" (175).

DuPlessis mobilizes these chaotic forces, paradoxically enough, for the redemptive task of making what Benjamin described in his "Theses on the Philosophy of History" as the "tiger's leap" beyond the "homogeneous, empty time" of normative historicism into the vital "presence of the now" (*Jetztzeit*).[105] In "Draft 24: Gap," disorder becomes a resource that yields in the "fracture" of normative time and speech a new "hinge" for revolutionary constellations of being—what DuPlessis, citing Benjamin, gleans in the "chips of messianic time":

> a seam
> > breaking inside existence
> a vent
> > that flanged
> through dark, and between
> > a wander, all awander
> > > fracture and hinge.
> One asks for meaning
> > and, faced with any bit of fleck along the crack,
> is eager: is it
> > in that spot, can one care
> for it, is it there?
>
> Now is the now. No matter what. No readiness
> for its ungrouted forms.
> Meaning is in its lack and in its bet,
> in trips that trigger rime.
>
> Let these be called the (underwired) "chips
> > of messianic time." (T, 158)

The linguistic wager that DuPlessis takes as poet in the aleatory drafts of her "ungrouted forms" and "trigger rime" would witness to the presencing of provisional truths in the "fleck" and "spot" of the *Jetztzeit*. Such disclosure happens in poetic discourse neither through one's intentional lyricism nor bardic metanarration. Rather, the tiger's leap into the now comes, for DuPlessis, precisely in the parapraxis of language itself down to the most minute trace of inscription, what in "Draft 15: Little" she calls, from the Hebrew, the "yod"—the smallest signifying element:

> Some clocks stopped but not
> other clocks, tick and tock and
> I was part of all that it,
> a lucky nothing
> not in the way of particular harm,
> half witness half witless
>> dot—a little
>> yod or yid
> amid the clamors of dawn,
> waking inside the whiteness,
> before anything is given—
> that is, taken.
> . . . . . .
> Not hero, not polis, not story, but it.
>> It multiplied.
>> It engulfing.
>> It excessive.
> "It" like X that marks the spot, that is, the spots,
> an ever wily while, a wilderness of hope.
> The spot of almost hopeless hope.
> Can barely credit it. (T, 100–102)

However belated in her authorial role—which DuPlessis ironically depicts here as "half witness half witless"—she nevertheless asserts a qualified faith in poetry's linguistic power to disrupt the normative continuum of universal historicism. Mindful of what it means to write poetry after Auschwitz, DuPlessis nevertheless would glean Benjamin's "chips of messianic time" from what Eliot more despairingly characterized in "*Ulysses,* Order and Myth" as the "immense panorama of futility and anarchy which is modern history."[106] Within the complexly mediated postmodern/postgenocidal/postmarxist registers that DuPlessis inscribes, the revolutionary moment of Benjamin's "material historicism" happens neither in the social solidarity of a "polis," nor in some saving ideological narrative of heroism and progress. Rather, such imaginary programs of universal historicism are arrested by the signifying yod of the poet's midrash as it punctuates the linear "story" of conventional historicism with the "truth" of language's symbolic procedures.

As one who possessed what Hannah Arendt described as the "gift of thinking po-
etically," Walter Benjamin remains a key precursor for contemporary writers who
would similarly inflect postwar poetics through the registers of contemporary philosophy and historical materialism. Moreover, the return of Benjamin as a cultural
signifier variously for the genocide of the Jews, the death of the Western
intellectual, the exile of Marxism, the disaster of state communism, and
so on—in its repetition—haunts contemporary poetics as a symptom of collective
trauma. Thus, Benjamin's "Theses on the Philosophy of History" not only underwrites *Toll* but also frames the poetic subject matter and technique of Carolyn
Forché's 1994 volume *The Angel of History*. Forché's book takes its title from Benjamin's ninth thesis—his famous meditation on Paul Klee's *Angelus Novus:*

> A Klee painting named "Angelus Novus" shows an angel looking as though he is
> about to move away from something he is fixedly contemplating. His eyes are star-
> ing, his mouth is open, his wings are spread. This is how one pictures the angel of his-
> tory. His face is turned toward the past. Where we perceive a chain of events, he sees
> one single catastrophe which keeps piling wreckage and hurls it in front of his feet.
> The angel would like to stay, awaken the dead, and make whole what has been
> smashed. But a storm is blowing in from Paradise; it has got caught in his wings with
> such violence that the angel can no longer close them. The storm irresistibly propels
> him into the future to which his back is turned, while the pile of debris before him
> grows skyward.[107]

Typically, reviewers of Forché's appropriated image have been content to state the
obvious: that she uses Benjamin's angel as a figure for the contemporary poet confronted by the fragmentation of everyday life in the twentieth century.[108] In fact,
however, Forché's relation to Benjamin's figure and the function it serves in her
writing are more complex and more provocative than such casual generalizations
would credit.

To begin with, both writers became fascinated with the angel when history itself reached a crisis point in their careers.[109] Benjamin acquired Paul Klee's 1920 wa-
tercolor *Angelus Novus* in 1921, and its iconic meaning would undergo major transformations in his writing up until his death in 1940. Benjamin, as early as 1922,
speculated about his forthcoming journal to be published under the same title as
Klee's painting. By 1933, the angel appears in his autobiographical parable "Agesilaus Santander." This earlier and more martial incarnation, with "wings . . . sharp
as knives," holds the figure of humanity "firmly in his gaze. . . . In order to pull him
along behind himself, on that path into the future on which he came and that he
knows so well that he traverses it without turning back, and without turning his

glance away from the one he has chosen."[110] The utopian agency personified in this angel shows an active commitment to historical becoming—one that limns Benjamin's biographical investments at the time in the Bolshevik revolution and the Soviet Union's first Five-Year Plan.

Benjamin's socialism would evolve in the direction of antifascism during the Popular Front years of the midthirties in such seminal essays as "The Author as Producer," which he presented in April 1934 at the Institute for the Study of Fascism in Paris, and in "The Work of Art in the Age of Mechanical Reproduction" delivered a year later for the French Communist Party at the Congress for the Defense of Culture. Nevertheless, Benjamin's avant-gardism would gradually distance him from the social-realist tendencies of the Comintern, while the Moscow trials and purges of 1936 through 1938 would further alienate him from the consolidation of Stalinist rule in the Soviet Union. Benjamin's tenth thesis, following on the August 1939 Soviet-German nonaggression pact, is quite pointed in its tirade against this strategic arrangement coming, he writes, "at a moment when the politicians in whom the opponents of Fascism had placed their hopes are prostrate and confirm their defeat by betraying their own cause" (I, 258). Thus in 1940, the representational shift in Klee's *Angelus Novus*—as Benjamin transforms it from active agent to passive victim of material history—anticipates his own suicide later that year on September 26, trapped as he was in flight from the Gestapo at Port-Bou on the closed Spanish border.

The repetition, then, of Benjamin's angel of history, as Forché foregrounds it in her third book of verse, sets up a grave resonance with disaster—one that mourns not only the personal tragedy that befell Benjamin but, by extension, the world-historical novum that ended in the Nazi extermination of the European Jews. Her choice sets up a comparative frame implicating Benjamin's fate in our own postmodern condition. For her part, Forché was uniquely positioned by the end of the 1980s as a writer of international social conscience and an award-winning American poet. Not unlike Benjamin, who faced mounting political and aesthetic dilemmas in the 1930s, Forché was similarly challenged in the 1990s with negotiating contradictory professional roles as a matter of institutional praxis. A 1975 winner of the prestigious Yale Younger Poets Award for her first book of poetry *Gathering the Tribes*, Forché went on in 1981 to receive the Lamont Poetry Selection Award of the Academy of American Poets for *The Country Between Us*. The book's widely read account of her experience as an Amnesty International witness in El Salvador was both praised and attacked for its mode of poetic testimony. In her critical reception, the clash between personal lyricism and history implicated her identity as poet at the heart of this pressing cultural divide.[111]

Working through the crisis of poetry's contested place in the public sphere, Forché would spend the next decade in redefining verse's relation to historical extremity. She made this intervention first, however, not in her role as an award-winning poet but as the editor of the anthology *Against Forgetting: Twentieth-Century Poetry of Witness*. Distinguishing between the "personal" versus the "political" poem, Forché foregrounded the former as always already mediated by the latter. Beyond subjective lyricism, the personal in Forché's account was not dismissed *tout court* but recoded as "one of the most powerful sites of resistance" to the "larger structures of the economy and the state [which] circumscribe, if not determine, the fragile realm of individuality." The cultural work of *Against Forgetting* promoted an international poetics committed to "the social": what Forché advanced as "a third term, one that can describe the space between the state and the supposedly safe havens of the personal."[112] Meanwhile, Forché was also composing a new volume of poems that would finesse the charge of personal lyricism leveled against *The Country Between Us*.

Published the year after *Against Forgetting*, Forché's 1994 volume *The Angel of History* would inflect her poetic voice through the kind of socially mediated textuality that she had promoted as an editor. "The first-person, free-verse, lyric-narrative poem of my earlier years," she writes in the "Notes" to *Angel*, "has given way to a work which has desired its own bodying forth: polyphonic, broken, haunted, and in ruins, with no possibility of restoration" (AH, 81). Like DuPlessis's fragmented poetics, Forché's verse also follows the compositional method of Benjamin's textual montage in the *Arcades Project*. While Forché's poem offers certain narrative lines of testimony gleaned from her travels in Beirut, the former Czechoslovakia, El Salvador, Hiroshima, and Paris, these scenic continuities are disrupted with textual citation gathered from her reading in Elias Canetti, René Char, Günter Eich, C. W. King, Gershom Scholem, Georg Trakl, Paul Valéry, and Elie Wiesel as well as the oral testimony taken from Claude Lanzmann's *Shoah* of Itzhak Dugin, Simon Srebnik, and Motke Zaidl.

Organized into a five-part format with a framing epigraph and "Notes" section, Forché's "polyphonic" long poem begs comparison with Eliot's *The Waste Land* and aspires, arguably, to that distinctive register of cultural authority. The postmodern difference, however, distinguishing Forché's moment from Eliot's has everything to do with the world-historical rupture of the Holocaust. Countering Eliot's anti-Semitic representations, Forché foregrounds the historical fate of the European Jews not only in her title but in Ellie's survival narrative, as well as the Sonderkommando stories of Dugin, Srebnik, and Zaidl. Forché also calls into crisis any metaphysical gesture toward the kind of theological consolation that, however tentative in *The Waste Land,* develops into a committed faith in Anglo-Catholicism proper in Eliot's subsequent career. While God speaks in Eliot's "What the Thunder Said," his silence during the Holocaust makes him a pathological deity for Forché after Auschwitz. If "le silence de Dieu," for Wiesel, "is Dieu," then for Ellie—Forché's roommate in the Hôtel-Dieu—"Le Dieu est un feu. A psychopath" (AH, 7). During her years of hiding in the Holocaust, "winter took one of her sons, and her own attempt to silence him, the other" (AH, 7). Her own children, her parents, aunts, uncles, friends—like the Jewish children of Izieu—have been "deported" to the fate of industrial murder, and it is the testimony of their absence that cries out in "le silence de Dieu." Unmourned and largely forgotten, they have passed to the other side of the boundary that Forché (re)marks in the symbolic hospital sign "NO ADMITTANCE":

> No—a little residue of nothing. And admittance, what does it mean? That they are / not going to blame themselves for anything. / But the deportees, no, there is nothing between the word and those who are not, who do not reviennent. / And if language is an arbitrary system, one must not go further than the sign NO ADMITTANCE / in the Hôtel-Dieu on the Place du Parvis Notre Dame. (AH, 9)

The ethicopolitical and metaphysical divide that the Holocaust introduces into Western history—which allows for "NO ADMITTANCE"—is not only the subject that Forché revisits and mourns in *The Angel of History.* But equally important, her long poem inscribes the trace of that novum in its formal procedures. Forché's citational poetic technique, which flows from her understanding of the postmodern condition after Auschwitz, culminates in her textual appropriation of Benjamin's *Angelus Novus.*

Recent commentary on Benjamin's description of Paul Klee's painting has been shaped by the allegory's epigraph, which excerpts Gershom Scholem's poem "Gruss vom Angelus" ("Greetings from Angelus") composed for Benjamin in celebration of his birthday in 1921:

> Mein Flügel ist zum Schwung bereit,
> ich kehrte gern zurück,
> denn blieb ich auch lebendige Zeit,
> ich hätte wenig Glück.

> My wing is ready for flight,
> I would like to turn back.
> If I stayed timeless time,
> I would have little luck.[113]

Informed by Scholem's instruction on Talmudic angelology, Benjamin's rendering of the *Angelus Novus,* emphasizes its ephemeral status as God's *malach* (messenger) both here as well as in his 1931 essay on Karl Kraus, Viennese author and editor of *Die Fackel (The Torch).* Concluding this earlier piece, Benjamin depicts the new angel as "one of those who, according to the Talmud, are at each moment created anew in countless throngs, and who once they have raised their voices before God, cease and pass into nothingness. Lamenting, chastising, or rejoicing? No matter— on this evanescent voice the ephemeral work of Kraus is modeled. Angelus—that is the messenger in the old engravings."[114] While Benjamin can still privilege the *malach's* "evanescent voice" in 1931, by 1940 the violence of history—"piling wreckage upon wreckage"—overtakes the Angelus, effectively canceling his role as God's liaison. Instead, he is swept up in an allegory of *catastrophe* that disfigures temporality, lending another turn—strophe *(strephein)*—to the trope of devastation and redemption in Messianic tradition. Futurity here spells dystopia, where, as Geoffrey Hartman puts it, "catastrophe becomes proleptic."[115] The new angel still intends to forward the messianic task of *tikkun* or mending the fragmented spectacle of modernism: indeed, "his mouth is open, his wings are spread." "But a storm is blowing from Paradise; it has got caught in his wings with such violence that the angel can no longer close them."

In Benjamin's last meditation on the *Angelus Novus* the metaphysical power of voice to mediate between the secular and the divine is suddenly arrested by a catastrophic visuality whose gaze befalls the thought, intention, and representation of messianic materialism as pure disaster. "This," Benjamin writes, "is how one pictures the angel of history": Klee's painting "shows" an angel "looking"; he is "fixedly contemplating"; "his eyes are staring"; "his face is turned toward the past"; "he sees one single catastrophe." Such a scopic *mise en abyme* exceeds both the imaginary and symbolic registers of experience, confounding them in what Jacques Lacan would designate as the Real: that which variously precedes, eludes, resists, and negates all imaginary identification and symbolic representation. If the Angel retains any Talmudic identity as *malach,* then his message remains unassimilable to the regime of communicative meaning. Instead, the messenger's gaze incorporates the force of the Real as a spectral address. Within the "pile of debris" of "what we call progress," it is the gaze of the Real that punctuates our imaginary investments in the symbolic repetition of modernism's "wreckage upon wreckage."

Lacan discusses the address of the gaze as it bears on repetition and the Real in his 1964 seminar II on *The Four Fundamental Concepts of Psychoanalysis.* In it, Lacan offers his reading of Freud's famous dream of the burning child that opens chapter 7, "The Psychology of the Dream Process," in *The Interpretation of Dreams.* Briefly, following the death of his child, a father hires an old man to say prayers over the corpse before burial. In the room next to where the body is laid out, the father falls asleep and dreams that his child comes to him and "reproachfully" exclaims: "Father, can't you see I'm burning?" The father awakens to discover that the watchman too has succumbed to sleep and, meanwhile, a candle had fallen by chance burning the arm of the corpse. Freud interprets the dream as the father's wish fulfillment that the child become alive once more thus delaying his reawakening to the reality of his death. Moreover, the impulse to dream is, in turn, motivated by a more fundamental desire pertaining to consciousness as such: that is, to sleep.

Lacan, however, reads the dream somewhat differently so as to discern a traumatic "nucleus" in the accidental encounter between the dreamer and the chance event. Appropriating Aristotle's distinction between the *automaton* and *tuché*, Lacan links the former—the dreaming father as *automaton*—to the Symbolic register insofar as his position in the dream is governed by the pleasure principle in the subject's compulsion to repeat (*Wiederholungszwang*) as manifest in language, bodily symptoms, and other processes of symbolization.[116] The return of the Real as *tuché* happens in the seemingly chance event, accident, or "missed encounter." Yet, the trauma of the father's dream inheres not so much in the external fall of the candle but in the internalized force of the child's address. "Is there not more reality in this message," Lacan asks, "than in the noise by which the father also identifies the strange reality of what is happening in the room next door?"[117] However "strange" the external scene of the burning child's corpse appears, the uncanny enigma of the child's address remains more traumatically unassimilable to signification precisely as it returns in the latent kernel and leftover otherwise screened in the *automaton*'s manifest representations. Not just a function of pleasure or wish fulfillment, the repetition of the father's failure of vision finds its origin, for Lacan, in the splitting of the subject through the missed encounter with the Real.[118] "That is why," Lacan writes, "it is necessary to ground this repetition first of all in the very split that occurs in the subject in relation to the encounter. . . . It is precisely through this that the Real finds itself, in the subject, to a very great degree the accomplice of the drive."[119]

Part of Lacan's project in the 1964 seminar on encountering the Real is, as he says there, "to grasp how the *tuché* is represented in visual apprehension" (FFC, 77). Inflecting his discussion of repetition and the split subject through Maurice Merleau-Ponty's *Le Visible et l'invisible*, Lacan observes the break and consequent negotiation between the point of view of the conscious subject as represented in its I/eye as opposed to the "phenomenal domain" of light as such, whose "depth of field" submits subjectivity to an "other" visual framing. Lacan identifies the privileged position of

the eye—as it orders the represented field of vision for conscious subjectivity—
with the I that Lacan relates to the Cartesian cogito as a "geometral point, a point
of perspective" (FFC, 86). One's intentional point of view as a conscious subject, for
Lacan, is itself always already positioned as a "stain" in the field of a radically other
gaze: one that Lacan describes as the "underside of consciousness" (FFC, 83). Thus,
"I am not simply," Lacan writes,

> that punctiform being located at the geometral point from which the perspective is
> grasped. No doubt, in the depths of my eye, the picture is painted. The picture, cer-
> tainly, is in my eye. But I am not in the picture.
>
> That which is light looks at me, and by means of that light in the depths of my eye,
> something is painted—something that is not simply a constructed relation, the object
> on which the philosopher lingers—but something that is an impression, the shim-
> mering of a surface that is not, in advance, situated for me in its distance. This is some-
> thing that introduces what was elided in the geometral relation—the depth of field,
> with all its ambiguity and variability, which is in no way mastered by me. It is rather
> it that grasps me, solicits me at every moment, and makes of the landscape something
> other than a landscape, something other than what I have called the picture. (FFC, 96)

During the course of his 1964 seminar, Lacan employs both an amusing personal
anecdote and a geometric diagram to portray further the splitting of the viewing
subject through a chance encounter (tuché) with a radically other gaze. To begin
with the story, Lacan recalls how in his youth he worked briefly with fishermen off
the coast of Brittany. One day at sea, Lacan's workmate, Petit-Jean, points out a
floating sardine can glittering in the sun, "a witness to the canning industry," and
makes a joke of it—a joke, that is, on Lacan. "You see that can? Do you see it?" says
Petit-Jean, "Well, it doesn't see you!" The jest, of course, signifies on how com-
pletely out of place and absurd Lacan the "young intellectual" appears in this ele-
mental scene of labor. But more to the point, Lacan writes, "if what Petit-Jean said
to me, namely, that the can did not see me, had meaning, it was because in a sense,
it was looking at me, all the same. It was looking at me at the level of the point of
light, the point at which everything that looks at me is situated—and I am not speaking metaphorically" (FFC, 95). The force of the joke befalls Lacan as an encounter
(tuché) that splits his presumed subjectivity, reducing it to an absurd jest or stain in
the gaze of the Real.

Schematizing the split subject in the scopic field, Lacan employs two superim-
posed triangles to represent the psychic economy of opposition and negotiation between the I/eye's double positioning as both subject and object of visual perception. The "subject of representation"—the I whose eye is privileged at the vertex of

the first triangle's visual field—is also positioned as stain at the base of the second triangle, which emanates from the gaze. It is in this visual splitting, Lacan writes, "at the level that I call the stain that the *tychic* point in the scopic function is found" (FFC, 77). One normally negotiates meaning and presence under the gaze of the Real in the mediating "image screen" of signification that Lacan locates midway between the subject's look and the force of the gaze. "Only the subject—the human subject," for Lacan, "the subject of the desire that is the essence of man . . . isolates the function of the screen and plays with it. Man, in effect, knows how to play with the mask as that beyond which there is the gaze. The screen is here the locus of mediation" (FFC, 107).

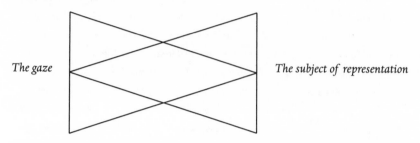

The gaze   The subject of representation

Although the Real is typically screened in our conscious and unconscious acts of symbolic representation, much of contemporary visual aesthetics—as Hal Foster argues in his reading of Andy Warhol, Gerhard Richter, Richard Estes, Richard Prince, and Cindy Sherman—stages the traumatic return of the Real precisely as a rupturing, tearing, and bleeding of light through the screen of serial repetition.[120] A similar breaching of signification by the Real, as we shall see, is powerfully rendered in the motif of the gaze as Forché presents it in *The Angel of History*. Returning to Benjamin's final allegory of the Angelus Novus, we can read it both as a passive figure for the kind of political paralysis Benjamin tragically encountered in 1940 *and* as an active agent for something that heralds the radically new of postmodern historicity. Viewed through the lens of the Lacanian Real, the Angelus Novus looks ahead to a world-historical novum emerging within the spectacle of modernity. The force of that futurity bears precisely on the Holocaust whose Final Solution would overtake Benjamin that same year. Significantly, the trope of vision—inscribed as an insistent repetition in Benjamin's text—is at once a symptom and screen for that unprecedented, collective trauma. Positioned as historical witness, rather than messenger, Benjamin's angel assumes a special agency through the testimony of his gaze. The brilliance of Forché's appropriation of the Angelus Novus lies in her sustained attention to that spectral address as it touches upon the Holocaust.

Registered in the angel's gaze, the Real returns in Forché's text as a ghastly illumination—a gnomon whose uncanny trace of light arrests the otherwise banal spectacle of postmodernity. Befalling the poet among the book's various settings—Paris, Beirut, Hiroshima, Puerto Diablo, Prague, Terezin, Sobibor, Chelmno—it is what she calls "The Testimony of Light" in part 4 of *The Angel of History* that possesses her own witnessing to the twentieth-century apocalypse. Not unlike the opening of *The Waste Land*, Forché's long poem signifies on and recodes the traditional associations we bring to the month of April, whose "yonge sonne" in the "General Prologue" to *The Canterbury Tales* is a reminder of rebirth, renewal, and regreening. Just as Eliot recodes this motif in "The Burial of the Dead," so too Forché's April musings on motherhood, paradoxically enough, awaken her to mortality. "When my son was born," she realizes, "I became mortal" (AH, 3). Yet, in the postgenocidal present that Forché inhabits, the deep, modernist structures of death and resurrection underwriting Eliot's mythic borrowings from the Cambridge anthropologists have shifted significantly after Auschwitz. As we have seen, "the administrative murder of millions," as Adorno theorizes it, "made of death a thing one had never yet to fear in just this fashion."[121]

In this new, spectral register of death-in-life, the legacy of the Holocaust leaves a visible trace on the visual field of postmodernity: a gaze whose luminous address disfigures the visual tropes underwriting Enlightenment values. Forché's landscapes are awash in the "bleached" aura of "white air" mirroring the "white veil of sea," whose low tide leaves behind "acres of light." Unlike the intensity of Eliot's "heart of light" found in the recollected hyacinth garden, Forché's visual landscape disperses a uniformly overexposed depth of field. Illumination no longer connotes the redemptive qualities of metaphysical values. Instead, it returns like an intrusive memory of trauma inflected by the fire imagery of the Nazi death camps and the nuclear flash of Hiroshima. Its visual synaesthesia deranges perception in a "white siren of sun" (AH, 55). Thus in "Elegy," testimony to the burning of the Jews at Sobibor and Chelmno, given by former Sonderkommando inmates Motke Zaidl, Itzhak Dugin, and Simon Srebnik, is set off by the image of a bottle in a coat pocket "half vodka half winter light" (AH, 69). Similarly, "The Testimony of Light" employs visual motifs to portray the nuclear victims of Hiroshima "in light pulsing through ash, light of which the coat was made" (AH, 55). Moreover, the "white roses" (AH, 14) of Paris after the birth of the poet's son—recalled in the book's title piece—become imbricated with Prague's *konvalinka*, the bouquet of "white tulips for the mother of God" (AH, 35) in "The Notebook of Uprising." Through the poem's metonymic chains of associated images, the "radiant white feathers" of the "white phosphorous bombs" beheld off the coast of Beirut resonate with René Char's quoted metaphor for writing: "Comment me vint l'écriture? Comme un duvet d'oiseau sur ma vitre, en hiver" (AH, 5). ("How did my writing come? As goose-down on my window in winter.") But they further inflect the poet's word through the repeated motifs of doves and geese associated with the plume cloud of the nuclear blast. Even the boy whom Forché encounters in the Rue Victor Considerant totes a "white toy M-16" (AH, 61). Like the prolonged "Nuit Blanche" that the poet regards in a "white window winter-locked," the work's entire world outlook is cast in the eerie, ghostlike shadings of a photograph negative. Just as "memory" is felt along the pulses, as a "wind passing through the blood trees within us," so too the light that befell the "[d]oves painted white on the stopped wind" of the Hiroshima blast (AH, 65) also reach into the "white rooms" that Forché occupies in present-day Paris.

Not just a source of light, the gaze that befalls Forché throughout *The Angel of History* demands the poet's response through its mode of address. The *tuché*, as a missed encounter with the Real, haunts the poet's dream fantasy of El Salvador in the arresting regard of the spectral other:

And just now it was as if someone not alive were watching,
　　so I asked if he'd suffered very much and he said *no.*

But when I came back from the border something odd happened.
It had been more than seventy days and I weighed nothing.
My bags were no heavier than usual but I couldn't lift them.
After a drink and some talk I went for a rest.
When I woke my room was filled with vultures.
They were hopping about the room, belching and vomiting flesh,
　　as you saw them at Puerto Diablo and El Playon.

Exactly as you saw them.

As if someone not alive were watching.
On the sill, the bureau, in the bath and on my body

So fat with flesh they weren't able to fly

And when I turned, there was nothing,
　　as someone asks, Is something wrong? (AH, 15)

The historical referent for this dream of death is rooted in the body dumps of the "disappeared" victims of El Salvador. However grotesque, Forché's visual fantasy screens the Real, whose invisible kernel falls outside the range of symbolic representation. We only approach its impossibility in the questioning address of an unseen, but all-seeing, gaze. Its query—"Is something wrong?"—is, of course, rhetorical because to acknowledge the address of the Real, for Forché's dreamer, is to be haunted by a most uncanny gaze: "as if," she writes, "someone not alive were watching."

Not only is "le Dieu," as Ellie has it, a "feu"—a literal psychopath but, more sinister, this mad, designing deity as Forché says, "is playing chess with us." Sexual violation dramatized in "The Game of Chess" section of *The Waste Land* appears here as well in the blank tropes of the "white socks," the "white towel" and calla lilies of the serial rape victim, whose photographs appear in section 3 of "The Recording Angel." The obscenity of her victimization, moreover, is set in a broader comparative frame, placing rape on a continuum with the "red maple" of nuclear annihilation as well as "the fresh claw of a swastika on Rue Boulard" (AH, 57). All of these scenes of brutality are imbricated in what Forché renders in "The Testimony of Light" as a novum: a new horizon of violence whose regard dawns in what Yeats anticipated in "The Second Coming" as "a gaze blank and pitiless as the sun":[122]

> Outside everything visible and invisible a blazing maple.
> Daybreak: a seam at the curve of the world. The trousered legs
>   of the women shimmered.
> They held their arms in front of them like ghosts.
>
> The coal bones of the house clinked in a kimono of smoke.
> An attention hovered over the dream where the world had been.
> *For if Hiroshima in the morning, after the bomb has fallen,*
> *   is like a dream, one must ask whose dream it is.* (AH, 72)

If Auschwitz and Hiroshima, for Forché, stage the dream fantasies of a divine "feu"—what Daniel Blumenthal calls the "Abusive God"—then their surreal scenes derange the conventional rituals by which we distinguish life and death: "Doves, or rather their wings, heard above the roof and the linens floating / Above a comic wedding in which corpses exchange vows. A grand funeral celebration / Everyone has died at once" (AH, 56). What Forché presents in her long poem is precisely the apocalyptic tone that witnessing takes after Auschwitz. Her achievement advances a distinctively postmodern point of view on the Holocaust: one that is split by the gaze of the Angelus Novus, whose regard bestows the address of the traumatic past. The force of history's extremity revisited upon the present, while uniquely felt in the Holocaust, complicates the continuities of tradition and identity not just for the survivors of genocide but also for those who bear the traumatic legacy of the Middle Passage, whose "heritage" I examine in chapter 3.

CHAPTER THREE

Harlem Dancers and the Middle Passage

African "heritage" remains as controversial a legacy for contemporary black poets to claim as it was for the "talented tenth" of the Harlem Renaissance. Today, appeals to an African-American aesthetic grounded in the authenticity, site specificity, and political commitment of African cultural nationalism are complicated by the increasingly hybridized conditions of postcolonial enunciation and textual performativity. Such discursive regimes are themselves powerfully shaped by the built environment of advanced capitalism: its transnational, mass-mediated, and increasingly electronic modes of cultural production, distribution, and commodification.[1] In these postmodern registers—where popular meaning has come to be negotiated—the "living proof" of what the black arts would actually look, feel, and sound like is not easily discerned. Nevertheless, critics and other cultural workers routinely gesture toward idealized standards of "blackness" in leveling aesthetic judgment and, more provocatively, in speaking on behalf of the African-American community.

The literary critic bell hooks, for example, assumes cultural power by invoking the authority of black experience so as to distinguish authors such as Paule Marshall from Coco Fusco and Adrian Piper. On the one hand, hooks valorizes Marshall for her reliance on "black expressive culture" while, on the other, she gives Fusco and Piper more qualified readings insofar as they negotiate—however much they may subvert—"white sensibilities." According to Fusco, such distinctions simply dismiss as inauthentic her otherwise complex and sophisticated recodings of racial representation. Similarly, Adrian Piper's performance art, Fusco maintains, is often "labeled less black"[2] than the work of those who, as hooks puts it, express racial experience in an "unmediated, direct engagement with an audience."[3] Degrees of authenticity in black aesthetic expression rest, in hooks's reading, on the historical difference between intrinsic and extrinsic traditions of black cultural address, with the former shaped by "ritual play" within the African-American community, versus the latter's masked performativity for an external, white audience: one whose genealogy reaches back ultimately to the plantation house. The very same performance, depending on the circumstances of its staging and intent, can be read as either ritual play or defensive masking. Conflating these two modes of address, however, reflects what hooks describes as the "madness" of "African-American postmodern identity"—a hybrid self that hooks stigmatizes as nihilistic insofar as it reflects "the absence of community, alienation from everyday reality, a fragmented individuality, and the loss of organized resistance" (LGIO, 210).

Against the "madness" of black postmodernity, hooks valorizes the "sense of immediacy" that comes from the "individual" self's "ritual re-enactment" of "specific aspects of black experience" (LGIO, 214). Following Peggy Phelan's strictures against the postmodern "circulation of representations of representations,"[4] hooks is skeptical of contemporary, mass-mediated networks as sites for lodging political contestations and recodings of popular culture insofar as they attenuate the roots of ritual performance. The contemporary culture industry, as far as she is concerned, is corrosive of live performance precisely because "the primacy of addressing the local is sacrificed to the desire to engage a wider audience of paying consumers" (LGIO, 214). Against that compromised scene of consumption, hooks valorizes the heritage of a more communal, more vernacular, less alienated version of the black aesthetic: one that she attributes, in retrospect, to the Harlem Renaissance. Harlem, as hooks retrieves it, not only marks a rebirth of black artistry but, equally important, serves as an imagined community: one that guarantees the claim to authenticity in the aesthetic representation of the black masses.[5] At stake in the Harlem Renaissance for contemporary African-American cultural expression is precisely what hooks gleans as the "voice of resistance" (LGIO, 21). Claiming that voice would empower intellectuals like hooks to speak from a collective subject position—one that would appropriate the first person plural "we" intoned on behalf of others. "Clearly," she concludes, "the performing arts have been crucial to the process by which we, as African-Americans, decolonize our minds and imaginations" (LGIO, 213).

As a place of memory (what Pierre Nora theorizes as a *lieu de mémoire*)[6] Harlem has long served as a symbol of racial solidarity, reaching back to Alain Locke's well-known trope for the "race capital" as a "laboratory of a great race-welding."[7] Yet, following Nora, we must question the contemporary desire to repossess such *lieux de mémoire* as symptomatic of a certain belatedness—an historic rupture stemming from modernity's remove from any social unity of common origin. "All *lieux de mémoire* are," Nora writes, "*objets mises en abîmes*" (HM, 297). Such places, sites, and figures of memory are "mixed, hybrid, mutant" (HM, 295), where the memory "passed down by unspoken traditions, in the body's inherent self-knowledge, in unstudied reflexes and ingrained memories" is "transformed by its passage through history, which is nearly the opposite" (HM, 289). This mutant, hybrid inmixture of textual history and embodied memory calls into question the Afrocentric desire to segregate what is imagined as intrinsic versus extrinsic to the black community. In fact, the "madness" of their inmixture—even in the Harlem Renaissance—is something that is neither politically disabling nor unique to postmodernity but instead constitutive of the black diasporic heritage.

For his part, Paul Gilroy reads the Afrocentric appeal to an originary, unifying heritage as itself a modern symptom of reaction to "the transformation of cultural space and the subordination of distance" that happens in the social economy of the Middle Passage:[8]

> The relatively simple understanding of cultural differences that supplied the Manichean cornerstones of the colonial world gave way gradually to an infinitely shaded, protean and unquiet system of differentiation and unequal cultural exchanges that might warrant the term post-colonial. . . . To read this complexity as the simple power of a latent but omnipotent Africanity, manipulating the superficial communicative codes that are manifest within white supremacy, is to trivialize the urgent question of cross-cultural trafficking and to obscure its potential and actual political effects. . . . In this post-colonial mood, there should be no sentimental celebration of pure alterity mechanistically producing pure culture as pure resistance.[9]

Unlike hooks's insistence on black vernacular expression as the sanctioned arena for asserting African resistance to Anglo-European domination, Gilroy resists such reductive Manichean understandings of social antagonism. Instead, the history of the Black Atlantic, as he conceives it, describes a more productive and more culturally dispersed domain in excess of any ritualized origins. Linguistic creolization, aesthetic polyphony, and the "cross-cultural trafficking" in the syncretism of social codes and commodities define the sly nuances always already at play in the performative staging of black identity. Similarly, Lorenzo Thomas would frame Afrocentrism as a discursive practice that is more "positional rather than merely polemical."[10] That is, he discerns Afrocentrism not so much in what hooks characterizes as the site-specific "rites of resistance" (LGIO, 211) of local and community-based performances, but rather in the broader, more global, and more worldly cultural agenda theorized by Alain Locke in "The New Negro." Thomas defines at least three elements in the makeup of American Afrocentrism. To begin with, he cites Locke's insistence on the catholicity in Afrocentrism's "mission of rehabilitating the race in world esteem" precisely through a formal mastery of Western cultural forms. Secondly, "the custodianship of the African American vernacular culture," Thomas avows, "is also a prominent Afrocentric principle" (EM, 101). And finally, Afrocentric modernism parts company with the cultural pessimism of the modern "waste land" of experimental modernism in favor of celebrating the millenarianism of what Nnamdi Azikiwe hailed as an African "civilization that is to be."[11]

In recent literary criticism, however, readings of the Harlem Renaissance based in binary modes of pitting Afrocentric against Western traditions persist in framing the era's cultural debates. Such dualistic assumptions underwrite Melvin Dixon's strategy of valorizing Langston Hughes by way of a somewhat dismissive critique of Countée Cullen. In "The Black Writer's Use of Memory," Dixon maintains that "poetic practice throughout tradition has charged the word Africa with meaning but not memory."[12] Reading the debate between Cullen and Hughes by way of Pierre Nora's model of a *lieu de mémoire,* Dixon contrasts the "racial amnesia" of Cullen's historical "book learning" with the authentic "memory of actual living" in Hughes, the Negritude poets of *mémoire,* and more recently Audre Lorde and Derek Walcott (HM, 24). Dixon's critical distinctions rest on a binary logic that splits black expressive memory from historical textuality. Dixon's divide in Harlem Renaissance poetics repeats hooks's recovery of Hughes as a key precursor of black vernacular aesthetics. Such privileging of memory before history recasts the blending of history and memory in Nora's framing of *lieux de mémoire.* Dixon's reading relegates Cullen to the kind of empty textuality that Wallace Thurman parodies in *Infants of Spring,* where he lampoons Cullen as a modern dilettante with his "eyes on a page of Keats, fingers on typewriter, mind frantically conjuring African scenes. And there would of course be a Bible nearby."[13] Yet to dismiss the poet of "Heritage" as a kind of black bookworm not only trivializes Cullen's literary achievement but, equally important, fails to account fully for the return of traumatic memory acted out in Cullen's reading of the African diasporic text.

Despite Cullen's infamous attack on the jazz poetics of Hughes's *Weary Blues* in his 1926 *Opportunity* review "Poet on Poet," his literary representation of racial memory, as Alan Shucard points out, is complex and conflicted. As Cullen's critics have shown, "Heritage" stages not only Cullen's "double consciousness" over race and religion, but also the ambiguity of his familial origins, and his clashing sexual identifications. Underscoring the poem's refrain "So I lie," Gerald Early suggests that the five occurrences of this pun on lying suspend any gesture toward a determinate reading of identity in the work.[14] Indeed, such a stylistically foregrounded network of lies voices a certain clash between the poem's *sujet d'énoncé* (subject of the statement), versus the speaking subject, the *sujet d' énonciation* (the subject of the enunciation). Viewed through a postcolonial lens, such a split presentation of self is symptomatic of what Homi Bhabha would attribute to the complex "cultural positionality" of the poem's "discursive embeddedness and address." In the postcolonial context, "the pact of interpretation," Bhabha writes,

> is never simply an act of communication between the I and the You designated in the statement. The production of meaning requires that these two places be mobilized in the passage through a Third Space, which represents both the general conditions of language and the specific implication of the utterance in a performative and institutional strategy of which it cannot 'in itself' be conscious. (LC, 36)

In "Heritage," that mediating Third Space positions the poet in diasporic relation to Africa, whose hybridity is inscribed in the work's ironic, double voicing of syntax and key signifiers.

With the very first line, the ambivalent performative of the poem's refrain "What is Africa to me?" marks the "double part" of that questioning as a *mise en abyme*.[15] Not unlike the "madness" that hooks will later attribute to black postmodernism, "Heritage" conflates the binaries presence / absence, memory / history, identity / difference, and heritage / diaspora. As a rhetorical question "What is Africa to me?" performs a statement of absence and distance owing to a diasporic history that renders the poet "one three centuries removed" (H, 24) from any identity conceived as origin, homeland, or essence.[16] Instead, Cullen presents black cultural memory in "Heritage" as imbricated with the "book" of colonial history: a textual legacy that Frantz Fanon would later explore in *Black Skin, White Masks*. For Fanon, the racial unconscious is less an essential blood knowledge than it is an acquired, cultural "sum of prejudices, myths, collective attitudes of a given group."[17] Similarly, the memory of Africa in "Heritage" amounts to little more than "A book one thumbs / Listlessly, till slumber comes" (H, 25). As a phenomenological mode of questioning, however, "What is Africa to me?" also invokes black memory as an openness to the disclosure of beings, inviting into a nearness the poem's "dark gods" (H, 27) of transformative otherness. Thus, the dialogic double part of Cullen's questioning is symptomatic of an African heritage that is both a repository of cultural memory and a discursive space produced by a Eurocentric history of primitivist inscription. On the one hand, the poem's textuality negotiates the stylized landscape of colonial desire, whose African exoticism is replete with the eroticized signs of "Jungle boys and girls in love" (H, 27). On the other hand, Cullen also witnesses to an existential heritage of lived racial affect figured in the "dark blood dammed within" the "chafing net" (H, 25) of the poet's repressed, colonized body. Repression is further inscribed in the poem's formalist resistance to the vernacular, jazz poetics of Langston Hughes.

Nevertheless, the "weird refrain" born of the contradiction between history and memory sutures the poet into the kind of hybridized madness that hooks will later attribute to black postmodernity:

> When the rain begins to fall;
> Like a soul gone mad with pain
> I must match its weird refrain
> Ever must I twist and squirm,
> Writhing like a baited worm,
> While its primal measures drip
> Through my body, crying, "Strip!
> Doff this new exuberance.
> Come and dance the Lover's Dance!"
> In an old remembered way
> Rain works on me night and day. (H, 26–27)

Hybridity happens in these lines not only in their ambiguous performance of black skin, but also in the imperative commands to "Strip!" and "Come and dance." To begin with, the "old remembered way" of black dance is itself a cultural hybrid whose primordial roots in African ritual and sacred performance have, since the Middle Passage, been grafted with the heritage of modernism's production, surveillance, and display of black bodies as commodity forms. On the decks of the slave ships, "in order to keep [slaves] in good health," James Arnold testified before the 1789 Parliamentary Committee for the Abolition of Slavery:

> it was usual to make them dance. It was the business of the chief mate to make the men dance and the second mate danced the women; but this was only done by means of a frequent use of the cat. The men could only jump up and rattle their chains but the women were driven in one among another all the while singing.[18]

From the auction block, nicknamed the banjo-table, to the Plantation Buck and Wing competitions at the Big House, to such urban performative sites as Congo Square in New Orleans and New York's Five Points, the heritage of African-American dance describes a mixed emancipatory and commodified performance. That hybrid heritage evolved through such touring companies as the Ethiopian Serenaders and The Creole Show. Formalized in musicals such as The Darktown Follies, dance was further popularized in the black ballroom scenes in Harlem (the Savoy and Alhambra), in cabarets like the Cotton Club and Small's Paradise, and finally staged for cosmopolitan audiences in such musical comedies as *Shuffle Along, Runnin' Wild*, and *Chocolate Dandies*.

Read through the Third Space of the Middle Passage, Cullen's dialogic imperative to come and dance simultaneously voices both an invitation to liberate the African body from Eurocentric repressions *and* a commanding interpellation of the black subject for Eurocentric commodification. On the one hand, the stripped black body repeats the molting of the poem's "silver snakes that once a year / Doff the[ir] lovely coats." Such doffing and stripping would shed the repressed, occidental self in transformative liberation of an Afrocentric identity. On the other hand, Cullen's poetic strip performance is mediated by his cultural positionality: that Third Space of "one three generations removed" from African essences. Here the command, rather than the invitation, to strip brings into play the surveillance of black skin as spectacle. The roots of this visuality, of course, reach back to the Middle Passage, where at auction, the commodity form of black skin was literally read for the signs of insubordination left from cat-o'-nine-tails scarring (BD, 101). Within the text of this heritage, the black body has come to signify what Frantz Fanon described as "a racial epidermal schema" (BSWM, 112).

Inflected by the visual field of the white world, "consciousness of the body," for the black subject, "is solely a negativing activity. It is," Fanon says, "a third-person consciousness" (BSWM, 110). This epidermalization of racial identity happens in the exchange between self and other as a third position of surveillance: a spectacle of corporeality that is underwritten by the deep "legends, stories, history, and above all *historicity*" (BSWM, 112) of a troubled racial past. In Fanon's biographical chapter "The Fact of Blackness," the force of that racial historicity becomes inescapably personal, particularly in the arresting interpellation he receives from a white boy's sudden exclamation: "Look a Negro!":

> In the train it was no longer a question of being aware of my body in the third person but in a triple person . . . I was responsible at the same time for my body, for my race, for my ancestors, I subjected myself to an objective examination, I discovered my blackness, my ethnic characteristics; and I was battened down by tom-toms, cannibalism, intellectual deficiency, fetishism, racial defects, slave-ships, and above all else, above all: "Sho' good eatin'." (BSWM, 112)

In Fanon's intimate account, he gives testimony to wearing literally on the skin the historicity of blackness for the white gaze. As a psychoanalytic theorist, Fanon reads this racial epidermal schema as a kind of "negrophobia" (BSWM, 160) through the

Imaginary register of Jacques Lacan's "mirror stage." In Fanon's formulation of negrophobia, the imago of blackness as visibly Other is essential to the construction
of white identity. "When one has grasped the mechanism described by Lacan,"
Fanon writes, "one can have no further doubt that the real Other for the white man
is and will continue to be the black man."[19] Similarly, Cullen lays bare the vexed
heritage of African-American identity as rooted in a hybridized social relation rather
than a racialized origin. By foregrounding the constructed rather than essential
"fact of blackness," Cullen's poem escapes the fixed, discursive space of colonial
authority along a temporal axis whose heritage serves even now as a resource for
contemporary diasporic aesthetics.

In its own moment, Cullen's hybrid inscription of black dance reflects the cosmopolitan splicing of racial identity codes that typified the broader, cultural representation of African-American performance practices as witnessed in Harlem Renaissance poetics. Specifically, Cullen repeats the grafting of primitivist and urban
motifs figured in the poetics and visual arts of Gwendolyn Bennett, and he even
takes his title from her 1923 poem "Heritage":

I want to see the slim palm-trees,
Pulling at the clouds
With little pointed fingers. . . .

I want to see lithe Negro girls
Etched dark against the sky
While sunset lingers.

I want to hear the silent sands,
Singing to the moon
Before the Sphinx-still face. . . .

I want to hear the chanting
Around a heathen fire
Of a strange black race.

I want to breathe the Lotus flow'r,
Sighing to the stars
With tendrils drinking at the Nile. . . .

I want to feel the surging
Of my sad people's soul,
Hidden by a minstrel-smile.[20]

Bennett's "Heritage" anticipates her 1926 cover illustration for *Opportunity*, after she witnessed Josephine Baker's celebrated *danse sauvage* in Paris the preceding year. In the three-year interim between the poem and the illustration, however, Bennett's aesthetic ideology evolves from what Sterling Brown described as the New Negro "discovery of Africa as a source of race pride" to a more cosmopolitan mixing of primitive and modern aesthetic codes.[21] Africa is conjured in "Heritage" through anaphora in the repetition of the poet's desire not just for the kind of stylized vision of exotic "palm-trees" derived from Claude McKay, but as a more holistic structure of feeling that involves the five senses. Bennett insists that she wants "to see lithe Negro girls / Etched dark against the sky," and to "feel the surging / Of my sad people's soul, / Hidden by a minstrel-smile." Moreover, her allusions to the moon's "Sphinx-still face" and "the Nile" advances the kind of cultural geography of African location witnessed, say, in Langston Hughes's celebration of the Nile in "The Negro Speaks of Rivers" as a body of water "ancient as the world and older than the flow of human blood in human veins."[22] Before Cullen, Bennett imagines the subversive "chanting / Around a heathen fire / Of a strange black race." Beyond such primitivist reminiscences, however, the poem is marked by a coded, and decidedly African-American, literary heritage. Bennett's "minstrel-smile," which hides "the surging / Of my sad people's soul" communicates the same double consciousness portrayed in Paul Laurence Dunbar's "We Wear the Mask." Three years later, her *Opportunity* cover art performs racial identity as a hybridized relation that subversively reinscribes the cultural differences between black primitivism and cosmopolitan whiteness.

In 1926, Bennett and Aaron Douglas were both awarded fellowships from the foundation of Albert C. Barnes, the wealthy collector of African and modern art. Bennett's award paid $100 per month toward a year's stay in Paris, where her studies at the Acadèmie Colorassi, Acadèmie Julian, and the Ecole de Panthèon continued her training in art begun in the early twenties at the Department of Teachers' College of Columbia University and Pratt Institute. Bennett's *Opportunity* illustration reflects the performative energies that she had witnessed in Josephine Baker's chorus-line antics in New York and in her avant-garde stagings in *La Revue Nègre*. In her visual art, Bennett presents the modern black dancer as both a more ecstatic and self-possessed version of Baker's cosmopolitan persona that signifies on, even as it masks, a primitivist self. The body language of the racially ambivalent figure silhouetted in white against a black background suggestively mimics the bold black celebrants modeled on the moves of Baker's *danse sauvage*. Aesthetic primitivism, of course, began with the importation of African, Brazilian, and Native American figurines, masks, and ritual objects that circulated in the flea markets and private

collections of Paris. The fetish of primitive otherness projected onto these artifacts
not only marked the avant-gardist imagination of Picasso, Leger, Apollinaire, Blaise
Cendrars, and the Zurich dadaists Hugo Ball and Tristan Tzara, but coincided with
the influx of African-American jazz culture and the emergence, as James Clifford
documents, "of a modern, fieldwork-oriented anthropology . . . at the Paris Institute of Ethnology and the renovated Trocadero museum."[23] Tzara, for example,
employed such ethnographic research in assembling his *Poèms Nègres* and in 1917
performed them at the Cabaret Voltaire in Zurich. However well intended, Tzara's
promotion of African and South Pacific culture betrayed a colonial relation in

tropes that infantilized and mystified non-Western culture. "Art in the infancy of time," he wrote, "was prayer."[24]

In critiquing the conjuncture of experimental modernism, primitivism, and ethnography, Clifford provocatively collages the icon of Josephine Baker in the celebrated banana skirt she first wore in the Folies-Bergère, a wooden figure from Angola and a costume design for Fernand Leger's 1923 "The Creation of the World," concluding that "the black body in Paris of the twenties was an ideological artifact" (PC, 197). Following Clifford, Paul Gilroy also reads Baker as a modernist minstrel that performed the Eurocentric demand for "escapist exoticism" (LGIO, 22). Similarly, bell hooks's take on Baker reduces her complex cultural positioning to the fetishized figure of colonial fantasy, the kind of stereotype of black sexuality that joins her as victim to Sarah Bartmann, Tina Turner, Iman, and Naomi Campbell.[25]

Such readings of Baker's cultural status in the twenties foreground her performance of the black body as a primitive fetish within the Imaginary registers of colonial fantasy. Yet, as we shall see, Baker's performance also witnesses to the traumatic Real in ways that are similarly inscribed in contemporaneous representations of black dance in Harlem Renaissance poetics of the 1920s. To begin with, in her Harlem lyric "Epitome," Ruth G. Dixon presents a modern figure whose blackness solicits the imaginary gaze of colonial "fancy" looking for the ideal figure of racial essence:

Emerges now a hero new,
A soul unknown,
To claim the horizon of your fancy.

Steps out from the dusky veil
A silhouette—black and stark,
Posing in the wake of your applause
All too thunderous.

You fawn, you worship, you adore;
You see a human god and goddess
Hitherto unknown.

They show a new and interesting life—
Souls of lust embroidered to your liking—
Not shaming gazing eyes
but feeding them,
Not piercing human hearts
But salving sores of pride.

You cry "Eureka!" and rejoice.
You've found at last the Negro!
Primitive! Beautiful! Untarnished
By the light of your civilization,
Unfettered by your laws
Of social decency.[26]

In "Epitome," Dixon lays bare the skewed cultural logic that instantiates the "dusky veil" of racial difference. The erotics of colonial fantasy in Dixon's account depend on a visual economy that projects an Imaginary figure of desire as Other. Addressed to the white audience, "Epitome" stages the spectacle of black skin as a dark fetish desired precisely because it is denied by the "laws" and "the light of your civilization." "Posing" on the "horizon of your fancy," the "black and stark" "silhouette" of the "Negro! / Primitive!" embodies but can never possess the "lust" of power, agency, and knowledge belonging to the racial privilege of "gazing eyes."

A more extreme, and perhaps less critical, example of this blend of exotic and tabooed sexuality is bodied forth in the Dionysian dancer that Byron Kasson and Lasca Sartoris encounter in the Black Mass of *Nigger Heaven* (1926). Part performance, part blood ritual, Carl Van Vechten's more violent version of the *danse sauvage* signifies on the stereotypes of racial primitivism:

> The girl—she could have been no more than sixteen—stood entirely nude. She was pure black, with savage African features, thick nose, thick lips, bushy hair which hovered about her face like a lanate halo, while her eyes rolled back so far that only the whites were visible. And now she began to perform her evil rites. . . . Byron groaned and hid his face in his hands. He could hear Lasca emitting little clucks of amazement. Standing before him, she protected him from the horror . . . while she watched. When he looked again, the light on the body was purple; the body was purple. The girl lifted a knife. . . . A woman shrieked. The knife . . .[27]

This spectacle glosses the literary and cultural codes of blood primitivism featured in Van Vechten's epigraph from Countée Cullen's "Heritage": "All day long and all night through, / One thing only must I do: / Quench my pride and cool my blood, / Lest I perish in the flood" (H, 27). "The horror" that Lasca watches but Byron cannot sustain signifies on Joseph Conrad's modernist tropes of primitivist Africa invoked earlier, however ironically, in Russet Durwood's description of Kasson's writing as "positively Conradian" (NH, 223). But it also reflects the internal textual coding of black dancing described from Mary Love's point of view as "primitive!" and "savage!" at "The Charity Ball" (NH, 164), where Byron and Lasca are figured as "panthers" (NH, 165). Moreover, the violent aposiopesis of the spectral knife that punctuates the Black Mass's "evil rites" looks ahead to the sadomasochistic turn in Lasca's seduction and betrayal as well as Byron's eventual undoing.

It would be a mistake, however, to position Baker within the register of Van Vechten's white, modernist imaginary. That kind of framing would fix her dynamic negotiation of black identity, reducing it to a passive icon within the visual field of the white public sphere. Foregrounding Baker's primitivist image from *La Revue Nègre* backgrounds the more complex, site-specific cultural work her improvisational performance art generated, globally, for diverse audiences throughout Europe, the United States, and South America. Moreover, interpreting Baker as a minstrel of the primitive eclipses her successful performances offstage in the roles not only of international celebrity but, more forcefully, of civil rights advocate and utopian visionary of cross-racial social coexistence.[28] As we have seen, for Harlem Renaissance artists such as Gwendolyn Bennett, Baker's hybrid mimicry of primitivist codes, mixed as they were with her mastery of Parisian cosmopolitanism, was an empowering role model in her own moment. But equally important, the force of Baker's performance has its source in a psychic register other than that of colonial fantasy.

A more considered, Lacanian reading of Baker's performative self-presentations would supplement Fanon's stress on the Imaginary representation of race by discerning not only how Baker was objectified visually in colonial desire but, equally important, how she reacted symptomatically to the force of the traumatic Real. In this vein, African-American recodings of colonial primitivism are discernible in the poetry of the Harlem Renaissance even before Baker acts them out in *La Revue Nègre*. Helene Johnson's "Bottled" (1923), for example, presents the double vision of a New York zoot-suiter who—like Cullen's narrator of "Heritage"—"strips and doffs" the artificial vestments and "[t]rick clothes" of the urban present in order to perform a "Dignified and proud" *danse sauvage:*

> And yesterday on Seventh Avenue
> I saw a darky dressed to kill
> In yellow gloves and swallowtail coat
> And swirling a cane. And everyone
> Was laughing at him. Me too,
> At first, till I saw his face
> When he stopped to hear a
> Organ grinder grind out some jazz.
> Boy! You should a seen that darky's face!

It just shone. Gee, he was happy!
And he began to dance. No
Charleston or Black Bottom for him.
No sir. He danced just as dignified
And slow. No, not slow either.
Dignified and *proud!* You couldn't
Call it slow, not with all the
Cuttin' up he did. You would a died to see him.

The crowd kept yellin' but he didn't hear,
Just kept on dancin' and twirlin' that cane
And yellin' out loud every once in a while.
I know the crowd thought he was coo-coo.
But say, I was where I could see his face,
And somehow, I could see him dancin' in a jungle,
A real hones-to-cripe jungle, and he wouldn't leave on them
Trick clothes—those yaller shoes and yaller gloves
And swallowtail coat. He wouldn't have on nothing.
And he wouldn't be carrying no cane.
He'd be carrying a spear with a sharp fine point
Like the bayonets we had "over there."
And the end of it would be dipped in some kind of
Hoo-doo poison. And he'd be dancin' black and naked and gleaming.
And he'd have rings in his ears and on his nose
And bracelets and necklaces of elephants' teeth.
Gee, I bet he'd be beautiful then all right.
No one would laugh at him then, I bet.[29]

Johnson's presentation of the Harlem street performer would convert what is otherwise an object of ridicule—"the darky"—into an agent whose self-possession of character is not only "[d]ignified and proud" but even militant in asserting a lethal prowess. Yet in its reliance on clichéd figures of Africa, the poem also tends to substitute one set of stylized representations for another. Primitivist costume displaces the urban garb. "Necklaces of elephants' teeth" take the place of "yaller shoes and yaller gloves." Nevertheless, there is a crucial moment in the passage from America to Africa that negates such all-too-familiar figures of Imaginary representation with an address that resists signification as such. Symptomatic in Johnson's account is her repeated insistence on the negative phrasings of "No / Charleston or Black Bottom for him. / No sir. . . . No, not slow either. . . . You couldn't / Call it slow, not with all the / Cuttin' up he did." Such repetition punctuates Johnson's testimony as she struggles to account for the address of the Real that exceeds the Imaginary fetish of dress (whether urban or African). In narrating the transformative effect of the performance on the dancer, Johnson also communicates its force through her secondary role of poetic witness. The gaze that addresses the poet shines in the dancer's face, but its origin is elsewhere: "over there" beyond the Symbolic order of conventional representation. The Real befalls Johnson as viewer in a "gleaming" regard whose address is traumatic for the witness: "You would a died," she insists, "to see him."

Not unlike the transformative otherness of Helene Johnson's street dancer, Josephine Baker's performance practice finds its origins and its particular symptoms of repetition in the traumatic Real. As a rising African-American star for a multicultural public sphere, Baker experienced, like Cullen, her audience's demand for the fetish of black skin as an encounter with sublime terror: "The first time I had to appear in front of the Paris audience," she recollects,

> I had to execute a dance rather . . . savage. I came onstage and a frenzy took possession of me; seeing nothing, not even hearing the orchestra, I danced! . . . Driven by dark forces I didn't recognize, I improvised, crazed by the music, the overheated theater filled to the bursting point, the scorching eye of the spotlights. Even my teeth and eyes burned with fever. Each time I leaped I seemed to touch the sky and when I regained the earth it seemed to be mine alone.[30]

Out of the psychically charged space of colonial desire—what Fanon characterized as the hybridity of Western negrophobia / negrophilia—Baker discovers identity, paradoxically enough, from the catachresis of cosmopolitan primitivism.[31] Yet to read her staging simply in terms of its exoticism would deny the complex tensions of agency and objectification acted out in her performance. Narrated from her own subject position, her dance has less to do with Imaginary fantasy than with what Lacan would describe as the gaze of the Real. The spotlight's eye is not coincidental with the point of view of the colonial audience. Unlike the colonial gaze, which looks for the primitivist fetish, the regard of the Real exceeds any representational closure. Its address scorches and burns with an extralinguistic intensity: one that searches out and elicits "crazed" emotions and "dark forces." That horizon of the Real exceeds both the imaginary investments of colonial desire and the range of symbolic expression available to experimental modernism and, more radically, splits conscious subjectivity with the force of what Lacan describes as a traumatic encounter. As we have seen, Lacan's reading of Freud's dream of the burning child locates the nucleus of the Real as what escapes conscious understanding precisely in

the child's burning reproach "Father, can't you see I'm burning?" Not just a representation of trauma, "this sentence," Lacan writes, "is itself a firebrand—of itself it
brings fire where it falls—and one cannot see what is burning, for the flames blind
us to the fact that the fire bears on the *Unterlegt,* on the *Untertragen,* of the real."[32]

In a similar encounter with the Real as "firebrand," what Baker experiences in
her "possession" is a kind of blinding sublime where both the framing of Miguel
Covarrubias's avant-garde set designs and the scene of her Parisian viewers alike
fall away. "Seeing nothing, not even hearing the orchestra," she testifies, "I danced."
It is only in a later moment that the ecstatic dance negotiates that gaze of the Real
through improvisation. The first moment, however, belongs to a "frenzy" whose
possession radically exceeds Baker's identity as an entertainer. The complex layering of the performative space that Baker traverses in its registers of the Imaginary,
Symbolic, and Real can be further discerned by way of comparison to Claude
McKay's inscription of the visual field as a network of possessing looks and gazes in
"The Harlem Dancer":

> Applauding youths laughed with young prostitutes
> And watched her perfect, half-clothed body sway;
> Her voice was like the sound of blended flutes
> Blown by black players upon a picnic day.
> She sang and danced on gracefully and calm,
> The light gauze hanging loose about her form;
> To me she seemed a proudly-swaying palm
> Grown lovelier for passing through a storm.
> Upon her swarthy neck black shiny curls
> Luxuriant fell; and tossing coins in praise,
> The wine-flushed, bold-eyed boys, and even the girls,
> Devoured her shape with eager, passionate gaze;
> But looking at her falsely-smiling face,
> I knew her self was not in that strange place.[33]

McKay's English sonnet foregrounds the visual field of performance as a space of
desire where subjectivity is negotiated in social relation to visible objects. During
the course of the poem's action, the viewing audience, jazz-club dancer, and poet-
observer variously emerge as perceiving subjects through the power to behold others as imaginary objects of desire. Possessing the gaze, however, is double edged as
every act of possession risks being possessed by the regard of the other. Ownership
of the gaze is further inflected by the mediating power of capital to reify the aura
of the visible according to the exchange logic of the commodity fetish.

The poem begins with the paying audience made up of "applauding youths" who include not only the consumers of the primitivist spectacle but also those on-lookers, the "young prostitutes," who are themselves for hire. Their consumption of the spectacle hinges on the imaginary fantasy of the "perfect, half-clothed body" of the dancer that is itself fetishized by "the light gauze hanging loose about her form." Desire in the poem is Dionysian and seizes "the wine-flushed, bold-eyed boys, and even the girls," with intensities that exceed the conventions of compulsory heterosexuality. However "devoured" by the "eager, passionate gaze" of the onlookers, the dancer's imaginary "shape" cannot redress the exchange of glances that undercuts the audience's mastery of the spectacle. The jazz-club audience must supplement its place in the scene's visual economy by literally paying attention to the dancer, by "tossing coins" at the stage. Similarly, the poet observer would possess the power of the gaze through the linguistic economy of figurative language, fixing the dancer as a "proudly-swaying palm / Grown lovelier for passing through a storm." "Looking," however, on the mask of the dancer's "falsely-smiling face," the poet finds that his aesthetic voyeurism is deflected by the agency of the other's gaze, which ultimately falls outside the scopic frame of primitivist spectacle. The final cogito or I of the poem's couplet presents a more radical perception of what the speaker "knew" to be "not in that strange place." Entering the register of the Real, the witnessing I testifies to what escapes the desiring eye through a glance that renders the bizarre spectacle of "that strange place" even more uncanny.

Similar to its extralinguistic horizon in "The Harlem Dancer," the return of the Real happens for Baker as a possessing address whose origin lies outside the frame of both her own performative self-presentations and her audience's imaginary expectations and desires. The repetition of the traumatic Real takes place throughout her career not just on stage but in the scenes she acts out in everyday life. Black corporeality in the visual field of the white other, as we have seen from Fanon, is inherently unsettling, but performing race as spectacle, for Baker, was particularly traumatic because of her mixed racial ancestry. Specifically, her grandmother's clashing Cherokee and African roots, coupled with the fact that her biological father, Eddie Carson, was a *bukra* "spinach"—a slang term for a Spaniard—made Baker acutely aware of the difference in her lighter pigmentation from that of her darker stepfather Arthur Baker and her half-brothers and sisters. Conversely, she felt herself to be darker than most of the New York chorus-line dancers. The vexed issue of race dogged Josephine Baker's early career as a vaudeville dancer for the Dixie Steppers and in breaking into the Broadway chorus line for *Shuffle Along*. "It rankled," writes biographer Phyllis Rose, "to be rejected as too dark by the New York show and by the Baker family when she was disliked in her southern vaudeville troupe and in her own family for being too light."[34] Beyond these domestic and professional encounters with miscegenation, however, the trauma of race's social relation was triggered early on in her childhood by the extremity of the St. Louis Riot of 1917.

Known as the "Pittsburgh of the West," East St. Louis at the time was the point of origin of twenty-seven railroads and a labor center for the Swift, Armour, and Morris stockyards and packing plants. With three hundred coal mines nearby, East St. Louis was also a major metals manufacturing center and home to Aluminum Ore Company and the Missouri Malleable Iron Company. From 1900 to 1917 the black population of East St. Louis had tripled, constituting a tenth of East St. Louis's 59,000 citizens. Resistance to the black migration of 1915–1917 was a pernicious element in the ideological campaign against the St. Louis "Black Belt" in the election 1916. Competition for jobs, coupled with popular controversy over integrated housing and the new force of the black vote, led to mounting tensions in May 1917 followed by the explosion of violent race hatred in July of that year. The climax came on Sunday evening of July 1 when a carload of white gunmen assaulted African-American neighborhoods in drive-by shootings that provoked blacks to respond in kind. By early morning, two white detectives had been killed. In retaliation, angry mobs of white rioters—cheered on by thousands of bystanders—set fire to blocks of black East St. Louis housing. Then they beat, tortured, shot, hanged, and burned hundreds of fleeing residents. The systematic nature of the violence was captured in the *St. Louis Republic*'s eyewitness testimony to racial mass murder:

> A crazed negro would dash from his burning home, sometimes with a revolver in his hand. Immediately revolvers by the score would be fired. He would zig-zag through the spaces between buildings. Then a well-directed shot would strike him. He would leap into the air. There were deep shouts, intermingled with shrill feminine ones. The flames would creep to the body. The negro would writhe, attempt to get up, more shots would be fired. The flames would eat their way to him, past him, and further along Railroad Avenue.[35]

One symptom of how formative this trauma was for Baker is plain to see in the very first sentences of her autobiography's opening chapter, which recast the optimism of Jo Bouillon's opening question about her early years. "My happiest childhood memory?" she muses:

> I really don't know, but I can tell you which was the worst. It marked me, first unconsciously and later all too consciously, for life. I think in ancient times they used to call it the power of destiny. (J, 1)

Baker's recoding of Bouillon's question about her "happiest moment" takes it as a pretext for narrating her "worst" moment, thus acting out an insistent need to repeat the return of a formative trauma that, by her own account, leaves its imprint with the "power of destiny." Trauma befalls Baker's already difficult childhood poverty in 1917 in a literal awakening to the uncanny nightmare of racial violence. Torn from sleep by the oncoming riot, Baker is driven with her family out of her home. Following her fleeing mother and siblings, she enters the scene of disaster. "What I saw before me as I stepped outside," she testifies:

> had been described at church that Sunday by the Reverend in dark, spine-chilling tones. This was the Apocalypse. Clouds, glowing from the incandescent light of huge flames leaping upward from the riverbank, raced across the sky . . . but not as quickly as the breathless figures that dashed in all directions. The entire black community appeared to be fleeing like ants from a scattered antheap. "A white woman was raped," someone shouted, and although I didn't understand the meaning of his words, I knew that they described the ultimate catastrophe. The flames drew nearer. As the choking stench of ashes filled the air, I was overcome with panic. (J, 2)

Other, specific atrocities and cruelties are recounted in Baker's eyewitnessing to the St. Louis riots that merge into a cumulative impression of apocalypse. Not unlike survivor testimony to the Holocaust, Baker's narrative depicts the end of the world as we know it in the fire, smoke, and ashes of a living hell. Implied in Baker's dehumanizing metaphor, which transforms the "entire black community" to so many fleeing ants, is the specter of genocide, suggested too in the literal "choking stench" of ashes, presumably from the public burning of the riot's victims.

It is precisely such searing knowledge of the traumatic Real—which as Lacan has it "brings fire where it falls"—that Baker encounters, symptomatically, in the "scorching" eye and burning "fever" of the *Revue Nègre* spotlights. The intensities of Baker's Afrocentric performance practice find their roots in her personal childhood trauma of the St. Louis Riot that itself is just one episode in a deeper history of institutional racism. If the quest for Afrocentric essences is actually produced in reaction to postcolonial, cultural exchanges—that, as Paul Gilroy has it, are only "half-grasped by incomplete concepts like creolization, syncretism and 'hybridity'"[36]—then trauma theory may well begin to recover the unsettling back story behind the performative mimicry of modern, African-American performance culture. In this vein, the "frenzy" of "possession" that drives Josephine Baker's stage artistry, the "primal measures" that haunt Countée Cullen's otherwise formalist verse refrains, "the gleaming" ecstasy that marks Helene Johnson's poetic witnessing, the "passionate gaze" that transfixes McKay's poet-observer of "The Harlem Dancer," and the lived affect of what Gwendolyn Bennett discerns in the "surging / Of my sad people's soul, / Hidden by a minstrel-smile" together testify, by way of a complexly mediated and "masked" performativity, to the traumatic legacy of the Middle Passage: "one three generations removed" from the black expressive culture of the Harlem Renaissance. Moreover, discerning that heritage is further complicated by the politics of racial and class discriminations that mark the reception of African-American poetics throughout much of the twentieth century. As we shall see in chapter 4, the continuing culture wars of our own moment are themselves haunted by the specters of modern political antagonism whose trauma, Slavoj Žižek has written, as "an impossible kernel . . . prevents a closure of the social field."[37]

CHAPTER FOUR

Specters of Commitment in Modern American Literary Studies

In the post–World War II decades, the new social movements that shaped African-American, feminist, postcolonial, gay / lesbian, and cultural studies not only changed the complexion of contemporary literary canonicity but also had certain recombinatory side effects on the makeup of canonical modernism. The older and more conservative story of high modernism's emergence between the world wars had pitted the period's genteel anthologies against the New Critical campaign to move T. S. Eliot and Ezra Pound from the intellectual margins of the modern canon to its center.[1] In retrospect, this traditional take on high modernism's displacement of the genteel tradition not only failed to account for the full diversity of modernist aesthetic production but, as Cary Nelson has argued, served politically as a strategy of cultural containment. "Once our image of the period," writes Nelson, "is contained and structured this way—once our sense of the discourses at work is limited to these choices—it is easy to feel that experimental modernism deserved to win this battle, for it is difficult to recapture the knowledge that these were not the only forces in play. But in fact they were not."[2] By now in the twenty-first century, Eurocentric high modernism is read in relation to, not transcendence of, the diverse social text of the interbellum public sphere.[3] For much of the twentieth century, however, the constituting paradigm of the high / genteel divide framed modernism's literary reception so as to obscure and repress the kind of cultural diversity that Nelson and others have recently recovered. But equally important, it also naturalized and sanitized the troubling ideologies of racism, sexism, classism, and anti-Semitism whose legacies haunt the high modernist and New Critical conjuncture between the wars.

In remapping the terrain of modernist literary reception, the revolutionary culture wars of our own moment have also unearthed certain specters of modernism long repressed at the heart of the key social antagonisms of the interbellum period. Whether emanating from the Old Left or Agrarian Right, such modernist revenants return in figures of social agency that are not just historical—not, that is, safely consigned to the past—but, more radically, "out of joint" in time. The "untimely" return of such hauntings, according to Jacques Derrida, involves, precisely, "a question of repetition: a specter is always a *revenant*. One cannot control its comings and goings because it *begins by coming back*. . . . [N]o one can be sure if by returning it testifies to a living past or a living future, for the *revenant* may already mark the promised return of living being."[4] The "ghostlier demarcations" of modernism—to borrow from the lexicon of Wallace Stevens—are doubly uncanny: they not only anticipate present aesthetic debate as itself a repetition of a forgotten political clash but, more enigmatically, they invoke a future whose utopia we have not yet grasped.[5] The present task of imagining new possibilities for revolutionary, literary representation necessarily conjures the specters that haunt modernism's repressed cultural politics.[6] In this vein, Ross Chambers has recently posed the question of "what it means for a culture to be haunted by a collective memory" of traumas that belong to the past.[7] Similarly, in examining the ethics of "consuming trauma," Patricia Yaeger has cautioned against the "greater terror, of not being haunted, of ceasing to feel the weight of past generations in one's bones."[8] Yaeger takes her metaphor of the past as haunting burden from Karl Marx's thesis on revolutionary repetition in *The Eighteenth Brumaire of Louis Bonaparte*. "The tradition of all the dead generations," Marx writes, "weighs like a nightmare on the brain of the living":

> And just when they seem engaged in revolutionizing themselves and things, in creating something that has never yet existed, precisely in such periods of revolutionary crisis they anxiously conjure up the spirits of the past to their service and borrow from them names, battle-cries and costumes in order to present the new scene of world history in this time-honoured disguise and this borrowed language.[9]

In Derrida's reading of Marx, the revolutionary moment hastens the new by invoking *and* parting company with "the tradition of all the dead generations." The anxiety, moreover, occasioned by such an inaugural rupture demands a symptomatic return to the familiar in the "conjured names" and "borrowed language" of traditional representation, lodged as defense against the trauma of that revolutionary break with the past.[10] Our own witnessing to such radical intensities, Yaeger concludes, becomes ethical insofar as it sustains the event's traumatic "weight" against the foreclosure of normative textual repetition: the borrowed names of historical containment.

In twentieth-century American literary culture, the modernist call to "make it new" underwent just such a containing, revolutionary repetition: one that domesticated modernism's radical energies and refashioned them in the more formal "costumes" of New Critical conservatism. In a somewhat unguarded boast that "the modernist canon has been made in part by readers like me," Hugh Kenner divulged the hegemonic, rather than heuristic agenda of modern canonicity.[11] Kenner's commercial troping in "The Making of the Modernist Canon" (1984), however ironic, points symptomatically to a thoroughly reified economy of valuation. Looking back on his graduate-student days under Cleanth Brooks at Yale, Kenner relates how he took up Ezra Pound in 1949 at the very moment when the Bollingen controversy threatened to destroy the poet's reputation by branding him as an anti-Semite and national traitor. "I was naive enough," he admits, "not to guess that I was mortgaging my future" against what at the end of the forties must have seemed a risky investment indeed (MMC, 372). Nevertheless, with the publication of *The Poetry of Ezra Pound* (1951), Kenner reflects that "Pound before long was a stock on the academic exchange: a safe 'subject' " for the next "two decades' academic expansion" (MMC, 372).

Much of that twenty-year bull market can be attributed not just to the revolutionary power of Pound's aesthetic but to inside traders like Kenner, who in the postwar academy, speculated on the sizable cultural capital already amassed by such literary magnates as Eliot, Pound, and Brooks. That story is normally told, as Kenner's is, in terms of a handful of "great men" (Yeats, Eliot, Pound, Joyce, Stevens, Williams) who fathered the modernist cultural revolution. Indeed, on Pound's insistence that "you have an obligation to visit the great men of your own time" (MMC, 373), Kenner dutifully made the pilgrimage in 1956 to Williams, Wyndham Lewis, and Eliot, among others with introductions from *il miglior fabbro*. Such "face-to-face" bondings led each of these literary mandarins, in Kenner's subsequent critical campaign, to emerge as a trademark brand of high modernism. Yet this familiar lineage of "major" individual talents rests on a deeper genealogy whose social foundations are grounded in a specific conjuncture of national, racial, sexual, and class formations that are politically charged. Kenner's large claim that "[i]nternational Modernism was the work of Irishmen and Americans" (MMC, 367), however correct in its take on the shaping of canonical modernism in the United States, betrays a key repression: one that elides the social diversity of the historical avant-gardes.[12]

Kenner's postwar promotion of high modernism buttressed the critical and ped-
agogical edifice that his mentor Cleanth Brooks promulgated between the wars. In
particular, Brooks's popular primer, *Understanding Poetry* (1938) codified for the
classroom the emerging New Critical theory of such seminal volumes as his own
influential study *Modern Poetry and the Tradition* (1939). In making his case for the
kind of "difficulty," "allusiveness," "ironic indirection," and "complexity" in modern poetry that T. S. Eliot had advanced in his 1921 essay "The Metaphysical Poets,"
Brooks campaigned against the regnant anthology markets of the 1910s and 1920s.
As Craig S. Abbott has shown, Fred Lewis Pattee's *Century Readings for a Course in
American Literature* (1919, 1926), Harriet Monroe's *The New Poetry* (1917, 1923, 1932),
Marguerite Wilkinson's *Contemporary Poetry* (1923) and *New Voices* (1919, 1921, 1928),
and the six editions of Louis Untermeyer's *Modern American Poetry* (1919–1950)
shaped a readership for poets like Robert Frost, Edna St. Vincent Millay, Lizette
Reese, Carl Sandburg, Sara Teasdale, Joyce Kilmer, Vachel Lindsay, James Oppen-
heim, Edwin Arlington Robinson, and such middlebrow talents as Katherine Lee
Bates, Richard Covey, Josephine Preston Peabody, Ina Coolbrith, Eugene Field,
Clinton Scollard, and other long-forgotten writers.

The subsequent, postwar policing of cultural modernism by the more restrictive
literary canon of high modernism also was meant to repress the revenants of ultra-
right political extremism, whose specters haunted Kenner's mentors from the
1930s—Cleanth Brooks and his collaborators in the Fugitive, Southern Agrarian,
and New Critical movements: Donald Davidson, John Crowe Ransom, Allen Tate,
and Robert Penn Warren, among others. This line of reactionary cultural politics
flourished right through the conservative renaissance of the Reagan-Bush era, reap-
pearing with the uncanny repetition of George W. Bush's presidency, and surviving to this day.[13] Although much work has been done on high modernism's various investments in, say, Eurocentrism, monarchist Anglo-Catholicism, and Italian
fascism, the specters of these ideologemes in their American reception and, indeed,
in the formation of postwar literary studies as such have been rigorously silenced.[14]
The academic foundation for high modernist studies was laid through New Critics
like Brooks, who offered the first courses in twentieth-century literature at Yale in
1947. That institutional base, however, lies on deeper underpinnings in the Southern Agrarian platform for an elite "squirearchy" of cultural domination.

As its twelve apologists advertised it in *I'll Take My Stand: The South and the
Agrarian Tradition* (1930), the Agrarian agenda was outspokenly political and, among
other things, reacted against the burgeoning American consumer market spearheaded by Henry Ford. Anticipating the Frankfurt attention to the emerging *kul-
turindustrie*, Southern Agrarian ideologues such as Donald Davidson—longtime

Vanderbilt mentor for the Fugitive movement—began to engage the question, as he posed it in his Southern Agrarian manifesto, "What is the industrial theory of the arts?"[15] Unlike, say, Walter Benjamin, Davidson was pessimistic about the new culture of mechanical reproduction. "Henry Ford's hired hands," he complained,

> do not hum themes from Beethoven as they go to work. Instead, the shop-girl reads the comic strip with her bowl of patent cereal and puts on a jazz record while she rouges her lips. She reads the confession magazines and goes to the movies. . . . The industrialists in art—that is, the Hollywood producers, the McFaden publications, the Tin Pan Alley crowd, the Haldeman–Julius Blue Books—will naturally make their appeal to the lowest common denominator. (ITS, 35)

It is against this denigrated and feminized version of the mass-cultural market that the campaign for an elite, high modern canon announces its classist and androcentric agenda.

Building on T. S. Eliot's implicit critique of the alienating social effects of mass industrial society in "The Waste Land," Southerners like Lyle H. Lanier looked forward to postwar critiques of advanced consumer society by analyzing what Hans Magnus Enzensberger would later characterize, from a Marxist vantage point, as the postmodern "industrialization of the mind."[16] Writing to the right of Enzensberger, Lanier in "The Philosophy of Progress," linked the Fordist techniques of factory production to the broader, ideological spread of consumer values throughout the social field: what Gramsci was simultaneously theorizing in *The Prison Notebooks* as "Americanism." "By 'industrialism,'" wrote Lanier, "is meant not the machine and industrial technology as such, but the domination of the economic, political, and social order by the notion that the greater part of a nation's energies should be directed toward an endless process of increasing the production and consumption of goods" (ITS, 148). Beyond Lanier's somewhat undertheorized reading of Fordism, this new mode of industrial and cultural production, in Gramsci's more sophisticated analysis, effected a crucial turning point in the progress of advanced capitalism: one that demanded a radical rethinking of both Second International economism and the cultural politics of vanguard Leninism.

More powerful than either the legacy of the Soviet Revolution or the rise of Italian fascism, Ford's new industrial mode of production stood, according to Gramsci, as "the biggest collective effort to date to create, with unprecedented speed, and with a consciousness of purpose unmatched in history, a new type of worker and of man."[17] What was revolutionary about Ford's approach was its adaptation of Frederick W. Taylor's time and motion studies to the semiautomatic production line. This technical regime, in Gramsci's account, reduced workers to replaceable cyborgs within a production process driven by capital and managed by a new administrative class.[18] But equally important, the gigantic scale of Ford's mechanical infrastructure, documented in Diego Rivera's expansive Detroit Industry murals of River Rouge, was also very costly to maintain. Consequently, it demanded not only a speed up in the labor process but also a reliable market for its mass products. Ford's decisive advance lay in researching and surveilling workers' habits of consumption as part of his productive calculus. "During the period in which we largely increased wages," Ford wrote, "we did have a considerable supervisory force. The home life of the men was investigated and an effort was made to find out what they did with their wages."[19] By targeting the domestic arenas and personal enclaves of consumption, he hastened the commodity form's penetration of everyday life, thereby setting the foundation for the postwar consumer society.

Significantly, the Fordist apparatus coupled a revolutionary principle of mechanization with a managerial strategy of planned consumption.[20] It is this conjuncture of the Northern industrial mode of production and the mass commodity market it serviced that Ransom, Brooks, and Warren anathematized as Southern Agrarians. The Southern critique of America's burgeoning consumer society, however, was doubly politicized in its proactive, anticommunist agenda. Not just a front for cultural squirearchy, Agrarianism aimed to turn the tide of the emergent socialist culture that was gaining considerable momentum in America between the wars. Indeed, Andrew Lytle, Allen Tate, and Robert Penn Warren proposed *A Tract against Communism* as the original title for the biting agrarian manifesto *I'll Take My Stand*. "We therefore look upon the Communist menace," they proclaimed in the volume's collaboratively authored "Introduction: A Statement of Principles," "as a menace indeed, but not as a Red one; because it is simply according to the blind drift of our industrial development to expect in America at last much the same economic system as that imposed by violence upon Russia in 1917" (ITS, xxiv). Thus, in the United States, the political struggle against the Comintern's Third Period push for a Soviet America would be spearheaded throughout the Depression era, by, among others, Donald Davidson, Frank Owsley, John Crowe Ransom, and Allen Tate.

Much of the Agrarians' reactionary social politics was theorized in essays published in the *American Review* (1933–1937), whose editor, Seward Collins, advanced an American version of Italian fascism. Sharing many of the key discursive markers of Southern Agrarianism and English Distributism, the native fascism that Collins espoused would support "the revival of monarchy, property, the guilds, the security of the family and the peasantry, and the ancient ways of European life."[21] Not unlike Collins's investments in tradition, family values, Eurocentrism, and what John Crowe Ransom called squirearchy, the Southern Agrarians—like the Distributists Hilaire Belloc, Herbert Agar, and Troy Cauley—also saw the economic blight of the Great Depression as heralding the death of capitalism that had split humanity into monopolists and proletarians. Agrarians like Frank Owsley campaigned to redistribute land to small growers held by "loan companies, insurance companies, banks, absentee landlords," and bankrupt planters.[22] Such redistribution would foster an agricultural middle class that would, nevertheless, be discouraged from buying the new technologies and consumer goods from the North by punitive import tariffs. Politically, in the pages of the *American Review,* there was strong resistance to the spread of democracy among the proletarian class through the Distributist plan to limit the franchise to property owners or to adopt the kind of hierarchic rule witnessed in Mussolini's Italy.

Given the deepening economic crisis of the Depression era, the *American Review* aligned itself with international fascism in reaction against the expanding democratic coalition of the Popular Front sponsored by the American left. In fact, the rhetorics of fascism and Southern white supremacy came together in such *American Review* contributors as Hoffman Nickerson, who in a 1935 essay entitled "Property and Tactics" argued that "[w]hat the fascist march on Rome did for the Italian nation, Vigilance Committees of angry citizens have done for many an American city. . . . That is the story of the original Ku Klux Klan . . . which restored white supremacy in the South. . . . Should the day come when the silver-tongued oratory of the Kerensky-Roosevelt type is not enough to guard our civilization from Communist chaos, then the intelligence and virility of Christendom will produce more fascist dictators . . . to diminish proletarianism and restore property."[23] Throughout the mid-1930s, the *American Review* ran articles that characterized Mussolini as "a man of tradition whom Aristotle or St. Thomas, or Machiavelli might without too great difficulty feel at ease."[24] Even more troubling, the journal featured articles contrasting Karl Marx the "jew, Mordecai" with Hitler, who restored "courage and hope" through the "resurrection of German National spirit."[25] By publishing their writings in the same venue as such anti-Semitic and profascist ideologues as Nickerson and Ross J. S. Hoffman, the Southern Agrarians, arguably, aligned themselves with these troubling cultural politics.

Although the Agrarians ridiculed the American left as mired in "propaganda"— their euphemism for social critique—Davidson, Ransom, Owsley, Tate, and the rest were no strangers to agitprop as evidenced in such *American Review* contributions as Donald Davidson's "The Rise of the American City" (1933), "Lands That Were Golden" (1934), "Regionalism and Education" (1935), "A Sociologist in Eden" (1936); Owsley's "Scottsboro, The Third Crusade" (1933), "The Pillars of Agrarianism" (1935), "The Old South and the New" (1936); Ransom's "Happy Farmers"

(1933), "A Capital for the New Deal" (1933), "Sociology and the Black Belt" (1934); Tate's "The Problem of the Unemployed" (1933), "Where Are the People" (1933), "A View of the Whole South" (1933), "Notes on Liberty and Property" (1936), "What Is a Traditional Society?" (1936). In standard versions of American literary and critical history, the social politics of Southern Agrarianism is either simply elided or contained in a *cordon sanitaire* from, on the one hand, the modernist poetics of the Fugitives and, on the other, the disciplinary formalism of New Criticism. Yet that figures such as Davidson, Ransom, Tate, and Warren, cut across these discrete, academic boundaries belies the supposedly apolitical transcendence that traditionally distinguishes literary from cultural studies.[26]

Consider, for example, the early career of, say, Cleanth Brooks. Typically viewed as a New Critic proper, Brooks is usually held at a formal remove from cultural matters by virtue of his close, "intrinsic" readings that are couched in sophisticated, theoretical registers. Nevertheless, the fact that Brooks was publishing in the midthirties in such reactionary journals as Collins's *American Review* reveals a certain positioning of his work within, not beyond, the political debates of his moment.[27] In fact, Brooks's reading of literary modernism is thoroughly implicated in an ideological, not just formal, critical stance. For example, in *Modern Poetry and the Tradition*, Brooks's constituting opposition between aesthetic "difficulty" and "sentimental" propaganda allowed him to valorize the high modernists under the first rubric and to denigrate, as its devalued "other," the poetics of Langston Hughes, Horace Gregory, Isidor Schneider, Genevieve Taggard, and the other contributors to *Proletarian Literature in the United States* (1935). "The characteristic fault," he charged, "of the type of poetry exhibited [in *Proletarian Literature*] is sentimentality. . . . It requires no special definition of the term to convict poems of Genevieve Taggard, Langston Hughes, and others in the collection of just this vice."[28] In hindsight, the force and authority of Brooks's critical judgment is attributable less, certainly, to the internal logic of his position (whose constituting binarism rests on a wholly arbitrary criterion of value)—less, that is, to his reading's intrinsic, critical rigor—but more to the enabling, extrinsic cultural politics of an era rocked by the crushing blow delivered to the American left by the 1939 Hitler-Stalin Nonaggression Pact. It is no accident that the rise of New Criticism, witnessed in works such as Brooks's *Modern Poetry and the Tradition* in 1939, is coincidental with the signing of the Soviet-German Nonaggression Pact that same year. The culture war waged throughout the 1930s between, on the one hand, the loose confederacy of conservative agrarians, protofascists, neoscholastics, and English Distributists and, on the other hand, American Marxism shapes the social text, argues John Fekete, that positioned "New Criticism as the ideological alternative to the Marxist criticism."[29]

One of the many careers that were ghosted by the New Critical campaign against the left is that of the recently recovered American poet, Edwin Rolfe. As a synecdoche of loss, the case of Edwin Rolfe reminds us of the disappearance not only of this major poetic talent but of an entire current in modern American culture. That the present recovery of the Rolfe canon should now elicit such widespread indifference is telling indeed. For, throughout his career, Rolfe's every literary act made a difference as a political intervention. Today, Rolfe's repression haunts the political unconscious of American poetics as a specter of revolutionary social forces that are no longer culturally permitted within the public sphere. That lapse in our collective self-knowledge is doubly impoverished when we consider how the course of Rolfe's career describes such a uniquely American life story.

To begin with, as a *nom du plume*, Edwin Rolfe describes an imaginary figure for the enabling cultural history that empowered the poet with a class-specific, social identity. A counterpart to Fitzgerald's Jay Gatsby—who "sprang from his Platonic conception of himself"—Edwin Rolfe, as a cultural signifier, is the poetic emanation of America's immigrant, working-class community.[30] For even before he became Edwin Rolfe, Solomon Fishman was a home-grown product of the American left. Fishman was the offspring of first-generation activists, who after emigrating from the Jewish community in Russia, became committed socialists and labor organizers in the United States. A member of the Young Communist League in the mid-1920s, Fishman published three agitational cartoons in the *Daily Worker* before going on to adopt the pseudonym Edwin Rolfe in the late twenties.

During this time, Rolfe was powerfully shaped by the examples, and socioaesthetic labor, of Michael Gold and Joseph Freeman, who in 1924 were mentoring what would become a new generation of politically engaged poets. "Some of us," Rolfe would later write, "took Michael Gold's 'Writers' Workshop' class at the Old Workers' School on East Fourteenth Street":

> We studied journalism and had fragmentary talks with Joseph Freeman. . . . Talking, lecturing, writing, they kept their ideas and convictions alive and growing when all others descended into bogs, were sidetracked, or deserted. It was Joseph Freeman who finally showed some of us our real direction, our real goal. . . . "Stop thinking of yourselves," he said, "as poets who are also revolutionists or as revolutionists who are poets. Remember that you are revolutionary poets."[31]

Such collective settings of creative writing were further inspired by cultural exchanges with Soviet envoys like Vladimir Mayakovsky, who toured the New York literary scene in 1925. Rolfe came of age as a revolutionary poet within a cultural conjuncture whose internationalist scope, diversity of gender, racial, and class perspectives, and blend of high, avant-garde, and populist styles are reflected in such publishing venues as the *New Masses* and the various little magazines sponsored by the John Reed Clubs and other communist and socialist organizations.

After a brief stint at the Experimental College at the University of Wisconsin–Madison, Rolfe wrote for the New York *Daily Worker*. Similar to Whitman, Rolfe took his identity as a poet, in part, from his early working experience as an urban journalist and later at midcareer as a war correspondent. Rolfe's first volume of verse, *To My Contemporaries* (1936), collects poems from the Depression era; some, such as "Asbestos," "Credo," and "Homage to Karl Marx," had been showcased earlier in journals like *New Masses, Dynamo, Partisan Review, New Republic, Daily Worker*, and in collaborative anthologies such as *We Gather Strength* (1933) and *Proletarian Literature of the United States* (1935). Reviewing the poet's first Dynamo Press volume, Joseph Freeman found strong poems that prompted his theoretical claims for the transpersonal foundations of poetic form. Freeman's critical assertion that the individual's concept of the artist as a free agent . . . is doomed to disappear with the passing of individualist civilization"[32] reflected Rolfe's "Credo" that:

> To welcome multitudes—the miracle of deeds
> performed in unison—the mind
> must renounce the fiction of the self
> and its vainglory. It must pierce
> the dreamplate of its solitude, the fallacy
> of its omnipotence, the fairytale
> aprilfools recurring every day
> in speeches of professors and politicians.
>
> It must learn
> the wisdom and strength and the togetherness
> of bodies phalanxed in a common cause,
> of fists tight-clenched around a crimson banner
> flying in the wind above a final, fierce
> life-and-death fight against a common foe.[33]

Contemporary readers will no doubt find such utopian faith in the imminent "passing of individualist civilization" somewhat anachronistic, echoing as it does certain orthodox forecasts of the Comintern's so-called Third Period that have been long discarded. Nevertheless, what is recoverable in much of Rolfe's early work is the arresting countermemory still to be found there: a voiced historicity that contra-

dicts the dominant postwar framing of American poetry through solipsistic narratives of the isolate self.[34]

Communal and proactive, "the mind" for Rolfe must inaugurate revolutionary
modes of collective social agency. "It must pierce / the dreamplate of its solitude"—
the Romantic poetics of sincerity that, as Jerome McGann has shown, would later
dominate postwar confessional verse.[35] But equally important, this active, theoretical agency simultaneously deflates "the fallacy / of its omnipotence," what Jean-
François Lyotard would later critique from the vantage point of postmodernity as
the tyranny of Enlightenment master narratives, including those that would idealize
the proletariat as the universal subject of history.[36] While Rolfe expresses the period's Popular Front solidarity against the peril of fascism, he also passionately affirms
the poet's power to critique the ideological "dreamplate" of empty political rhetoric,
whether coming from the left or the right. Rolfe's "credo" subordinates the cultural
representation of political commitment—"the fairytale / aprilfools recurring every
day / in speeches of professors and politicians"—to concrete social praxis, not the
other way around. Admittedly, the radically utopian and communal impulses inscribed here, and that everywhere mark proletarian poetics, make alien and unsettling claims on us at first. Few readers of contemporary American verse will feel entirely comfortable with following Rolfe in simply giving up the "fiction of the self."
But this very resistance to embracing "the togetherness / of bodies phalanxed in a
common cause" points symptomatically to the personal bias of postwar confessionalism, whose residual power still reigns over poetry's contemporary milieu.

Subjective lyricism and the poetics of solipsism, however valorized in the postwar era, for Rolfe's generation seemed an illusory, even dangerous, luxury. Disen-
gaged from political struggle, such bourgeois discourses of the self appeared out of
step with the free world's resistance to the onslaught of international fascism. Reading the poem against its historical moment, we may begin to see how our own contemporary allegiance to possessive individualism is not so much a "natural" as it is
a historically contingent credo. What a closer attention to the social contexts both
of this body of literature and its reception serves to demonstrate, then, is that our
assessment of a work's literary significance does not necessarily rest on universal
foundations of aesthetic judgment. On the contrary, as we move back and forth between the pre- and postwar periods, such sharp disagreements concerning poetry's
formal resources and pragmatic functions clearly show that whatever standards of
taste and distinction we import into our readings of poetry are subject necessarily
to certain contingencies of value.[37] The shock of radical difference that we confront
in proletcult verse—a difference that transgresses nearly everything we have been
disciplined to expect from poetry—highlights how our personal reading habits are

themselves not just "normative" but always already positioned in relation to particular critical genealogies—always already mediated, that is, by our own immersion in history.

That judgments of poetic taste involve social, not universal, acts of valuation is
something Thomas McGrath's 1955 "Foreword" to *Permit Me Refuge* foregrounds in
accounting for the formal transitions Rolfe's poetry underwent, particularly in his
successful efforts during the Red Scare "to name the new thing that a degenerate
age had created."[38] Some four decades later, Cary Nelson's cogent preface to the
definitive, *The Collected Poems of Edwin Rolfe* (1993) underscores that historicizing
recognition. Transcoding the reception of Rolfe's formative stances for a very different cultural moment and a very changed readership, Nelson acknowledges that
"[n]o effort to make Rolfe's poetry an appropriate subject of historical inquiry can
avoid asking whether his work represents a past that remains usable now" (CP, 3).
The particular historicity witnessed in Rolfe's verse, I would argue, has crucial cultural value precisely as a compelling countermemory to the ahistoricism dominating the postwar containment of twentieth-century verse, first through the formal
constraints of American New Criticism and later in the solipsistic impulses shaping
academic verse traditions from the 1960s onward.

Against that better-known version of American poetry, Rolfe's career preserves
three definitive moments of a quite different literary history that is now seldom
seen. His three published volumes, *To My Contemporaries* (1936), *First Love and Other
Poems* (1951), and *Permit Me Refuge* (1955), give voice to a democratic tradition of
international socialism that evolves respectively through the Popular Front years
of the Depression era, the Spanish Civil War, and the postwar Red Scare. Not insignificantly, the recovery of Rolfe's poetry restores a set of literary coordinates by
which we can plot that progressive aesthetic legacy not only as the forerunner of
the feminist, antiwar, and black aesthetic movements of the Vietnam era but,
equally important, as the harbinger of a cultural poetics beyond the triumph of
multinational capitalism, whose social barbarism dominates our moment.

Not insignificantly, the return of Edwin Rolfe coincides with current scholarship
that is revisiting the historical passages that join Popular Front culture and the
Spanish Civil War to the underground aesthetics of the McCarthy era, to the New
Left of the 1960s and, more recently, to the New Social Movements of the post-
Vietnam period. But equally important, to read Rolfe now is also to reread the very
much unfinished business of classism, racism, sexism, and fascism that the poet
struggled against throughout his career. Across the great divide of history that sep-
arates Rolfe's moment from our own, his poetry makes pressing claims not only on
our habits as readers of American verse but on our present political reflexivity as

such. For it is cultural memory that is supremely at stake both in the repressive 1950s—the decade that decisively censored Rolfe's publication—and in the reactionary resurgences of the contemporary period. Rolfe is an uncanny figure in modern American poetry, for through him we begin to recognize just how far the same ideological agenda that repressed Old Left poetics persists even now in the received disciplinary protocols shaping our own naturalized habits of reading. Recovering Rolfe in the era of advanced capitalism is thus imbricated in a broader cultural task, whose politics entail, as Alexander Kluge and Oskar Negt have theorized, an active remembering: a "working through of the suppressed experience of the entire labor movement that has been mutilated by the bourgeois public sphere."[39] Witnessed in Rolfe's writing is the erasure of the progressive counterpublic sphere that his generation conceived out of the Great Depression and sought to defend in the Spanish Civil War and later during the postwar inquisitions of the McCarthy era. Reading Rolfe now recalls troubling historical defeats: defeats that are hardly over and done with but live on as they "exert pressure," according to Kluge and Negt, "on the ability to remember" (PSE, 95).

Part of the trouble in our cultural recall of modern American poetics is politically determined by the culture wars of the 1930s, where the formal innovations and social representations of proletarian poetics were countered by a conservative wave of critical reception. The clashing ideologies of the Great Depression pitted cultural workers of the American left against the Southern Agrarians. Contrary to the Agrarian, Fugitive, and New Critical campaign to silence proletarian verse—to dismiss it as agitprop doggerel—the poetry of Edwin Rolfe testifies to the rich, working-class aesthetic that flourished throughout the interbellum decades.[40] As an organic intellectual in Gramsci's sense, Rolfe in the 1930s voices the lived experience of urban starvation in "Season of Death," industrial disease in "Asbestos," political martyrdom in "Witness at Leipzig," local activism in "Unit Assignment," collective labor unrest in "Not Men Alone," and international solidarity in "Winds of Another Sphere." Inscribed in these works is not just the defining social poetics of the Great Depression, but the structure of feeling of what it was to be alive and active in the class struggle against global capital and international fascism.

In representing the Great Depression, Rolfe adapted a blend of realist and surrealist pictorial techniques inspired, in part, by Mexican muralists such as David Alfaro Siqueiros, whom Rolfe salutes in "Room for Revolutionaries." Similarly, "Georgia Nightmare" employs surrealism to expose the violence of Southern lynching as a surreal, civic horror. Called to witness the grotesque murder of a "black man [who] strangles above a sea of eyes" (CP, 60), Rolfe penetrates beyond the Southern spectacle of racial violence to risk social identification with "the black man," he affirms, "who looks like me" (CP, 69). The surrealist estrangement of the poem's visual field—found here in the image of "crazy mountains / crazily moving" with "a million faces leering in the sun" (CP, 69)—develops into a more sophisticated technique of poetic defamiliarization in Rolfe's definitive volume on the Spanish Civil War, *First Love and Other Poems* (1951). Real life in "City of Anguish," for example, assumes hallucinatory intensities in Rolfe's portrait of Republican Madrid's epic resistance to the air and artillery bombardment by the combined assault of Franco and the forces of the German Condor Legion in the summer and fall of 1937. On the streets of Madrid, the human evidence of war everywhere marks the urban scene in the literal signs of a dismembered history:

> The solitary foot
> deep-arched, is perfect on the cobbles, naked,
> strong, ridged with strong veins, upright, complete . . . (CP, 132)

Amidst such grotesque *objets trouvés*, the poet cringes in the moment suspended between artillery assaults, orchestrated metaphorically as "the pause in the idiot's symphony, prolonged / beyond the awaited crashing of cymbals," until "the swastika'd baton falls! and the clatter of / thunder begins again" (CP, 132).

Rolfe's aesthetic strategy in *First Love* recodes not just our perceptions of Spain but also the social meanings it signifies in the popular imaginary. In "Entry," the poet deploys a series of negations of what Spain represents as a "land of / postcard ruins" (CP, 130) for the capitalist tourist market. Rolfe's Spain is "No land of flamenco. . . . No land of oranges, or olive groves . . . nor gitanos and guitarristas" (CP, 130). Within the secured space of global capitalism, such static and fetishized cultural signifiers fix Spain as a spectacle of tourism, consumption, and imperialist nostalgia. Against that reified version of Spanish national identity, "Entry" deterritorializes Spain along a temporal axis of revolutionary change. As a literal front line in the historic clash between the forces of fascism and communism, capitalism and socialism, global imperialism and regional resistance, "Spain," Rolfe writes, "is yesterday's Russia, tomorrow's China / yes, and the thirteen seaboard states" (CP, 130).

Ten years after, Republican Spain remained for Rolfe's generation at once the triumph of that historical consciousness and, paradoxically, the haunting memory of its defeat. As a veteran, Rolfe lost close friends to the Republican cause and he knew first hand that "[w]ar is your comrade struck dead beside you, / his shared cigarette still alive in your lips" (CP, 135). As poet laureate of the International Brigades, Rolfe gave voice to the sacrifices of the war dead in poems such as "Death by Water," "Epitaph (for Arnold Reid)," and "Elegy for our Dead." Yet unconsoled by his own language, he notes that for all his verbal eulogizing, "Deeds were their last words" (CP,

143). The resurrection of the Republic's martyrs, figured in the war's Hispanic verse as well as in Rolfe's own elegies, happened. But it did not happen in the poet's hopeful, organic metaphors of rebirth that would transmogrify graves into seed beds "that sun can reach and rouse to luminous birth" (CP, 144). Instead, the dead—as specters of ultimate political commitment, of deeds rather than words—make haunting demands on the poet throughout the Cold War decades.

"In the Time of Hesitation," an uncollected poem of the 1940s, finds Rolfe suspended between the defeat of the Spanish Republicans and basic training at Camp Wolters, Texas, for World War II: a war that might have been prevented, in his view, had the free world responded decisively to the staging ground of fascism in Spain. Possessed by the memory of dead companions, Rolfe realizes that his true "comrades-in-arms" are not the green recruits around him—those "children / too young to look into her [war's] eyes of furious-fire"—but the victims of that earlier conflict the international community failed to win, whose martyrs are now "dust wherein the million half-remembered faces / and million haunted eyes accuse without voices, / repeating the agonized question: When? When?" (CP, 202). Eroded by time, those "half-remembered" ghosts make the task of cultural memory more urgent as a pressing political necessity. "We must remember," the poet insists, in "Postscript to War," "cleanly why we fought, / clearly why we left these inadequate shores / and turned our eyes, hearts, Spainward" (CP, 160).

Yet as time passed, the memory of the international brigades, eulogized in such poems as "War Guilt," became harder to bear. Reversing the ontological order of things in "Brigadas Internacionales," the dead assert their sacrifice as more vital than the diminished thing of mere survival. Here, that otherworldly chorus "proclaim[s] in pride: We saw. We acted. Fought. / We died, while others in cowardice lived on" (CP, 198). Living on as a veteran of the Loyalist cause—first under the political harassment of Congressman Martin Dies and the House Un-American Activities Committee in the aftermath of World War II and, later, through the inquisition and betrayals of McCarthyism in the 1950s—Rolfe and his faith in the very viability of a socialist politics were severely tested.

During the Popular Front years, the organic politics of class solidarity had provided foundational certainties, inspiring the poet in, say, "Marching Song of the Children of Darkness" to "fight man's inhumanity—the monstrous synthesis / arrayed against him, in chaos, in malice" (CP, 165). Later, however, the problem of capital's global and complexly organized Third Wave in the postwar years becomes paralyzing in poems such as "In Praise Of." Here, instead of the "bodies phalanxed in a common cause" of "Credo" (CP, 59), we find "dark forces phalanxed" against the isolate, surviving revolutionary: "the spiked fist, the assassin's knife, the horses' / eyeless hooves above as he fell under" (CP, 223). Such powers of political repression are both literally and psychologically crushing for "[t]o understand the sum of all this terror," Rolfe writes, "would a priori have meant defeat, disaster." "Born of cold panic," the "error" of living on into the 1950s renders the haunting memory of those who had died well a poignant rebuke to mere survival.

Despite Rolfe's self-recriminations, perhaps the sign and force of his continuing political allegiances in the McCarthy era reside in his record of publication and reception or, rather, the lack of one. Even in the thirtieth anniversary year of the commencement of the Spanish Civil War, one could still note Rolfe's continuing exile from the republic of letters.[41] An MIA in the Red Scare culture wars, Rolfe's body of verse from the 1950s nevertheless remains the most arresting and prophetic account of McCarthyism and Cold War angst that we possess in American poetry. Not unlike the fate of the Spanish War dead, the disappearance of Edwin Rolfe, the author, marks the crypt of cultural memory struck from the text of modern American letters. The return of Rolfe makes for an uncanny read: invoking, as his writing does, revenants of social experience that have long been repressed rather than worked through. Witnessed in Rolfe's poetry of the 1950s are the at once estranging and familiar specters that prevailed in the McCarthy era and that persist, arguably, in the reactionary resurgence of the New Right and in the phantom emanations of neofascism, domestic xenophobia, ultranationalism, homophobia, classism, racism, and sexism haunting America's contemporary political unconscious.

The revenant of Red Scare paranoia, for example, returns with remarkable affective force in Rolfe's long poem "All Ghouls' Night." Rolfe's horrific portraits of Joseph McCarthy and the rituals of the House Un-American Activities Committee (HUAC) hearings recall, in their personifications of America's postwar inquisition, the dark mastery of Goya's "Black Paintings": "Compounded of deceit / and avarice and horror, / shrieking I am the state, / Ghoul unleashed his terror, / destroyed all loveliness" (CP, 221). Similarly coded metaphors of McCarthyism predominate in Rolfe's late oeuvre as in "Bal Masqué," a surreal meditation on HUAC surveillance. Here at the "Gala Event," the accused must "line up like living puppets / carved in a crazed alchemist's dungeon / and colored with his mad imaginings; / line up like children awaiting the terror / of the giant stranger's question" (CP, 237). In this distorted public sphere—"where privacy is publicly outlawed . . . where even an innocent unguarded eye / means sudden expulsion, the culprit sent, / clutching his emptiness, to banishment" (CP, 237)—the poet, likewise, must perform a practiced dissemblance before the "big Band Leader," who nevertheless "knows us all, / sees through the subtle masquerade / the lie of each elaborate disguise" (CP, 239).

Ultimately, "Bal Masqué" locates the ontological roots of HUAC inquisition in the modernist registers of death-in-life that Eliot plumbs, say, in *The Waste Land*. The arresting metaphor of the *danse macabre* that Rolfe portrays in "Bal Masqué"s' ballroom automatons offers a postwar version of the kind of spiritual torpor and paralysis with which we are familiar in "The Hollow Men":

> The wound is the magic signal to begin.
> Thus tapped, each rigid dancer moves
> her tapering limbs, his trembling fingers.
> The heart would beat, if there were a heart,
> and breathing, if there were breath, sigh out
> with pleasure if it knew what pleasure was.
> But since this ballroom is unique,
> heart and breath and pleasure hang
> on the silent music, the motionless baton,
> the rigid poise of the dancers, whose eyes
> are drained of sight, whose ears of sound. (CP, 238–39)

Appropriating the same repetition of conditional clauses that Eliot employs in the despairing opening lines of section 5 ("What the Thunder Said") of *The Waste Land*, "Bal Masqué" exposes the lifeless, "rigid poise" of the 1950s as the end result of a world orchestrated by total state surveillance.

In his last uncollected and unpublished poems, Rolfe's dramatic monologue and epistolary forms parody the mad masquerade of political passing in the McCarthy era. Poems such as "Are You Now or Have You Ever Been," "Letter," and "A Letter to the Denouncers" dwell on the destinies of those who "cooperated" with the House Un-American Activities Committee in "recanting" their former lives and naming onetime comrades. In portraying the social casualties of the Red Scare, the poet reveals the ill fate of moral collapse, ethical compromise, and spiritual defeat that went hand in hand with the loss of the core social commitments forged two decades earlier in the Depression era. "Are You Now or Have You Ever Been" ironically reverses the discursive conventions and civic rituals of committee inquisition. The poem takes its title, of course, from the key question put to all those who were subpoenaed to appear before the committee. In the early days of the Martin Dies Committee, the question was simply, "Are you a member of the Communist Party of the United States?" To undermine this line of interrogation, the Party launched the countermeasure of automatically canceling one's membership upon having to respond, so that one could truthfully answer "No" without risk of perjury. Making the line of questioning retroactive allowed the committee, in turn, to circumvent this ploy.[42] The famous nickname of this query, the so-called sixty-four-dollar question, reflects the committee's theatrical politics borrowed from the spectacle of game shows that came into their heyday with the advent of television. In Rolfe's poetic drama, the accused confesses to the crime of succumbing to "a moment of pity / a vulnerable second of sympathy" (CP, 254). "My defenses were down," the speaker pleads to the multiple charges of having supported clemency for six black defendants, having made a modest donation for refugee relief, and having demonstrated for rent control. Rolfe's poem stages how simple altruism, human empathy, and social solidarity in the 1950s put one supremely at risk, framed as they are here as grounds for state sedition.

Tellingly, this defendant's plea for leniency internalizes the Cold War cultural logic that placed communal ethics and social commitment at odds with domestic conformity, self-reliance, possessive individualism, and traditional family values:

> but please believe me
> everything I did was done through weakness if you will
> but it's strange how weakness of this kind snowballs
> multiplies
> before they approached me with that innocent petition
> I was may it please the court exactly
> like you like every other man
> I lived my own life solely suffered
> only my own sorrows and enjoyed my own triumphs
> small ones I grant you
> asked nothing from
> gave nothing to
> any man
> except myself my wife my children. (CP, 254)

The ideological clash between the privatized, nuclear family and the democratic polis persisted throughout the postwar era and could be heard, for example, in the 1996 Republican Presidential Convention when nominee Bob Dole insisted that "it takes a family" to raise a child, thereby signifying his party's antagonism to the rhetorical figure of community featured in Hillary Rodham Clinton's 1996 book *It Takes a Village: And Other Lessons Children Teach Us.*

In a similar dramatization of the Red Scare's shaping of everyday life in the 1950s, "Letter" blurs the boundary between the public and domestic confessional in a husband's note to his spouse explaining the circumstances of his own impending committee summons. Employing the epistolary conventions of intimacy, privacy, and sincerity, Rolfe draws the reader into sympathy with the father's ethical concern for his family's well-being, faced with the impending fiscal hardships and civic scandal of committee interrogation. Here he advises his spouse to "send the children up to Jim's in the country" so as to avoid "the cruelty of their classmates, possibly even their teachers" (CP, 256). Such familial care is ironically undercut, however, in the letter's final instructions, which are telling in their social and self-betrayals:

> And third—and this is most important—
> find out who those people were—
> the people who asked me to sign that letter,
> who asked me for that small contribution,
> who prompted me to join the demonstration.
> By the time I return
> I want to know them better
> I have lots of questions to ask
> many things to find out
> and they're the ones I have a hunch
> who can tell me everything I want to know. (CP, 256)

In its turn to black humor as a psychic defense against Red Scare repression, Rolfe's late verse resists his moment's pervasive cultural pressure to disavow communal allegiances in favor of the socially restrictive simulacra of civic normalcy, sexual conformity, and upward class mobility, as well as gender and race subordination that were all sanctioned in the new phenomenon of the suburban nuclear family.[43] As an ideological figure of containment, the white, middle-class, patriarchal household of the 1950s—as promoted, not insignificantly, by the spectacle of television and the burgeoning mass media—served as the domestic counterpart to America's emergent foreign policy doctrine of containment of global communism: the "malignant parasite" diagnosed as early as February 22, 1946, in George Kennan's so-called Long Telegram of eighty-thousand words from Moscow to the State Department.[44] Moreover, as a habitus of social reproduction, the all-American family effectively displaced alternative identities whose social foundations rest on class, gender, sexual, and racial difference.[45] Adopting the solicitous address of postwar advertising and bureaucratic speaking, Rolfe hails the would-be subject of upright civic virtue as itself a paranoid figure of state surveillance: "Sir, as you start for work each morning, please, / check your clothes-closet for skeletons, / your dreams for inconsistencies, / the radio in your car for microphones" (CP, 258). Not dissimilar to the kind of black humor we have come to value in Kenneth Fearing's caustic,

Depression-era verse, Rolfe's amusing parodies of middle-class phobias baffle the extreme, psychopolitical states of postwar cultural suspicion, paranoia, and terror otherwise registered in "Bal Masqué" and "All Ghouls' Night."

In an era when poetic formalism served the New Critical mission of neutralizing socially committed verse, Rolfe's use of fixed forms to voice his most subversive commentaries on American life marks a key appropriation of traditional measures for political protest. Indeed, at the level of form, the rhyming couplets of "Little Ballad for Americans—1954" perform an implicit parody of the kind of poetic artifice that, in the fifties, defined the conservative New Critical hegemony in academic verse. Rather perversely, Rolfe turns such formalism against itself not only to capture the reigning paranoia of the Red Scare:

> Student, student, keep mouth shut and brain spry—
> Your best friend Dick Merriwell's employed by the F.B.I.

but also, to push succinctly the mass-mediated spectacular logic of McCarthyism to its dehumanizing conclusion:

> Give full allegiance only to circuses and bread;
> No person's really trustworthy until he's dead. (CP, 260)

Similarly, in "Pastoral—1954," formalism drives home the point in Rolfe's ironic collapsing of two antithetical cultural moments, thereby clarifying the political divide separating Republican Spain from Republican America:

> Who used to lie with his love
> In the glade, far from the battle-sector,
> Now lies embraced by a lie-detector
> And can not, dare not, move. (CP, 259)

In such savvy formalist measures, Rolfe masterfully marks the break between the passionate thirties and the paralyzed fifties: between the organicism of international socialist commitment and the paranoia of state surveillance. Part of why Rolfe matters to twentieth-century American poetry is the sheer endurance of his political stances that bridge the interbellum and postwar decades. Moreover, Rolfe's evolving continuity of poetic strategies counters the persistent critical tendency to periodize modern poetry as a discrete domain cut off from contemporary American verse. In this shaping of American poetics, the postwar years typically belong to New Criticism, whose ahistorical formalism prevails up through the advent of the Beat and Black Mountain movements anthologized in Donald Allen's *The New American Poetry* (1960). For too long that narrative of academic contain-

ment has backgrounded Rolfe's crucial linkage of the politically engaged project of
Depression-era verse to the haunted cultural poetics of McCarthyism and the Cold
War era.

New Criticism not only effaced the socialist poetics of American verse between the
wars, but imbricated class with racial repression in its broader political agenda of
promoting cultural squirearchy. Lodged against Northern industry—whose Fordist,
planned economy threatened to bestow more democratic cultural representation
on a diversified buying public—the Southern Agrarian nostalgia for an idealized
plantation life resisted the leveling of social distinctions that subordinated blacks
and other ethnic groups of the American laboring class to what Ransom described
as the "Anglophile sentiment" (ITS, 3) of the traditional Republic. In theorizing the
South through what Benedict Anderson might describe as an "imagined community"—the narrative "fraternity" of a "deep horizontal comradeship"[46]—Ransom
charged that the newly industrialized South had "forgotten" its true self: its agrarian rootedness in "physical earth" and its "primary joy, which is an inexhaustible
source of arts and religions and philosophies" (ITS, 9). Promulgating a brand of
Southern nationalism, Ransom sought to deploy Southern nostalgia for an idealized and largely imaginary rural tradition in ideological resistance to the forces of
social modernization that went hand in hand with the cosmopolitan spread of industry and big city life.

  As spokesperson for a Southern intelligentsia, Ransom noted the damaging
influences of capitalization and the "American progressive doctrine" on Southern
living. His aim was to "reverse this order and find that the Southern idea rather
than the American has in its favor the authority of example and the approval of theory" (ITS, 3). Such a politics of "underdevelopment"[47] defended the kind of conservative cultural order espoused in T. S. Eliot's earlier framing of high literary tradition within the "mind of Europe": a key precedent for Ransom's own campaign
for "European principles of culture."[48] Positioning Southern Agrarianism as heir to
the "heredity" of Western culture, Ransom warned that "the European principles
had better look to the South if they are to be perpetuated in this country" (ITS, 3).
But more to the point, such Eurocentrism was lodged in his polemic, against what
he stigmatized as the twin "Americanisms" of "Progress and Service." In tropes that
imbricate nationalism, race, and gender, Ransom linked the former, "masculine"
ideology of progress to the biblical typology of "Adam's Curse" of unbridled am-
bition and the willful domination of nature. But more telling was Ransom's critique of progressive social service, which he described as the "feminine form" of
the Northern, urban economy. Ransom's tirade against the Popular Front of the

Depression era revealed his own ideological melting pot of racism, sexism, classism, and ethnocentrism, against which he positioned the "European principle of culture" in differential relation. Couched in misogynist and xenophobic stereotypes, "service," Ransom wrote, "means the function of Eve, it means the seducing of laggard men into fresh struggles with nature. It has special application to the apparently stagnant sections of mankind, it busies itself with the heathen Chinee, with the Roman Catholic Mexican, with the 'lower' classes in our society" (ITS, 10).

Read as a reactionary nationalism, the Agrarian cause marks not just a turning away from the industrialized "new South," not just a recovery of an older confederacy "deeply founded in the way of life itself—in its tables, chairs, portraits, festivals, laws, marriage, customs."[49] But more troubling, the cultural logic of this Southern ideologeme rests on the differential rubric of race as its constituting ground of imaginary group identity. Not surprisingly, Southern squirearchy's regime of the same—what Tate defended as "white rule"—depends on an enabling community of others made up of its former slave class. Thus, the Southerners' critique of Northern industrialism, their campaign for a refined Eurocentric and Anglophilic canon, and their attempted restoration of a hierarchic cultural order were all inextricably interwoven with the specific historicity of the African Diaspora coupled with the colonizing discourses and material praxes that would sustain white supremacy.

The "social organization" of what John Crowe Ransom described as Southern squirearchy entailed a cultural logic where "people were for the most part in their right places." But what did it mean, we may well ask, to be positioned in one's rightful place within a slave system? "Slavery," as far as Ransom was concerned, "was a feature monstrous enough in theory, but, more often than not, humane in practice" (ITS, 14). Ransom's apology for a "humane" slavery, of course, is baldly oxymoronic and breaks down under squirearchy's commodification of persons as capital. Implicitly assumed here is what Ransom's colleague Frank Lawrence Owsley explicitly theorized: that the slave plantation is the "right place" for African Americans because of their racial inferiority, primitivism, and savagery. Owsley was not only quite blunt about the bottom-line realities of such a chattel economy, noting that the North depleted the South of "nearly $2,000,000,000 invested in slaves." But more outrageously, he openly stigmatized African Americans as subhuman brutes, "some of whom," he charged, "could still remember the taste of human flesh and the bulk of them hardly three generations removed from cannibalism" (ITS, 62). It was precisely against this racial stereotype of the barbarous other that the South's own self-image as the latter-day exemplar of Western culture—the "seat of an agrarian civilization" (ITS, 71)—was founded. In a symptomatic linkage of the American South to a venerable lineage of such precursor, slave-holding states as ancient Greece and the Roman republic, Owsley rationalized slavery through the same cultural tradition that founds the Western canon. "The Greek tradition," he wrote, "became partly grafted upon the Anglo-Saxon and Scotch tradition of life. However, it was the Romans of the early republic, before land speculators and corn laws had driven men from the soil to the city slums, who appealed most powerfully to the South" (ITS, 70).

Although less blatant in its racial stereotypes than Owsley's savage representations, Robert Penn Warren's "The Briar Patch," exploited Booker T. Washington's version of the Tuskegee work ethic to resist the emerging "New Negro" intelligentsia of the 1920s and to confine African Americans to the lumpenproletariat and semiskilled working classes. Black theorists of the New Negro movement such as Alain Locke had five years earlier promoted the Roaring Twenties' renaissance in African-American cultural expression celebrated in the salons, cabarets, and lecture halls of Harlem, Durham, Washington, DC, Atlanta, Hampton, Nashville, and Lincoln. Pockets of entrepreneurial success—as in, say, Durham's prosperous North Carolina Mutual Life Insurance Company and its Mechanics and Farmers Bank—coupled with growing black enclaves in the professions and academy were sowing the seeds for the growth of an African-American bourgeoisie. And it was precisely against this emerging professional class that Warren advocated "an emphasis on vocational education for the negro" (ITS, 250). This proletarianization of the emerging black professional class, moreover, was joined to the racial subtext of Warren's resistance to its call for social equality in, and desegregation of, the privileged spaces of the Southern public sphere—schools, restaurants, hotels, concert halls, etc. Warren sought to legitimate his take on desegregation by stigmatizing it as the agenda of the black "radical."

Linking his position to Booker T. Washington's famous Atlanta Exposition speech (1895) of the previous century, Warren allowed that when Washington "lifted his hand and said, 'We can be as separate as the fingers, yet one as the hand in all things essential to mutual progress,' the hand he raised, in the eyes of such a radical, was the hand of treason" (ITS, 254). Similarly, Warren argued against the integration of white trade unions, noting that while the American Federation of Labor had opened its ranks to blacks in the Atlantic City Convention of 1919, "there is a vast difference between that paper victory and a workable system which would embody its principles" (ITS, 257). Through the clever argument that Northern industry was relocating to the South simply to capitalize on cheap black labor, Warren maintained that African Americans would be better served under the South's traditional sharecropping economy.

Writing to the left of Warren, W. E. B. Du Bois had already critiqued the exploitation of Pan-African labor worldwide. But differing from Warren, Du Bois's solution did not call on blacks to give up the new forces of industrialization to "white capital." Moreover, he challenged the force of racial propaganda installed throughout the modern culture industry, which drives home capital's global wedge against labor. As early as 1925, in his contribution to Locke's *The New Negro* anthology, Du Bois had theorized that the "propaganda of poet and novelist, the uncanny welter of romance, the half knowledge of scientists, the pseudo-science of statesmen—all these, united in the myth of mass inferiority of most men, have built a wall which many centuries will not break down."[50] The same propaganda of the African American's racial inferiority was patent in Warren's patronizing claim that "the Southern negro has always been a creature of the small town and farm. That is where he still chiefly belongs, by temperament and capacity" (ITS, 260).

For Warren, belonging to Southern squirearchy also meant an espousal of "a certain individualism" from which it sprang (ITS, 257). In his idealized version of the agrarian economy, racial oppression and class subordination were obscured by such mystifying ideologies of earthy self-reliance and communal "personalism." "The rural life," he concluded, "provides the most satisfactory relationship of the two races which can be found at present . . . in all cases—owner, cropper, hand— there is the important aspect of a certain personal contact" (ITS, 262). Not coincidentally, Warren's defense of Southern sharecropping as the best and most humane social alternative for African Americans came after three decades of the so-called Great Migration of blacks to the urban North, which had the effect of eroding the South's cheap labor market. In fact, the real economic subordination of blacks served the interests of both wealthy Southern planters and poor whites despite their class differences.

Contrary to Warren's rosy picture of Southern living, blacks had little incentive to eek out a subsistence wage under a racial caste system that also restricted them to separate and unequal facilities, disenfranchised them through discriminatory voting statutes, de-skilled them in education, and exposed them to constant harassment and lethal levels of physical abuse. As a matter of fact, in response to these gross social inequities, some 170,000 African Americans made the exodus out of the South during the first decade of the twentieth century, while 450,000 followed suit in the 1910s, peaking in a flood tide of 750,000 black émigrés during the 1920s. One form of institutional racism that belied Warren's consoling myth of "personal contact" among owner, cropper, and hand was the covert system of black peonage practiced throughout the rural South. Although outlawed as early as 1867 and confirmed by a Supreme Court declaration of 1905, it was common for local judges and sheriffs to take blacks convicted of minor violations and contract them out to local plantations, where they were submitted to slave labor conditions for indefinite periods of time. Worked far in excess of their nominal fines, such prisoners were in some instances murdered, as on John Williams's 2,700-acre plantation, in local attempts to cover up this chattel economy. Chain gangs, prison camps, and urban vagrancy stockades compounded the inhuman conditions to which municipal offenders, 90 percent of whom were black, were sentenced.[51]

However disenfranchised at the voting booth, Southern blacks nevertheless could vote with their feet by moving on to the urban, industrial North. Outmigration was heaviest in such "Cotton South" states as Georgia and South Carolina, where African Americans were victims of longstanding racial violence. Between 1882 and 1930, for example, 1,663 African Americans were lynched by mobs of whites within the Cotton South alone, with another 1,299 legally executed on frequently trumped-up charges.[52] In Georgia, African Americans were terrorized by such infamous cases as Atlanta's mob violence of 1906. There, some ten thousand armed whites had rampaged through the streets of the city, torturing, mutilating, and shooting blacks during the harrowing weekend of September 22. Similarly throughout the Southern countryside, "legal" convictions of black Georgians on charges of capital punishment frequently degenerated into brutal spectacles that staged the message of racial subordination in the cruelest terms. In rural Georgia, writes John Dittmer, "there is truth in H. L. Mencken's statement that lynching often replaced the merry-go-round, theater, brass band, and other diversions found in the city."[53] Such was the case in Statesboro, where Paul Reed and Will Cato were sentenced to the gallows on the charge of murdering a white planter. Before the sentence could be carried out, however, a crowd of some ten thousand spectators violently seized the two prisoners from the custody of sixty-eight state militia, chained them to a stump, doused them with twenty gallons of oil, and burned them to death to the cheers of the mob.[54]

Not just a form of local entertainment, the Southern spectacle of racial violence communicated in no uncertain terms the blunt message of the black underclass's social subordination at the very moment when new political antagonisms—coupled with revisionary representations of race and an emergent, cultural Pan-Africanism—were shaking the foundations of white, Southern squirearchy. More is at stake here than a simple antiquarian glimpse back into the record of rural lynchings in the Deep South. For such racial subordination in social practice was also linked to the ideological labor of the very figures who inaugurated the academic institution of modern literary studies. No less a founder of the Fugitive and New Critical movements than Allen Tate, in fact, advanced a rationale for enforcing "white rule" and "white supremacy" by any means necessary, including lynching. "I argue it this way," he wrote in Seward Collins's 1934 volume of the *American Review:*

> the white race seems determined to rule the Negro race in its midst; I belong to the
> white race; therefore I intend to support white rule. Lynching is a symptom of weak,
> inefficient rule; but you can't destroy lynching by fiat or social legislation; lynching
> will disappear when the white race is satisfied that its supremacy will not be ques-
> tioned in social crises.[55]

Such is the unsanitized conjuncture of racial and class oppression whose Agrarian specter haunts the later, New Critical campaign for an idealized, Anglo-European cultural order. Southern, white supremacy, though explicitly repressed in the Fugitives' New Critical incarnation, nevertheless marked its critical tenets based, as they were, on the repression of history, social critique, and multicultural diversity.

Beyond its promotion of the modernist literary canon, the New Critical agenda had wider cultural ambitions that—tied to the cultural elitism of the high modernists—sought to intervene in the shaping of everyday life in twentieth-century America. For example, Brooks and Warren would complain in the fifties that modern readers, as consumers of pop culture, showed little interest in or capacity for close textual reading. "Instead, they listen to speeches, go to church, view television programs, read magazine stories, or the gossip columns of newspapers."[56] Framed as it is here in the preface to the 1958 edition of *Understanding Poetry,* Brooks and Warren's project in this widely adopted primer was arguably not just to popularize a set of rules for honing reading skills but, equally important, to intervene in the shaping of the postwar culture. Operating at the academic margins of this new public sphere, Brooks and Warren nevertheless sought to secure it as what Pierre Bourdieu would describe as a privileged "habitus" of social distinction.[57] As an institution not just of knowledge but of power and domination, the literary canon that Brooks and Warren promulgated in *Understanding Poetry* would reproduce the social logic of squirearchy, where as Ransom had earlier written, "[P]eople were for the most part in their right places." Thus, of the ninety-four poets anthologized in the 1938 edition of *Understanding Poetry* not one is black; less than a handful are female; and not a single poet of the American left is preserved.

To "save the text" of New Critical pedagogy, which is still an enduring, if not dominant, reading and teaching practice in the academy, is to keep its underlying specter at bay. One would have to argue that the canonical assumptions shaping *Understanding Poetry* reflect a moment where black literature, women's literature, and socially committed literature were simply absent from America's public culture between the wars. In the instance of race, to take just one of these social

exclusions, one would have to argue that Brooks and Warren's erasure of black poetics was a disinterested oversight or blind spot toward race, not a willful silencing
of racial discourse. Moreover, one would have to maintain that the New Critical
core doctrine of eschewing from the study of literature proper (1) "paraphrase of
logical and narrative content," (2) "study of biographical and historical materials,"
and (3) "inspirational and didactic interpretation" does not implicate that doctrine
in a strategic politics of cultural containment and social repression.[58] Yet, from the
hindsight of our postmodern vantage point, none of these rationales is at all satisfactory. Indeed, the New Critical marketing of canonical protocols of reading in
primers like *Understanding Poetry* implicates it in a seamless, ideological continuity
reaching back to the Southern Agrarian cause.

In fact, the cultural work of Brooks and Warren's anthology would go far toward
turning the tide back against the previous decade's push to promote an African-
American aesthetic in such precursor volumes as Louis Untermeyer's *Modern American Poetry* (1925) and Alfred Kreymborg's *Lyric America* (1930).[59] Within the African-
American community, intellectuals like James Weldon Johnson had valued black
culture on a par with white. "The status of the Negro in the United States," he
wrote in the classic preface to *The Book of American Negro Poetry* (1922), "is more a
question of national mental attitude toward the race than of actual conditions. And
nothing will do more to change that mental attitude and raise his status than a
demonstration of intellectual parity by the Negro through the production of literature and art."[60] Putting Johnson's cultural strategy into literary practice, Countée
Cullen, in his "Foreword" to *Caroling Dusk* (1927), rather self-consciously positioned
his text within an authoritative African-American literary continuity. Here he cited
its foundational precursors, including James Weldon Johnson's inaugural volume
The Book of American Negro Poetry (1922), as well as Robert Kerlin's *Negro Poets and
Their Poems* (1923), and Newman Ivey White's *An Anthology of Verse by American
Negroes* (1924). Cullen's tactic was to popularize new black talents by joining them
to a reputable body of "modern Negro poets already established and acknowledged, by virtue of their seniority and published books, as worthy practitioners of
their art."[61] Thus, he linked Dunbar's dialect poetry and Johnson's sermon forms
to Helene Johnson's "colloquial verses" and Hughes's blues lyrics, while noting
Sterling Brown's fusion of vernacular idiom with sonnet forms.

Cullen revised somewhat the task of the black artist as Johnson had defined it
five years earlier. "What the colored poet in the United States needs to do," Johnson had argued, "is something like what Synge did for the Irish" (ANP, 40). Cullen,
however, parted company with Johnson's nationalist paradigm as an inadequate,
ideological limit to the emerging diversity of the new black canon. He resisted

any "attempt to corral the outbursts of the ebony muse into some definite mold to which all poetry by Negroes will conform" (CD, xi). In this vein, Cullen foregrounded the role of black authors in advancing experimental modernism and the international avant-gardes. As examples, he cited Jessie Fauset's debts to the Sorbonne and Lewis Alexander's reliance on tanka and haiku forms. But equally important, Cullen shrewdly articulated Anne Spencer's "cool precision" to the new wave of imagist poetics, popularized in America by Amy Lowell. Differing from the often phallocentric bent of high modernists like Pound, Cullen, as a black bisexual editor, was open to the revisionary gender role inscribed in the poetry of Alice Dunbar-Nelson, Angelina Weld Grimké, and Gladys May Casely Hayford. He not only promoted art that challenged stereotypical relations between the races but published works that subverted Victorian sexual norms.

All of this effort, however, was lost on Brooks and Warren, who as arbiters of institutional literary tastes, simply erased the sophisticated linkages Cullen and many others had forged between literary modernism and the emerging black canon. Today, the standard "professional" gesture—which returns even now as an uncanny revenant in the classroom, at academic conferences, and even in print— is to dismiss such racism through the claim that modernists "didn't know better": that they were somehow innocent or unconscious of their racially motivated politics, that such racism was simply a reflection of modern culture. This would be an understandable defense if modernism in its own moment was not as dialogic and contested a cultural terrain as our own period's panorama of competing social interests. Indeed, as recent recovery projects have shown us, American culture was if anything even more politically inflected between the wars than it is today.

Despite the theoretical revolution of the post-Vietnam era, Brooks's cultural politics proved a remarkably durable foundation for canonical institutions in the postwar era. Transmitted through such contemporary apologists for the Western canon as say, Allan Bloom, E. D. Hirsch, Arthur Schlesinger, Jr., Diane Ravitch, Dinesh D'Souza, and Hilton Kramer among others, the Eurocentric cultural mission originally forged in the high modern–New Critical conjuncture of the 1930s made inroads via the Reagan and Bush presidencies into the Department of Education and National Endowment for the Humanities with the appointments of William Bennett and Lynne Cheney. Throughout the 1980s, both Bennett and Cheney exploited their government positions as bully pulpits to espouse the "transcendent" values of Western Humanism.[62] Not surprisingly, their foregrounding of "great" literature backgrounded the same multicultural constituencies that were marginalized in the formalist agenda of New Criticism. For his part, Cleanth Brooks remained unwavering even at the end of the twentieth century in advocating a consistent, Anglo-European cultural platform. Even as late as 1991, in a *Partisan Review*–sponsored panel address entitled "The Remaking of the Canon," Brooks reflected back on his early schooling in a mostly male, white-only, "classical academy" in West Tennessee. There, Brooks recounted that his education naturalized the tradition of the "great" books as the unspoken norm. Although he pointed out that there was no semantic term for the canon as such, he admitted that "we read such books as Caesar's *Commentaries on the Gallic Wars,* Cicero's *Orations,* Ovid's *Metamorphoses,* Xenophon's *Anabasis,* and the first three books of Homer's *Iliad.*" Moreover in the 1990s, Brooks quite frankly admitted that, as a Depression-era teacher, he sought to reproduce this classical standard of taste with Robert Penn Warren in their *Understanding Poetry* text for modern students, who, he claimed, "could not distinguish between a good book and a bad." As a defender of those same canonical values, Brooks still intoned the revenant of the old-line Southern Agrarian platform, inveighing on behalf of the Western Humanist tradition against the regime of science and vocational trends in the academy, as well as today's multicultural challenges to the Eurocentric canon of "great" books.[63]

Repudiating those whom he maligned as the "New Revolutionaries" in feminism, Marxism, psychoanalysis, deconstruction, queer theory, and so on, Brooks sought even at the close of the twentieth century to return literary studies to a prelapsarian moment where all "political, historical, and sociological information" would be excluded from its disciplinary purview.[64] In the 1930s, Brooks's colleague Robert Penn Warren had sought to discredit and exile the "black radical" from the interbellum *Republic of Letters;* six decades later, Brooks's target remained the heretical subject of critical theory. Replayed there, albeit in a more guarded rhetoric, was the specter of what John Crowe Ransom had defended as the Eurocentric and Anglophilic tradition espoused by T. S. Eliot against the expanded social field of democratic representation forged by the new social movements of our postmodern moment. By the century's end, however, one could no longer buy into the disciplinary formalism of the New Right—one could no longer bank on its supposed transcendence of social struggle—without also conjuring the specter of its barbarous cultural legacy. Meanwhile, despite that campaign for a return to the "classical academy," avant-garde and "confessional" writers such as Djuna Barnes and Anne Sexton forged experimental modes of writing inflected by the trauma of everyday life. Their aesthetic interventions, as we shall see in chapter 5, offered a new multiplicity of gendered subject positions outside the range of modern containment culture.

CHAPTER FIVE

The Enigma of Witness

Domestic Trauma on and off the Couch

The strange, biographical case of Djuna Barnes, the author, remains a stubborn contradiction to our moment's recovery of Barnes the Left Bank avant-gardist who championed a lesbian discourse boldly subversive of German fascism—and, more broadly, modern patriarchy. Against that utopian persona, what are we to make of Barnes's lifelong enthrallment to a self-proclaimed classicist, royalist, and Anglo-Catholic like T. S. Eliot? Not Natalie Barney, Gertrude Stein, or Baroness Elsa von Freytag-Loringhoven, but "only Tom Eliot," Barnes said of her literary godfather, "had my permission to write something in one of my books!"[1] Apparently, Barnes's identification with her male mentors was lifelong. During a rare foray from her almost total reclusion after age fifty at 5 Patchin Place, Djuna Barnes was taken on a shopping trip to Altman's to buy some slippers. Bringing her purchase up to the register, Barnes, in Andrew Field's account, "wanted to pay by cheque but had no identification with her.—'I am Djuna Barnes. I was a friend to T. S. Eliot and James Joyce.' To which the saleslady replied:—That's very nice, lady, but do you have a driver's license? Barnes was indignant. She drew herself up so she was tall again.— 'Do I look like the sort of person who would have a driver's license?'"[2] Although not herself a driver, Barnes nevertheless presents here her driving obsession with public recognition, literary reputation, and canonical authority, all inflected through phallic identification with the licensed, master signifier of desire, the literary figure of T. S. Eliot. Her investment in modernism's major apologist for canonical hierarchy was not just a literary alliance but, as symptom, reflects Barnes's troubling streak of elitism, racism, and homophobia.

In addition to Barnes the subversive Left Bank lesbian, there is the "historical" Barnes, who according to her literary amanuensis Hank O'Neal, not only alienated virtually everyone she met but, curiously, kept a book of phone listings organized by sex, race, and religion (LP, 8); who joked continuously about "pansies and buggers"; who claimed "to hate lesbians and [to be] rather unfeeling towards women" (LP, 30); who allowed that Carl Van Vechten's 1933 portrait "made me look just like a nigger" (LP, 151); who regretted selling her papers to the McKeldin library because "hoards of niggers were pawing through them all the time" (LP, 163); who frequently remarked, "How odd of God to choose the Jews" (LP, 176). We are used to such sexual, racial, and anti-Semitic slurs in the careers of the "great" modernists like, say, Ernest Hemingway, T. S. Eliot, F. Scott Fitzgerald, or Ezra Pound. No one, of course, would want to contend that these expatriates ever intended to subvert the rule of phallocentrism. In Barnes's example, how are we to square the reactionary with the writer? Are such remarks allowable as the salty, Rabelaisian manner of a streetwise New Yorker and latter-day Left Banker? Or do they instead manifest a profound ambivalence and self-loathing that steadily drove Barnes into the closet of psychic repression?

Pursuing the psychological determinants of Barnes's career may help us better understand the Djuna Barnes who was her own worst Angel of the House, who believed that "if I did anything wrong, if I took a pencil that didn't belong to me, if I was dishonorable in any way, in any fashion, then I would be unable to write a word" (LP, 80–81). Such self-censorship not only curtailed Barnes's output over the last four decades of her life but was projected retroactively in the desire that, as she wrote in a letter to her publisher du Sautoy, "I could wish a great number of my writings had managed to avoid being written" (LP, 112–13). More than late literary anxiety, however, Barnes's compulsion to destroy her own creations reached back to the 1920s, when, uncomfortable with her first volume of verse *The Book of Repulsive Women,* she recounts how "I collected as many copies as I could find and burned them in my mother's backyard" (LP, 98). Like Franz Kafka, she left orders to her executor that her remaining manuscripts, notebooks, drafts, correspondence, and papers be burned upon her death and, fearful that this writing would outlast her, set much of it ablaze herself.

Obsessed, apparently, with controlling the reputation of her "great" individual works, most notably *Nightwood,* she relentlessly contained and repressed what Roland Barthes would describe as the "epistemological slide"[3] of her writing's textuality not only in literally burning the plurality of forms it took, but in censoring its "activity of production" as her text moved off the shelf and into the writing of others, out of the closet and onto the stage, beyond the reclusion of "her mother's backyard" and into the public sphere of the social Other. Seldom do Barnes's critics theorize the sharp contradictions between the historical Barnes and her lesbian personae. Most of her readers do not pay sustained attention to the issue of Barnes's authorial relation to her writing; instead the question goes begging or is simply elided. In Shari Benstock's reading, the entire psychoanalytic terrain of Barnes's life is bluntly repudiated as the "crass efforts at psychoanalysis indulged in by most commentators on her life and work." Such a rhetorical move allows Benstock to go on to suggest that "the informing despair of Nightwood might be interpreted beyond the biographical details of her own life."[4] This critical strategy of "saving the text" serves to sever the historical Barnes from her lesbian discourse. Thus Susan Sniader Lanser writes that "[t]he problem lies, then, not in attempting to reconcile the historical Barnes with the textual voice of Ladies Almanack but in having thought the two equivalent."[5] Karla Jay and Elizabeth Meese, however, have complicated our view both of Barnes's troubled relationship to the Left Bank salon culture that she satirized in Ladies Almanack and of her self-reflexive sadomasochism in Nightwood.[6]

The critical operation of separating Barnes's life from her art rests on a loaded binary opposition that foregrounds the letter of Barnes's feminism at the expense of her biography. While the former assumes the privileged status as discourse, the latter is backgrounded as some historical essence falling outside the text. This convention of reading the historical Barnes out of her writing illustrates in her critical reception what Foucault defines as the "author principle" insofar as it installs a utopian version of the Left Bank lesbian as a more palatable literary figure for an affirmative feminist culture. In choosing this formation as a productive site of intervention in Barnes criticism, the point would not be to valorize some raw version of her personal intention, as that would simply reverse the original binary, thereby restoring an equally fictive version of authority. Instead, the challenge would be to recast the figure of the historical Barnes as itself a culturally mediated construct released from what criticism has closeted as the eccentric lapses of the private self. In foregrounding the textuality of Barnes's biography in relation to her literary work, the pressing critical task would then identify the common narrative underpinnings that link the former with the latter, not sever them. Here a new discursive formation emerges precisely through the lines of continuity between Barnes's literary and nonliterary selves.

The stakes of textual autobiography escalate when we move into the work that obsessed Barnes throughout her later life, namely, her closet drama The Antiphon (1958). In rationalizing her destruction of a now "lost" sequel to The Antiphon, Barnes claimed it bore too close a resemblance to its original and that "[i]t is very important not to repeat one's self" (LP, 50). This symptomatic proscription against repeating one's self, however, itself belies a lifelong struggle among her biographical and literary personae: one that enacts a repetition compulsion, whose recurrent family romance from *The Book of Repulsive Women* through *The Antiphon* acts out Barnes's resistance to and internalization of herself as an Oedipal subject. Shaped by an Oedipal "sex/gender system," the patriarchal family—which Barnes dwells on at length in her early short stories, in *Ryder* and in *The Antiphon*—is, as Freud theorized it in his 1923 study *The Ego and the Id*, the site where the phallocentric order of Western culture is reproduced in the unconscious lives of individual women and men. Setting aside the question of Freud's own investments in Victorian sexism, the Freudian sex/gender system, as Juliet Mitchell, Christopher Lasch, and Gayle Rubin have observed, provides a crucial descriptive framework for the feminist critique of patriarchy. "One is not born a woman," as Simone de Beauvoir reminds us, "but, rather, becomes one."[7] For, anatomical difference conditions the imaginary distinction between the male and female genders in the symbolic registers of cultural practice.

In theorizing women's gender identification, Freud advanced an explanatory account of the passage through Oedipus that remains controversial. According to Freud, a girl in the pre-Oedipal stage moves from a same-sex investment in the mother to a heterosexual cathexis focused on the father, and later male substitutes for him. In Jacques Lacan's revisionary reading of Oedipus, the phallus (not the biological penis) serves as the signifier of desire marking through its displacements the movement of lack at the heart of language's Symbolic order. According to Lacan, the rite of passage through Oedipus and its seemingly universal proscription against incest serves to foreclose the undifferentiated psychosis of early infancy's polymorphous, pre-Oedipal realm. In the Imaginary register of the "mirror stage" the infant's bodily individuation from the mother leads to a further recognition of separation and lack that instantiates the compensatory, linguistic substitutions and sign exchange of language's Symbolic order. For Lacan, the Oedipal *Nom du Pere*— as the recognition of difference, separation, and lack in being—inaugurates a salutary, psychic castration insofar as it also initiates one's becoming by means of linguistic symbolization. So far so good, but where does the actual incest victim fit into this scheme? How does one assume identity in the Symbolic order if one's actual father is in perverse denial of this Oedipal framework and shatters it with the traumatic force of the Real?

In both *Ryder* and *The Antiphon* Barnes presents a crisis facing the incest victim's exile from the patriarchal order underwritten by the Oedipal paradigm of the Law of the Father. Not insignificantly, Barnes's writing troubles the *Nom du Pere* with portraits of perverse fathers who confuse Imaginary and Symbolic paternity. To begin with, Wendell Ryder—who is based on Barnes's real father, Wald Barnes—receives very mixed messages about gender differentiation from his mother, Sophia, who compares him to her granddaughter:

> "She has always been you," Sophia answered; "I have seen you from the seed," she continued, "and I have seen her, and you are exactly alike, except"—she made a period in the air with one of her Jesuitical hands—"that she is unhung, and you are slung like a man; it will make the difference."[8]

Wendell would supplement the biological difference of the genital binary "slung / unhung" by becoming the potent Symbolic father figure in the family's reproductive order. Tellingly, however, Ryder confuses the categories of the Imaginary and the Symbolic; that is, he conflates the penis and bodily reproduction with the Symbolic function of the phallus. In chapter 10 "The Occupations of Wendell," Barnes rather perversely acts out the role of the family patriarch as he attempts at every turn to seduce his two wives Amelia and Kate-Careless into the role of mother with "that tool / Known . . . as 'Wonder'" (R, 69): "For this he shope, with craft, an oxen bone / That with pleasure might his Kate groan" (R, 70). Thus, in the absence of the natural "wonder," Wendell tries to colonize his wives sexually through raping them with an artificial phallus. Against Freud's contention that women resolve penis envy through "having" children to supplement castration, Barnes depicts Wendell as the one who needs children as Imaginary figures of phallic authority. Indeed, he would "stack a deck of daughters and of sons" (R, 68). "What need have I of such a cognomen as 'Cock of the Walk,'" he asks, "when the evidence of it sits at my table with sixteen legs?" (R, 215). Wendell's compulsive investment in the father's imaginary reproduction—whose natural evidence sits on display at his table "with sixteen legs"—resists the "cognomen" or phallic function of the Name of the Father (*Nom du Pere*), whose Nom / No would enforce the prohibition on incest through the assumption of castration as the precondition for entry into the sociolinguistic order of the Law of the Father.

But while Wendell finds a certain Imaginary empowerment in biological fatherhood, "screaming oneself into a mother," as Amelia confides to Julie, "is no pleasure at all" (R, 117). This imbalance in sexual roles—the theme that "women die, unequally / Impaled upon a sword they scabbard to" (R, 93)—as Marie Ponsot shows, is a recurrent motif throughout the entire corpus of Barnes's writing from *The Book of Repulsive Women*, through *Ryder*, *Nightwood*, and *The Antiphon*, and in such late poems as "Quarry."[9] The sexual politics of compulsory maternity, however, not only poses potentially grave biological risks for a woman but positions her, more often than not, as wanton in patriarchal judgment. Originally published in the avant-garde journal *transition,* Ryder's fifth chapter, "Rape and Repining!" seemingly depicts sexual violation as an inevitable fact of nature, announcing, "What ho! Spring again! Rape again, and the Cock not yet at his Crowing!" (R, 26). The apparent lesson of what James B. Scott tellingly calls "this delightful chapter" is that "nature is irresistible, to give birth is to extend the reign of death by another generation."[10] Yet Scott's somewhat androcentric reading not only "delights" in a sexual politics that Barnes explicitly parodies but entirely misses her critique of the way woman is positioned as both "natural" victim and sexual commodity within a patriarchal sex / gender system of cultural exchange. That oppressive positioning is doubly traumatic, moreover, in the case of the incest victim.

The nature / culture distinction that underwrites Scott's interpretation has been the subject of feminist critique by anthropologists such as Marilyn Strathern and Carol MacCormack. "Nature / culture discourse," as Judith Butler argues, "regularly figures nature as female, in need of subordination by a culture that is invariably figured as male, active, and abstract. . . . The sexual politics that construct and maintain this distinction are effectively concealed by the discursive production of a nature and, indeed, a natural sex that postures as the unquestioned foundation of culture."[11] Similarly, the target of Barnes's subversive parody in "Rape and Repining!" is the cultural construction of woman's sexuality as the natural object of male possession, surveillance, and gift exchange. Whether inflected by comic or tragic narratives, however, the lesson of what Adrienne Rich would call "father-right" linking *Ryder* to *The Antiphon* repeats the experience of the historical Barnes. Wald Barnes's seduction of his daughter Djuna, which is the subtext of *Antiphon,* reenacts the narrative of marital rape in *Ryder.* Yet, more symptomatically, in *Antiphon* the latent trauma of incest leaves its trace variously in the linguistic distortions and gaps that punctuate the verbal character of the play; in the extensive editorial cuttings that both Barnes and Eliot made to the explicit presentations of the event; in the pattern of censorship marking the history of its stage productions; and in its general silencing in the reception of Barnes's oeuvre.

Such textual repressions are symptoms, arguably, of the domestic extremity of Barnes's somewhat gothic childhood trauma. As Lynda Curry shows in recovering Barnes's cuts to act 2 of *Antiphon,* Barnes excised the explicit narrative of how Titus Higby Hobbs—an incarnation of Wendell Ryder and Barnes's actual father, Wald Barnes—failed in his attempt to rape his daughter Miranda and thus make her the "[i]nitiated vestal to his 'cause.'"[12] Nevertheless, she becomes a sexual victim to the father as Titus "[h]auled her, in an hay-hook, to the barn; / Left her dangling; while in the field below / He offered to exchange her for a goat / With that old farm-hand, Jacobsen" (SP, 290). Miranda's ritual rape by a "cockney thrice her age"—a vicarious stand-in for Titus—structures the triad of father / rapist, daughter / sacrificial "ewe," and mother / madam that makes a "doll's room a babes bordel" (SP, 292). "Yes," Barnes told James B. Scott, "Ryder and Titus, they are my father. Where did the basic story come from? From my life. . . . Ryder is my father. And Titus" (D, 185). The forced, incestuous exchange of the daughter between men acts out a certain perversion of the *Nom du Pere*, whose symbolic and cultural orders are founded on the proscription—the tabooed Nom / No—against incest.

As the universal archetype of outlawed sexuality, incest troubles the deep logic of differentiation constituting the symbolic Law of the Father. In *Ryder*'s fifth chapter, "Rape and Repining!" Barnes stages a subversive parody of how patriarchy reinstantiates identity through difference precisely in judging the incest victim as anathema: sentencing her to the abjection of the undifferentiated. Once a "simple Rustic Maiden . . . with Knowledge nowhere" is ravished, Barnes queries in a parody of her male prosecutor, can "the Law frame her Maidenly again" (R, 26)? Barnes's trial scene lays on the daughter the vexed charge of both being the natural object of paternal lust and retaining the virginal status of the father's "Original Approval." Such an impossible embodiment characterizes not only the incest victim but woman's uncanny place as (m)other within and outside patriarchy. Negotiating the catachresis of the maiden / madonna dilemma leads inevitably to loss—to the daughter becoming "no better than her Mother, and her Mother's Mother before her! Soiled! Despoiled! Mauled! Rumpled! Rummaged! Ransacked!" (R, 26).

The incest victim as defiled—not dutiful—daughter threatens the Oedipal underpinnings of men's regulation of women's economic value as "gift," "True Coin," and "Known Sum." Found guilty within the Father's Law, Barnes's incest victim is submitted to a second, verbal assault from a patronizing prosecutor:

> You have but one Life, yet in one Night you have changed the Complexion of All Nights, thus pilfering from the community, which has honoured you as True Coin, only to discover you Counterfeit, thereby changing a Known Sum into a Sum needing Recount. Have you not, therefore, made the whole of Society a Dupe, and shall we not, for that, have you in the Just Distaste we evince to the Forger? You Mint with your false Metal, Metal as false, so that from now on, we must watch our Change, lest there be Lead in it, or such Alloy as might make us sadly out at Pocket. (R, 33)

While *Ryder* maintains a comic distance that lampoons the patriarchal inscription of women's sexuality within the binary economy of True Coin / false Metal, *The Antiphon* more traumatically stages how incest unravels the differential logic constituting the Oedipal Law of the Father. For Deleuze and Guattari, of course, the "private" sphere of domestic family life is continuous with the broader, public regime of the Father. Both the "interior colony" of family life and the totalitarian rule of the boss, the hero, the leader, the public figurehead flow from the logic of

> the transcendent Phallus, and the exclusive distribution that presents itself in girls as desire for the penis, and in boys as fear of losing it or refusal of a passive attitude. . . . Oedipus creates both the differentiations that it orders and the undifferentiated with which it threatens us. . . . Oedipus informs us: if you don't follow the lines of differentiation daddy-mommy-me, and the exclusive alternatives that delineate them, you will fall into the black night of the undifferentiated. (59, 78–79)

In her writing, Barnes vacillates between this conflicted scene of Oedipal sexuality and the nightwood of the undifferentiated. On the one hand, as incest victim Barnes is always already positioned outside the domestic scheme of differentiations maintaining Oedipus. In *Ryder* she undermines the authority of Father-right through parodying the violence that otherwise maintains it. On the other hand, however, the historical Barnes internalizes that same sexual politics as she denigrates the "black night of the undifferentiated" in her symptomatic homophobia, sexism, racism, and self-loathing. Barnes's extreme acts of self-censorship literally incinerate precisely that writing otherwise devoted to versions of undifferentiated sexuality in excess of the Oedipal frame.

Theorizing the consequences of early traumas similar to those of Barnes's childhood, Alice Miller writes that "[t]he unremembered plight of *being at someone else's mercy* and being abused by a loved object is perpetuated either in a passive or an active role, or alternately in each."[13] Miller's psychoanalytic take on the effects of childhood abuse provides a suggestive framework for rereading the sadomasochistic dynamic that underpins Barnes's lesbian feminism as well as the divided aesthetic politics shaping her depiction of other marginalized subcultures. *Ryder, Nightwood,* and *The Antiphon* embrace the anti-Oedipal, "black night" of the undifferentiated—insofar as they demystify patriarchy both in and beyond the domestic sphere. Nevertheless, Barnes's own internalization of Oedipus deconstructs any one-dimensional reading of her various personae and their social meanings. On the one hand, for example, we could read the recurrence of animal motifs in her work as a deterritorialization of the Oedipal paradigm much as they function in Kafka's fiction, where, according to Deleuze and Guattari, "To become animal is to participate in movement, to stake out the path of escape in all its positivity, to cross a threshold, to reach a continuum of intensities that are valuable only in themselves, to find a world of pure intensities where all forms come undone, as do all the significations, signifiers, and signifieds, to the benefit of an unformed matter of deterritorialized flux, of nonsignifying signs."[14] On the other hand, the very same animal

motifs, as in Robin Vote's celebrated embrace of a dog at the end of *Nightwood*
appear not just as a deterritorialization of Oedipal sexuality but also as a reterrito-
rialization of nature in the name of Oedipus, repeating as it does Wendell's bestial-
ity, which colonizes nature for patriarchy in *Ryder*, not to mention Basil's Beast motifs found in *The Biography of Julie von Bartmann*. Similarly, while Jane Marcus reads
Nikka the black, former bear wrestler of the Cirque de Paris as a parody of the
"phallic negro," how are we to insulate this portrait of the inscribed African subject
from the denigrated, undifferentiated "niggers" who Barnes feared would "paw"
through her manuscripts? Such a radically divided inscription of social representation stems, arguably, from the domestic trauma that splits Barnes's literary and biographical selves.

Avowing and disavowing the undifferentiated psychosis of the black night of the
anti-Oedipal, Barnes's modernist project, however conflicted, finds its postmodern
counterpart in the more explicitly performative confessionalism of Anne Sexton. If
personal trauma returns with a vengeance to silence Barnes the author, Sexton conversely becomes an author by making a vocation and career out of interminable
confession. "I can be deeply personal," Sexton once said, "but I'm not being personal about myself."[15] How are we to understand such a statement? For the most
part, Sexton's critics take her confessional aesthetic at face value as the straightforward, however stylized, account of the private self. In the postwar period, poetry
as a sullen art of the personal self was lodged largely against the "impersonal" poetics of T. S. Eliot and experimental modernism generally. "These poems," wrote
M. L. Rosenthal, "seemed to me one culmination of the Romantic and modern tendency to place the literal Self more and more at the center of the poem."[16] In retrospect, Rosenthal's opposition of personal and impersonal poetics seems an over-
simplified framing of what Helen Vendler would begin to characterize as the
"Freudian lyric" some three decades later.[17] Sexton herself, as her quote implies,
confesses to truths that she does not own and that are not reducible to any naturalized or fixed essence of personal experience. As she writes in her poem dedicated
to her first creative writing workshop leader, John Holmes, "At first it was private / Then it was more than myself."[18]

Viewed today, the critical reception of confessionalism appears as a disciplinary
symptom of containment aimed at simplifying and normalizing Sexton's otherwise
complex and subversive poetics. Beyond personal confessionalism, however, what
are we to make of the important cultural work Sexton's verse performed from the
late 1950s into the mid-1970s? What is the excess she inscribes that is "more than
myself"? We might begin by questioning the confessional subject as someone who

testifies to the naked facts of his or her experience in some wholly unmediated and spontaneous discourse of truth. Michel Foucault, in contrast, theorizes that the "truthful confession"—beginning in the Middle Ages—goes to the heart of the "procedures of individuation by power."[19] One would have to have "an inverted image of power," Foucault maintains, to think that confession liberates one from power into freedom (HS, 60). On the contrary, confessional discourse, Foucault writes, "unfolds within a power relationship, for one does not confess without the presence (or virtual presence) of a partner who is not simply the interlocutor but the authority who requires the confession, prescribes and appreciates it, and intervenes in order to judge, punish, forgive, console, and reconcile" (HS, 62). In reading the history of sexuality at the *fin de siècle,* Foucault examines how modern psychoanalysis adapts rituals of confession—reworking them through specific interpretive techniques and practices of confessional labor—to produce a *scientia sexualis:* a "complex machinery for producing true discourses on sex" (HS, 68). Foucault further questions whether this new *scientia sexualis* is "but an extraordinarily subtle form of *ars erotica* . . . the Western, sublimated version of that seemingly lost tradition" (HS, 71). Beginning in the nineteenth century, this new, modern science of the erotic institutes the "pleasure of analysis" precisely as the taking of "pleasure in the truth of pleasure, the pleasure of knowing that truth, of discovering and exposing it, the fascination of seeing it and telling it, of captivating and capturing others by it, of confiding it in secret, of luring it out in the open—the specific pleasure of the true discourse on pleasure" (HS, 71).

In this vein, it is telling that the rhetorical context inaugurating Sexton's writing career, is produced out of the highly cathected bond shared by analyst and analysand. Sexton, that is, only began to write at the urging of her psychiatrist Dr. Martin Orne, who took Sexton on as a patient in 1956 after she had attempted suicide at age twenty-eight. "Early in therapy," Orne has reported, "I focused on Anne's developing her skills, suggesting among other things that she begin writing about her experiences in order to help other patients. This idea struck a responsive chord in her, and we were able to work on it together without her immediately getting so discouraged as to reject it."[20] Curiously enough, Dr. Orne tends to lapse, as he does here, into the first person plural "we" when talking about Anne Sexton. Although Sexton's career as a confessional poet was not based on any explicit collaboration, one can glean—from the symptoms of Orne's accounts—the powerful injunction she received from his suggestion received in the analytic transference that she write. Thus confessionalism, for Sexton, begins not with the privacy of the self but precisely in the locus of the psychoanalytic Other. Writing on the hysteric's discourse, Jacques Lacan notes that "because it is produced in the locus of the Other, it is first of all for the subject that his [or her] speech is a message. By virtue of this fact even his demand originates in the locus of the Other, and is signed and dated as such. This is not only because it is subjected to the code of the Other, but also because it is marked by this locus (and even the time) of the Other."[21]

If, as Slavoj Žižek argues, the hysteric internalizes the desire of the social Other, we should begin as Lacan suggests, with that signed and dated locus which for Sexton's confessional poetics stems from the transference and countertransference of the analytic dialogue. In a profound sense, Sexton's dual careers as an analysand and confessional poet were iatrogenic—confabulated, that is, from the analytic dialogue between patient and psychiatrist. In fact, Sexton presented herself as a kind of tabula rasa of lack in her first analytic session. As Orne observed, she exhibited a

> "profound lack of self worth" unable to think of any positive abilities or qualities within herself. . . . When I pressed her to think hard about what she might be able to do, she finally revealed that there was only one thing that she might possibly be capable of doing well—to be a good prostitute and to help men feel sexually powerful. It was clear that in her case, goals were not a place to start to find positive facets to bolster a sense to self. (M, xiii)

Although Sexton initially gave Orne almost nothing to go on, it was enough to diagnose her as a hysteric. Other symptoms followed, as Orne began to note Sexton's tendency to move in and out of trance and fugue states, her chronic depression, insomnia, her conversion symptoms, profound dissociation, and lesions of memory. Such symptoms, however, may have themselves been partially produced in therapy as Orne directed Sexton's readings in Freud and Breuer's *Studies on Hysteria* while deepening and confirming his own diagnosis. Indeed, insofar as hysteria is a mimetic condition based in imitation, it would be hard to tell what would not fall under its umbrella. Sexton, Orne concluded, "was hysteric in the classic sense: like a chameleon, she could adopt any symptom" (M, 39), and, in fact, Orne had to have her discharged from Westwood Lodge, where she began to pick up signs of psychosis from her interaction with the schizophrenic patients there.

Later in 1957, the year in which Joanne Woodward starred in *The Three Faces of Eve*, Sexton began to present a promiscuous alter personality named Elizabeth (a cryptonym that Sexton understood as a cipher for "a little bitch"—what Sexton's father Ralph Churchill Harvey allegedly called her when he was drunk and abusive [M, 56]). "Elizabeth" urged Orne to put Anne under hypnosis as a way of recovering memories of possible incest child abuse. Orne, who would later author several essays criticizing the use of hypnosis as evidence in court proceedings, refused and did not want to encourage Sexton down the rocky road of multiple personality syndrome (MPS).[22] A later advisory board member of the False Memory Syndrome Foundation, Orne discouraged Sexton from considering her recovered memories of child incest at the hands of both her father and aunt as actual events. Adhering to the orthodox Freudian line of resisting seduction theory, Orne urged Sexton to consider such memories as the products of infantile sexual fantasy.

Thus the diagnosis of hysteria licensed Sexton's repertoire of creative writing, symptomatic behaviors, and her performative scenes of acting out. Equally important, what Orne tended to deny Sexton in the analytic scene—that is, the technique of hypnosis, the encouragement of MPS, and the recovered memories of incest child abuse—had the effect, arguably, of producing what Foucault would characterize as "the formation of a 'reverse' discourse" precisely of those blockages in the power / knowledge arrangements of Orne's therapeutic techniques. Viewed through a Foucauldian lens, Sexton's confessionalism emerges not just from her personal intention, sincerity, or authorial genius but also from the mediating locus of the Other, where literature and psychoanalysis converge. Symptomatically, perhaps, Orne conflates Sexton's new identity as a writer with his own creative role in launching her career as a contemporary poet.

> In the beginning, her poems obviously needed much additional work, but they were clearly pieces with a compelling communication and a flair that Anne and I could discuss—a meaningful project on which she could begin to build a foundation. . . . She was able to obtain and use the necessary criticism and feedback she received in these sessions to improve her work in a way that is very unusual early in an artist's career. Once Anne was assured that she really was able to write poetry, she almost could not stop. Writing poetry became a driving force. Thus began an incredibly rocky but strengthening period in Anne's life. Little by little, she began to deal with the practical problems of correspondence, of submission and resubmission, of reviewing and rewriting. (M, xiv)

Soon Sexton would move up through the ranks of the literary establishment beginning with her workshop with John Holmes at Tufts, where she would meet Maxine Kumin, to similar seminar settings with W. D. Snodgrass, and later Robert Lowell at Boston University. In each of these stages, Sexton would respond to the demand of the Other to produce the hysteric's discourse. Supplementing Orne's therapeutic role with the literary father figures of Holmes, Snodgrass, and Lowell, Sexton staged her own brand of hysterical poetics for the social Other, whose audience expanded rather quickly beyond the academic and therapeutic settings of the writing workshop to embrace a broad popular audience after she won the Pulitzer Prize in 1967.

Much has been made of the immediacy of Sexton's literary success. "Sexton's progress in Holmes's workshop in 1957," writes Maxine Kumin, "was meteoric."[23] Of his first encounter with Sexton a few months later, Robert Lowell remarked: "She had met Snodgrass that summer and become a 'confessional' poet overnight."[24] The intensity of that confessional persona was contagious, possessing readers and fellow poets alike. Meeting Sexton in 1961 at the Radcliffe Institute, Barbara Swan has reminisced, "Anne had moved into my world like a tornado. She shook it up, rattled it, possessed it like a demon."[25] Part of Sexton's possessing charisma derived from what Alicia Ostriker has described—by way of the carpe diem tradition—in terms of literary seduction. "From the beginning," writes Ostriker, "Sexton saw readers and audiences as potential intimates. . . . Indeed the condition of her poetry is the presence of an audience, whom she needs to need her; Sexton's vocation as a poet was determined to an extraordinary degree by an assumption of and dependence on readerly empathy."[26] Ostriker's account of confessional seduction, however, remains problematic insofar as it reduces Sexton's relation to the language of the Other to an interpersonal relation between poet and audience.

But equally important, *seduction,* as Ostriker herself observes, is a troubling term for empathic identification, evoking as it does the hotly contested origins of psychoanalysis in "seduction theory" and the trauma of father-daughter incest.[27] Does the force of Sexton's charismatic seductiveness stem from a personal narrative of sexual trauma, or does she tap zones of sexual fantasy that are universal? In the poet's critical reception, of course, both sides of the "seduction" controversy over Sexton's status as an analysand and confessional poet have been bitterly debated. The disavowal of Sexton as a literal incest survivor is a typical move for such critics as J. D. McClatchy, who finesses the referential truth of Sexton's traumatic memories of incest by claiming that "since fantasies become memories, it becomes impossible and useless beyond a certain point to distinguish between 'events' that happened and fears or desires imagined so strongly that they might as well have happened."[28] More recently, reading Sexton through the lens of "trauma" theorists such as Judith Herman and Cathy Caruth, Cassie Premo Steele finds compelling evidence that seduction, for Sexton, meant child sexual incest both with her father, Ralph Churchill Harvey, and her maternal great-aunt Anna Ladd Dingley. As Steele argues, "Reading Sexton's poetry today, after more than 20 years of research concerning the signs, aftereffects, and possibilities of healing from childhood sexual abuse, we can see that there is ample evidence that Sexton was a survivor of traumatic childhood sexual abuse."[29] This long-standing literary clash over how to read Sexton repeats the Freudian controversy over the diagnostic sentence in the analytic scene. Did Sexton present symptoms of childhood seduction or fantasies of infant sexuality? "If you ask me either as a psychiatrist or as a scientist," concluded Dr. Orne, "I would have to say I am virtually certain that it never occurred" (M, 58). On the other hand, Sexton's longtime friend, the psychiatric social worker Lois Ames, reached just the opposite conclusion: "I could never believe anything but that Anne was a victim of child sexual abuse by both Nana and her father" (M, 58).

The clash over Sexton's personal status as a victim of domestic abuse is further complicated by the fact that Sexton, unlike Djuna Barnes, never decided in her own mind whether her recovered memory of incest was based in fact or fantasy. Leaving open rather than foreclosing this question of desire, Sexton looks forward to Jane Gallop's controversial position that the daughter's incestuous fantasy is, paradoxically enough, produced by the "seductive function" of patriarchy's prohibitive law against incest. At once soliciting and barring the daughter's desire, the incest taboo veils the father's desire for the daughter—thus protecting him from the acknowledgment of sexual difference—and thereby maintains his power within the phallocentric logic of the patriarch:

> If the phallus is the standard of value, then the father, possessor of the phallus, must desire the daughter in order to give her value. But the father is a man (a little boy in the anal, the phallic, phase) and cannot afford to desire otherness, an other sex, because that opens up his castration anxiety. The father's refusal to seduce the daughter, to be seduced by her (seduction wreaking havoc with anal logic and its active/passive distribution), gain him another kind of seduction (this one more one-sided, more like violation), a veiled seduction in the form of the law. The daughter submits to the father's rule, which prohibits the father's desire, the father's penis, out of the desire to seduce the father by doing his bidding and thus pleasing him. . . . Briefly, the veiled seduction, the rule of patriarchal law over the daughter, denying her worth and trapping her in an insatiable desire to please the father, is finally more powerfully and broadly damaging than actualized seduction. As surprisingly widespread as incest may be, the veiled seduction traps all women in its vicious circle.[30]

Gallop's most provocative claim, perhaps, is that the daughter's dilemma in relation to the seductive law of phallocentrism is "more . . . broadly damaging" than actual incest. The universal situation of women's vexed place before the Law of the Father, she argues, is more generally traumatic than the minoritizing event of sexual seduction. Certainly, Sexton understood the complexity of her overdetermined relation to the father's seductive function and portrayed it as both an alluring cathexis and source of trauma. To cast Sexton in the minoritizing role of incest survivor not only reduces the poetry to a biographical referent but, equally important, forecloses any chance of fully assuming the agency of the daughter's desire in excess of the father's law of seduction. Moreover, the foreclosure of personal confessionalism also re-presses Sexton's insistence—gleaned from her psychoanalysis—on the complex in-terplay among language, fantasy, and the trauma of the primal scene.

Throughout her career Sexton portrays poetry's power to adjudicate fantasy and trauma as a nexus possessing universal, not just minoritizing, pertinence: en-compassing precisely what, as she avowed in verse, was "more than myself." While criticism has debated both sides of the seduction issue, surprisingly little attention has been paid to the question of how trauma as such is worked through in Sexton's relationship to language. In a well-known letter Sexton wrote to Anne Clarke, she links her bouts of mental illness not just to moments of despair but also to her "thrilled" discovery of "language"—specifically, the discourse of psychic extremity:

> Language has nothing to do with rational thought. I think that's why I get so horribly
> furious and disturbed with rational thought.
> Language is the opposite of the way a machine works.
> Language is poetry, maybe? But not all language is poetry. Nor is all poetry
> language.
> That's the trouble with me.
> Language is (i.e.) when I said "I have room. . . ."
> Who me? Sailing around like crazy in LANGUAGE whatever it is and then
> brought up short by reality (what is it, really?).[31]

In interpreting this letter, Ostriker concludes that Sexton "places the issue of human intimacy at the center of her writing, both thematically and as the source of poetic language itself" (SC, 7–8). Ostriker's rhetoric of centers and sources returns the poet's inaugural discovery of "language" to the humanist origins of confes-sional "intimacy." But if we read Sexton's comments on language through the hindsight of poststructuralist thought, they yield precisely the opposite conclusion. Here the poet's manic discovery of language reflects what Foucault discerns in modern *scientia sexualis* as "the specific pleasure of the true discourse on pleasure." Moreover, in pursuing such a discourse of pleasure, Sexton's understanding of lan-guage as such did not entail a return to the word's genesis in subjectivity, thought, or personal intention. Rather, she pursues language in its prior and extrinsic rela-tion to these intrinsic beginnings. "From the moment discourse ceases to follow the slope of self-interiorizing thought," Foucault writes, "and, addressing the very being of language, returns thought to the outside; from that moment, in a single stroke, it becomes a meticulous narration of experiences, encounters, and improb-able signs—language about the outside of all language, speech about the invisible side of words."[32] As early as 1958, Sexton held that subjectivity, empathy, and confessional intimacy followed from language, not the other way around. In therapy, she told Martin Orne:

> If I write RATS and discover that rats reads STAR backwards, and amazingly STAR is wonderful and good because I found it in rats, then is star untrue? . . . Of course I KNOW that words are just a counting game, I know this until the words start to arrange themselves and write something better than *I* would ever know. . . . I don't really believe the poem, but the name is surely mine so I must belong to the poem. So I must be real. . . . When you say "words mean nothing" then it means that the real me is nothing. All I am is the trick of words writing themselves. (M, 82)

Martin Orne, no doubt, gave Sexton permission to write and provided the impetus for her poetry as a form of therapy. Nevertheless, Sexton's profound engagement with language as such had a life far in excess of any iatrogenic empathy she received from him. In "Said the Poet to the Analyst," she boldly asserts that "my business is words." But even before the claiming of that profession in the first line, the title sets out the primacy of enunciation in the performative key word "said." It is a mistake, she claims in her first stanza's simile, to consider poetic discourse as therapy where words are to be "counted like dead bees in the attic." Signified meaning, instead of being prior to language, is produced from one signifier's relational difference from another: from one word's power to "pick / out another, to manner another." If identity, likewise, is constantly produced out of the word's metonymic relation to the signifying chain of other words, then the psychoanalytic meaning of one's experience is likewise contingent upon the dynamic production of the self in language.

Consequently, as Lacan insisted, the analyst's role should not be confused with that of the "subject presumed to know." "In particular," Lacan writes in *Seminar VIII: The Transference*, "the analyst has to know that the criterion for his correct positioning is not whether he does or does not understand. It is not absolutely essential that he understands: I would even say that up to a certain point, if he does not understand, this would be preferable to too great a confidence in his own understanding."[33] It is the claim to analytic understanding that Sexton resists in the analyst's "business," as she has it, of "watching my words." Analytic meaning in her final metaphor in stanza two is more radically overdetermined by linguistic excess:

> Your business is watching my words. But I
> admit nothing. I work with my best, for instance,
> when I can write my praise for a nickel machine,
> that one night in Nevada: telling how the magic jackpot
> came clacking three bells out, over the lucky screen.

But if you should say this is something it is not,

then I grow weak, remembering how my hands felt funny

and ridiculous and crowded with all the believing money. (CP, 12–13)

While the analyst's "business" would discern the patient's cure, Sexton as analyst and, more radically as poet, wagers her identity on the "magic jackpot" of sheer linguistic excess: the understanding that the poetic "I am," as Sexton came to realize in her analytic sessions, "is the trick of words writing themselves."

In addition to Martin Orne, Sexton's other mentor whose business turned on watching her words was John Holmes, her first creative writing instructor. But while Orne interpreted Sexton's words, Holmes more forcefully tried to repress them, advising Sexton not to publish her poems on what she described as "the commonplaces of the asylum." In "For John, Who Begs Me Not to Enquire Further," Sexton discerns her teacher's own psychic defenses owing, as Diane Middlebrook has explained, to the trauma her example called up in him. For John Holmes had had his own share of tragedy. A former alcoholic, Holmes also had to reckon with the traumatic memory of his first wife, who in committing suicide had rather methodically cut her wrists and bled to death over his poetry manuscripts. In any case, the poem's key figures for verse straddle art and life in such paradoxical tropes as the "awkward bowl" and "cracked star." Similar, perhaps, to Wallace Stevens's defense of poetry's "necessary fiction," Sexton presents her apology for poetry's "complicated lie" through the figure of oxymoron:

And if you turn away

because there is no lesson here

I will hold my awkward bowl,

with all its cracked stars shining

like a complicated lie,

and fasten a new skin around it

as if I were dressing an orange

or a strange sun. (CP, 34)

Critics have commented on the explicit Oedipal allusion in Sexton's title, signifying on Jocasta's plea that Oedipus not inquire too deeply into the mystery of his tragic fate. For the most part, however, Sexton's readers repeat Jocasta's example;[34] that is, Sexton's critics tend to swerve away from traumatic truths the poet alone was given to witness. As poet, Sexton takes as her epigraph for *To Bedlam and Part Way Back* (1960) Schopenhauer's letter to Goethe where the philosopher points to Jocasta's example as a universal repression: "But most of us carry in our heart," he writes, "the Jocasta who begs Oedipus for God's sake not to inquire further." Beyond her thematic rejoinder to Holmes's repression, Sexton—like Djuna Barnes—more radically troubles the frame of sexual differentiation that Oedipus otherwise instantiates. Sexton not only projects Holmes as the incestuous mother but reverses the relationship in her birth image of wrapping a "new skin" of flesh around "a strange sun," whose homonym signifies on the son who is also husband. The catachresis of Jocasta's Oedipus is further explored in the rather intimate mirroring of "my face, your face" featured in the poem's concluding line. Less an affirmation of human empathy between student and teacher, "my face, your face" marks not just an uncanny mirroring of self and other but a more radical implosion of difference. The poem's central metaphors of the "cracked mirror" and "cracked stars" similarly collapse and fracture the discrete subject positions of fathers and daughters, sons and mothers into an undifferentiated primal scene. What Sexton exposes in the poem is not just the pre-Oedipal—"your fear, anyone's fear"—but the ways in which aesthetic idealization is always already a compensatory gesture. Indeed Sexton performs that disturbing recognition by invoking it in her astral metaphor of the "star" encrypted as it is in her verse with its opposite figure of "rats": the poet's key trope for traumatic abjection.

The palindrome "rat's star" makes its appearance as early as 1958 in Sexton's analytic sessions with Martin Orne, and by 1962 Sexton features it in "With Mercy for the Greedy" as a central figure for poetic language and its relation to traumatic experience, specifically the poet's abortion two years earlier. Addressing the poem to her dear friend Ruth Soter, who counseled Sexton to take confession, the poem, according to Diane Middlebrook, "sets up two parallel kinds of 'mercy': the one available to Ruth through religious practices, and the one she herself achieves through writing poetry. Both derive their power from confession" (M, 122). Sexton's emphatic direct address to Soter ends the poem so as to underscore her newfound aesthetic credo:

> My friend, my friend, I was born
> doing reference work in sin, and born
> confessing it. This is what poems are:
> with mercy
> for the greedy,
> they are the tongue's wrangle,
> the world's pottage, the rat's star. (CP, 63)

Reading this passage through the two "parallel kinds of 'mercy,'" Middlebrook reduces Sexton's emphasis on language to spiritual confessionalism. "Like Soter's cross," she writes, "Sexton's metaphors are vehicles of Spirit" (M, 123). Middlebrook's critical desire to find a reparative aim in Sexton's confessionalism is a symptom that several of Sexton's readers share. Nevertheless, the linguistic energies of the poem actually work against that redemptive impulse. In fact, Sexton's diction—"tongue's wrangle" and "pottage"—arrest Soter's religious brand of confessionalism. Instead, the wholly secular cast of such discordant and cacophonous word choices forcefully resists that kind of idealization.

Seldom are Sexton's poetic figures merely "vehicles" for preexistent spiritual belief, ideology, or existential insight. On the contrary, as analysand and poet, Sexton arrives at the meaning of her experience, her identity, and her psychic truth by means of language, not the other way around. Meaning happens, she insists, only when "the words start to arrange themselves and write something better than *I* would ever know." The paradox of language's "complicated lie" is encoded in Sexton's palindrome of the "rat's star" as a persistent trope throughout her canon. Rats, as Diana Hume George and Suzanne Juhasz, among others, have shown, signal symptoms of abjection, self-loathing, horror, fear, and despair in Sexton's poetry. Similar to Middlebrook, however, both George and Juhasz project a reparative reading onto the rat's relation to the verse. They interpret the palindrome "rats live on no evil star" as a redemptive synecdoche for the career. Thus, "the poem for Sexton," writes Juhasz, "is an important agent in her quest for salvation: for a way out of the madness that the rat's vision engenders, a way that is not suicide."[35]

Yet, as we know too well, Sexton's verse corpus never wholly transcends the poet's terminal madness. Although Sexton's possessing rats made her a star, the course of her career, nevertheless, led inexorably to suicide. How, then, are we to understand her insistence on the agency of the letter at stake in the reversible figure of the rat's star? How are we to interpret her fascination with language portrayed in what Sexton, at one point, thought of as the title for her 1969 volume *Love Poems* and later chose as the title for the poem "Rats Live On No Evil Star" published in *The Death Baby* (1974) just nine months before she took her life? How can we discern in the rat's star the key to Sexton's dynamic relationship to language, a relationship that is not reducible to reparative idealization? If there is a redemptive dimension to Sexton's trope of the rat's star, it is inscribed precisely in her aesthetic's oppositional relation to radical abjection: what Sexton knew to be "anyone's fear."

The critical challenge, then, is to comprehend the dynamic relationship in Sexton's poetics between negation and reparation so as to account psychologically for both the rat's possessing force and the star's linguistic cure. Although Sexton's critics tend to read her poetry through the lens of Freudian theory—emphasizing the theme of Sexton's Oedipal relation to her male mentors and ultimately her father,

Ralph Churchill Harvey—the poet's fascination with the rat's star leads, arguably to the more primordial terrain that Melanie Klein and her followers traced back to the pre-Oedipal trauma of early childhood experience. In her 1929 essay "Infantile Anxiety Situations Reflected in a Work of Art and in the Creative Impulse," Klein extends in the aesthetic dimension her revision of Freud's Oedipus undertaken the previous year in "Early Stages of the Oedipus Conflict" (1928). Freud, of course, held that Oedipus "may justly be regarded as the nucleus of the neuroses,"[36] and in *Inhibitions, Symptoms, and Anxiety* (1926) hypothesized infantile anxiety situations as signaling castration fears in the phallic phase and the loss of the maternal object. Klein, however, insisted that "castration by the father is a modification, in the course of development, of the earliest anxiety situation," which she located in prior phases of infantile fantasy marked by anal and oral sadism.[37] In "The Importance of Symbol Formation in the Development of the Ego" (1930), Klein writes, "My whole argument depends on the fact that the Oedipus conflict begins at a period when sadism predominates. The child expects to find within the mother (a) the father's penis, (b) excrement, and (c) children, and these things it equates with edible substances. . . . In my experience sadism reaches its zenith in this phase, which is ushered in by the oral-sadistic desire to devour the mother's breast (or the mother herself) and passes away with the earlier anal stage" (LGR, 219). Such early sadism, in turn, sets off the infant's anxiety that acts of dismemberment and cannibalization will be repaid in kind and revisited on the self.

Not insignificantly, it is this early scene of traumatic fantasy that, according to Klein, has a key role to play in language acquisition and aesthetics. Klein supplements the thesis put forward by Ernest Jones in "The Theory of Symbolism"—namely, that the pleasure principle determines the child's "pleasure and interest" in the process of symbolization. Parting company with Jones, however, Klein advances a different motivation based precisely in the pre-Oedipal anxieties of oral and anal sadism:

> Since the child desires to destroy the organs (penis, vagina, breast) which stand for the objects, he conceives a dread of the latter. This anxiety contributes to make him equate the organs in question with other things: owing to this equation these in their turn become objects of anxiety, and so he is impelled constantly to make other and new equations, which form the basis of his interest in the new objects and of symbolism. (LGR, 220)

In Klein's revision of Jones's position, anxiety is as powerful a force as pleasure for the child's early processes of symbolization, language usage, fantasy, and thought as such. But, while a "sufficient quantity of anxiety is the necessary basis for an abundance of symbol formation" (LGR, 221), Klein adds that overwhelming anxiety—as she demonstrates in her most famous clinical case involving the autistic child Dick—can result in a breakdown and even paralysis in symbol formation. Similarly, in "Infantile Anxiety Situations Reflected in a Work of Art and in the Creative Impulse," Klein makes a key, related point about the necessity of displacing anxiety through symbolic expression.

In this 1929 essay, Klein analyzes the symptoms of depression that overcame the painter Ruth Kjär as related in the Karin Michaelis article "The Empty Space." The title of Michaelis's essay refers to the artist's predisposition to melancholy and feelings of emptiness. Kjär's melancholy reached a crisis point when her brother-in-law, a famous artist, removed a painting on loan to the house. The literal "empty space" where the painting had been displayed also called up the psychic void in Kjär that increasingly came to haunt her. Not until Kjär fills that vacuum with artwork of her own creation does she discover her gift for painting and the cure for her melancholia. In accounting for the analytic meaning of Kjär's empty space, Klein insists—following Freud—that a "complete analysis" must penetrate to the roots of the symptom: the primal scene. "Now the new demand upon the analyst," she writes, "is this—that analysis should fully uncover these anxiety situations right back to that which lies deepest of all. This demand for a complete analysis is allied to that which Freud suggests as a new demand at the conclusion of his 'History of an Infantile Neurosis,' where he says that a complete analysis must reveal the primal scene" (LGR, 212).

To begin with, Klein observes that the subjects for much of Kjär's artwork were portraits of women. She goes on to read Kjär's recovery as a dispersal of the anxiety she experienced from the fantasy of the "terrifying" maternal object. Not insignificantly, Klein theorizes that the imago of the "terrifying mother" is threatening precisely to the degree to which she cannot be seen. "When the little girl," Klein writes, "who fears the mother's assault upon her body cannot see her mother, it intensifies the anxiety. The presence of the real, loving mother diminishes the dread of the terrifying mother, whose image is introjected into the child's mind"(LGR, 217). It is only through the symbolic expression of her art that Kjär finds the means of making reparation to this terrifying mother, thus curing the intense anxiety situation of the primal scene.

Not unlike Ruth Kjär, Anne Sexton began her career as an artist in response to an overwhelming anxiety situation whose force exceeded symbolic expression. The unseen and unknown trauma of the primal scene underlies several of Sexton's best works, and she renders its enigma particularly compelling in her early poem from her first volume, "What's That":

"What's That"

Before it came inside
I had watched it from my kitchen window,
watched it swell like a new balloon,
watched it slump and then divide,
like something I know I know—
a broken pear or two halves of the moon,
or round white plates floating nowhere
or fat hands waving in the summer air
until they fold together like a fist or a knee.
After that it came to my door. Now it lives here.
And of course: it is a soft sound, soft as a seal's ear,
that was caught between a shape and a shape and then returned to me.

You know how parents call
from sweet beaches anywhere, *come in come in,*
and how you sank under water to put out
the sound, or how one of them touched in the hall
at night: the rustle and the skin
you couldn't know, but heard, the stout
slap of tides and the dog snoring. It's here
now, caught back from time in my adult year—
the image we did forget: the cranking shells on our feet
or the swing of the spoon in soup. It is as real
as splinters stuck in your ear. The noise we steal
is half a bell. And outside cars whisk by on the suburban street.

and are there and are true.
What else is this, this intricate shape of air?
calling me, calling you. (CP, 26)

A somewhat obscure poem in the Sexton canon, "What's That" is seldom discussed in her critical reception. Indeed, what can one say about the mysterious "it" that seems to combine a half-forgotten childhood setting imbricated with the uncanny beckoning of "something" at once so surreal and so deeply repressed that it is almost unreadable? As if to punctuate the uncanny familiarity of what Sexton avows is "like something I know I know—," she adopts the characteristic end-stopped dashes that also lend emotional intensity to Emily Dickinson's verse. Obviously, that something has significant purchase on Sexton's psychic life, all the more so because it is largely unavailable to her conscious knowing. The tropes through which she attempts to understand it—a "broken pear," say, or the "fat hands" that "fold together like a fist or a knee"—actually resist the poet's cognitive mastery.

"What's That" is a possessing poem precisely insofar as its uncanny question escapes conscious understanding. As poet, Sexton renders the haunting quality of the unclaimed object not only at the level of theme but, equally important, in the poem's formal techniques. First, to capture the mystery of childhood perception, she relies on the rhetorical figure of synaesthesia that she gleaned, no doubt, from Theodore Roethke's regressive poetics. The surrealistic turns of Sexton's troping invokes the poem's enigmatic something as "a soft sound, soft as a seal's ear, / that," in the poet's even more encrypted figure, "was caught between a shape and a shape and then returned to me." That strange something is at once a "soft sound" and an invasive "image we did forget": one that, as Sexton insists, "is as real / as splinters stuck in your ear." Second, the poem also turns on several reversals in point of view and address. "What's That" presents—but does not answer—its riddle from two vantage points that are temporally distinct. The question is posed by both the mature poet and her remembered childhood persona. Voiced from both perspectives, the title can be read in the form of an interior monologue and, at the same time, as addressed to the reader. The narrative frame of "What's That" opens out from the confessional lyricism of the opening stanza to the next stanza's direct address to the reader: "You know how parents call." By the end of the poem, poet and reader are in turn addressed by a third figure, an "intricate shape of air" "calling me, calling you." In this way, Sexton sutures the reader's position at the point of the difference in what the child witnesses but does not understand—in the sound "you couldn't know, but heard."

One way to discern the discourse of the Other in "What's That" is to set it beside a later and more widely read poem, "In the Beach House," which similarly evokes the memory of summers at the shore with the parents. In "What's That," Sexton hides, as a child, from the "sound" of her parents' call to "come in" out of the water and into the house, the domestic setting where she half recollects "how one of them touched in the hall / at night: the rustle and the skin." Later, after years of analysis, Sexton revisited the childhood setting recalled in "What's That"—her mother's beach house on Squirrel Island, Maine. "In the Beach House" delves deeper into the encrypted trauma lying at the heart of "What's That." Composed in 1965, "In the Beach House" recovers an explicit and more intrusive memory of what Sexton described in her 1971 interview with Barbara Kevles, in terms of the primal scene:

> About three or four years ago my analyst asked me what I thought of my parents hav-ing intercourse when I was young. I couldn't talk. I knew there was suddenly a poem there, and I selfishly guarded it from him. Two days later, I had a poem, entitled, "In the Beach House," which describes overhearing the primal scene. In it I say, "inside my prison of pine and bedspring, / over my window sill, under my knob, / it is plain that they are at / the royal strapping." The point of this little story is the image, "the royal strapping." My analyst was quite impressed with that image and so was I, al-though I don't remember going any further with it then. About three weeks ago, he said to me, "Were you ever beaten as a child?" I told him that I had been, when I was about nine. I had torn up a five-dollar bill that my father gave to my sister; my father took me into his bedroom, laid me down on his bed, pulled off my pants and beat me with a riding crop. As I related this to my doctor, he said, "See, that was quite a royal strapping," thus revealing to me, by way of my own image, the intensity of that mo-ment, the sexuality of that beating, the little masochistic seizure.[38]

The sexual drama of the Oedipal triangle overheard in this recollected primal scene links the "unspeakable sounds" of "In the Beach House" to the "soft sound" in "What's That." However thematically akin, the two poems nevertheless rely on different aesthetic strategies of probing the deep memory of childhood trauma. "In the Beach House" offers an explicit recovery of what is questioned but nevertheless repressed in "What's That."

Reading these two poems in relation to each other inevitably raises questions of aesthetic valuation and the poet's cognitive mastery of her material. Certainly, "In the Beach House" is the more widely discussed of the two, but that neglect, para-doxically enough, may be an index of the aesthetic power to be found in "What's That." Is "In the Beach House" more successful than "What's That" because it more consciously inscribes the primal scene in the figure of the "royal strapping"? Or, is "What's That" a more compelling poem precisely because the poet has less conscious ownership of the psychic "truth" the poem otherwise encrypts? Does Sexton, in fact, "know" what lends force to the primal scene beyond what she other-wise views as a "corny" (PR, 86) psychoanalytic take on the masochistic pleasure derived from the well-known Freudian formula of "A Child Is Being Beaten." Is there a dimension of the primal scene inscribed in both poems that eludes her con-scious understanding in her 1971 interview?

Both "In the Beach House" and "What's That" testify in different ways to what the child "couldn't know, but heard." So arresting is that witnessing, however, that it not only escapes the poet's conscious knowledge but also that of her critics. One symptom of the possessing force of the unconscious in "What's That" is the critical silence that marks the poem's reception. Another symptom is the critical tendency to repress what lies encrypted in the poem's "screen memory" of Sexton's conscious childhood memory of her mother's summer beach house. Surprisingly, Diana Hume George, an otherwise astute reader of Sexton's Oedipal poetics, misses Sexton's profound psychoanalytic witnessing that is otherwise screened by the everyday associations in "What's That." Instead, George reduces the poet's deep memory of the primal scene to ordinary domestic nostalgia. As critic, George reinforces that swerve from the poem's unconscious truth by projecting readerly empathy onto her own audience precisely in her symptomatic reliance on direct address—a usage that is otherwise quite rare in critical writing. "You know," George writes,

> how parents call from those sweet beaches anywhere, *come in, come in,* even if you have long since grown into the parent who calls instead of the child who tries not to hear. Sexton remembers those sweet beaches, those voices, more clearly than most people do, and she gives back to us, a gift "caught back from time." The "image we did forget" is the one she remembers; the "half a bell" now silenced for most of us, she hears. . . . Sexton's ability to be enveloped by that intricate shape of air made her happiest when she was; it also caused her to be vulnerable to a special sort of sadness: "in my heart I go children slow." (OA, 119)

What George neglects in reading the poem's "half a bell" of recollection is, arguably, memory's Other half. In fact Sexton writes, "The noise we steal / is half a bell." What, however, is the other half of this childhood theft in that "noise" that, she says, "is as real / as splinters stuck in your ear"?

The "noise we steal" in the primal scene is, arguably, a theft from the mother's body, which according to Melanie Klein, is prior to and indeed incorporates the child's fantasy of parental coupling. Following Freud's hypothesis in "On the Transformations of Instinct as Exemplified in Anal Eroticism" that "the products of the unconscious—spontaneous ideas, phantasies and symptoms—the conceptions *faeces* (money, gift), *baby,* and *penis* are ill-distinguished from one another and are easily interchangeable,"[39] Klein writes that "the little girl has a sadistic desire, originating in the early stages of the Oedipus conflict, to rob the mother's body of its contents, namely, the father's penis, faeces, children, and to destroy the mother herself" (LGR, 217). Such sadistic impulses are reflected in the child's fantasies of the primal

scene. In Klein's rendering, the primal scene is marked by the trauma of cannibaliz-
ing the mother's breast and father's penis and, in turn, being devoured by them:

> According to the child's earliest phantasies (or "sexual theories") of parental coitus,
> the father's penis (or his whole body) becomes incorporated in the mother during the
> act. Thus the child's sadistic attacks have for their object both father and mother, who
> are in phantasy bitten, torn, cut or stamped to bits. The attacks give rise to anxiety
> lest the subject should be punished by the united parents. (LGR, 219)

Parental coupling, overheard in both "What's That" and "In the Beach House," intrudes so forcefully on the memory of the adult poet precisely because it is underwritten by the kind of infantile fantasy that Klein uncovered in her clinical work.
Not insignificantly, both poems associate childhood memories of the primal scene
with the mother's house, a setting Sexton elsewhere in her poem "Housewife" explicitly links to the body of "fleshy mothers." Underlying Sexton's sexual fantasy of
participating in the "royal strapping," then, is the terror of a more primordial anxiety situation owing to the infant's fear of coupling parents who are perceived as
"extremely cruel and much dreaded assailants" (LGR, 213).

Sexton's psychic defense against that primitive anxiety is inscribed in the final
stanza of the poem through the rhetoric of prosopopoeia:

> Have mercy, little pillow,
> stay mute and uncaring,
> hear not one word of disaster!
> Stay close, little sour feather,
> little fellow full of salt.
> My loves are oiling their bones
> and then delivering them with unspeakable sounds
> that carry them this way and that
> while summer is hurrying its way in and out,
> over and over
> in their room. (CP, 160)

As Paul de Man defines it in his well-known essay, "Autobiography as De-Facement," prosopopoeia relies on "the fiction of an absent, deceased, or voiceless en-
tity, which posits the possibility of the latter's reply and confers upon it the power
of speech. Voice assumes mouth, eye, and finally face, a chain that is manifest in
the etymology of the trope's name, *prosopon poien*, to confer a mask or a face
(*prosopon*)."[40] Prosopopoeia in Sexton's poem sets up a linguistic chain of verbal
substitutions that function as a kind of psychic defense. Prosopopoeia buffers

against the anxiety of the primal scene imbricated as it is with both the violence of infantile sadism and the child's terror of horrific retribution. "In the Beach House" screens out the "unspeakable sounds" of the parents' "royal strapping" overheard "over and over / in their room" by repeatedly invoking personifications of and direct address to the girl's "little pillow," "little sour feather," and "little fellow." In the passage through that metonymic signifying chain—from pillow to feather to little fellow—the child's masturbation mimics the parents who are imagined as wrapped around the bedpost and bedstead. But Sexton's prosopopoeia involves not only sexual pleasure—"the little masochistic seizure" that Sexton recalls through her analytic sessions—but also a psychic escape from the terrifying "disaster" of infantile anxiety.

Responding, perhaps, to the sustained psychic labor of her analytic sessions, Sexton's return to the primordial, infantile fantasy of oral and anal sadism underwriting her early verse becomes increasingly more explicit in the subsequent volumes after *Live or Die* (1966). In her 1971 volume *Transformations,* for example, Sexton's fantasy of eating and being eaten by the mother is given uncanny license in her imaginative rereading of such Brothers Grimm fairy tales as "Hansel and Gretel":

Little plum,
Said the mother to her son,
I want to bite,
I want to chew,
I will eat you up,
Little child,
Little nubkin,
sweet as fudge,
you are my blitz.

.   .   .   .   .   .

Oh succulent one,
It is but one turn in the road
and I would be a cannibal! (CP, 286–87)

As in "What's That" and "In the Beach House," prosopopoeia and direct address buffer the poet from the fantasy of cannibalism, but by now Sexton also delivers that primal scene in blunt, violent declaratives that assert her passion to "bite," "chew," and "eat up" the other. In her next volume *The Book of Folly* (1972), Sexton in turn addresses the mother as "my milk home": "I ate you up. / All my need took / you down like a meal" (CP, 314–15). Such cannibalistic impulses are reversed in *The Death Notebooks* (1974), where Sexton imagines herself passively "at the dog's party."

"I was their bone," she writes, "I had been laid out in their kennel / Like a fresh turkey." If Sexton idealizes the mother's breast as the good object—"a sweet nipple, a starberry" (CP, 397)—she also imagines its absence, in harrowing moments, as a fantasized threat from the "rat inside me / the gnawing pestilential rat" (CP, 418).

Insofar as confessional poetry, like autobiography, relies on what Lacan called the "full" speech of psychoanalysis to mediate its disclosures, it can never wholly sustain the kind of consoling, readerly empathy that Sexton's critics would like to claim for her verse. As de Man famously concludes, "the restoration of mortality (the prosopopoeia of the voice and the name) deprives and disfigures to the precise extent that it restores" (RR, 81). Such linguistic disfiguration is encrypted in Sexton's favorite palindrome of the "rat's star," which witnesses to the alien and alienating encounters the poet attributed to language: to moments, as she says, "here in my white study / with the awful black words pushing me around" (CP, 592). Part of why writing, and indeed psychoanalysis, failed to cure Sexton's melancholia has to do, perhaps, with Klein's more traumatic understanding of psychic "incorpora-tion." Emphasizing the persistence of early childhood phantasy in adult experience, Klein did not assume the kind of normative, developmental view of psychic phases and stages that would underwrite the therapeutic aims of American ego psychol-ogy in the 1950s. In reviewing the Kleinian formulations of the paranoid-schizoid, depressive, and reparative modes of infantile phantasy, Hanna Segal writes, "Klein chose the term 'position' to emphasize the fact that the phenomenon she was de-scribing was not simply a passing 'stage' or 'phase' such as, for example, the oral phase; her term implies a specific configuration of object relations, anxieties and de-fences which persist throughout life."[41]

Differing from Freud's theory of melancholia as an act of "internalizing" and thus preserving the "incorporated," lost object, Klein's model of "introjection"—for Judith Butler—submits the lost object to a further trauma occasioned by the in-fant's aggressive, sadistic, and specifically cannibalistic phantasies of devouring loss.[42] The persistent psychic returns of the paranoid-schizoid position—whose rad-ical reversals of love and hate, benevolence and hostility, protection and destruc-tion play havoc with the ego's relation to its earliest part-objects—also belie the aim of achieving any normative, prescriptive, and thus terminal self-possession of iden-tity by means of the redemptive logic of symbolic reparation. Indeed, as Jacqueline Rose—following Lacan—has observed, Klein's positing of a third stage of symbolic reparation demands at once "too much and too little of an ego whose role it is to master the anxiety out of which it has itself been produced." Reparation thus bears a "mysterious" relation to melancholia insofar as it is always already predicated as a kind of negotiated defense against what it purports to cure. For Rose, the radical negation that marks the Kleinian field proves salutary, paradoxically enough, "in the trouble it poses to the concept of a sequence" and as a "bar . . . to what might elsewhere (and increasingly) appear as normative and prescriptive in the work and followers of Melanie Klein."[43] Part of the value of Sexton's career is its resistance to the normalizing containment of identity that otherwise marked much of contemporaneous psychoanalytic discourse of the postwar decades in America. Although black words did not offer a therapeutic cure, finally, for the poet's traumatic autobiography, language did serve to translate the gnawing anxieties of Sexton's psychic rats into a cultural discourse that, curiously, made her a public star.

A further dimension of understanding Sexton's achievement has to do precisely with accounting for the phenomenal success she enjoyed in performing the rat's star of madness for a broad popular audience. What gave Sexton's verse such a forceful purchase on the public mind of her moment? To her credit, Sexton's persona staged precisely what Michael Hardt and Antonio Negri describe as the "mixed constitution" of an emerging "hybrid subjectivity": one that reflects the new times of postmodern, postindustrial, and postdisciplinary society. Such "hybrid subjects," they write, "may not carry the identity of a prison inmate or a mental patient or a factory worker, but may still be constituted simultaneously by all of their logics. It is factory worker outside the factory, student outside school, inmate outside prison, insane outside the asylum—all at the same time."[44] Similarly in the 1950s, Sexton effects a radical transformation of her various postwar personae—as hysteric, housebound agoraphobic, manic-depressive, survivor of domestic trauma, and the rest—by collapsing their minoritizing boundaries into new and increasingly universal models of hybridized subjectivity. As a public intellectual on the cusp of the postmodern, Sexton deterritorializes the disciplinary institutions of postwar American culture. Moving beyond personal confessionalism, her poetry traverses and escapes the sentence of the psychiatric diagnosis, the marriage oath of the nuclear family, the religious creed against abortion and suicide, and the interpretive judgment of her critical reception.

Sexton's defining figure for this double possession of and by the new hybrid identity of postmodernism is the "witch" whom she celebrates in her signature poem, "Her Kind":

I have gone out, a possessed witch,
haunting the black air, braver at night;
dreaming evil, I have done my hitch
over the plain houses, light by light:
lonely thing, twelve-fingered, out of mind.

A woman like that is not a woman, quite.
I have been her kind.

I have found the warm caves in the woods,
filled them with skillets, carvings, shelves,
closets, silks, innumerable goods;
fixed the suppers for the worms and the elves:
whining, rearranging the disaligned.
A woman like that is misunderstood.
I have been her kind.

I have ridden in your cart, driver,
waved my nude arms at villages going by,
learning the last bright routes, survivor
where your flames still bite my thigh
and my ribs crack where your wheels wind.
A woman like that is not ashamed to die.
I have been her kind. (CP, 16)

In "Her Kind," Sexton takes back the evening's undifferentiated "black air." She re-claims the "twelve-fingered," carnivalesque dreamworld that Djuna Barnes con-jures in *Nightwood*. As a witch—the traditional political figure, according to Juliet Mitchell of "unconscious feminism"—Sexton rides her broomstick as the lonely "Thing." Not unlike Lacan's formulation of *das Ding*, "Her Kind" inscribes the trace of the Real in what is prior to and outside the Law of the Father, whose symbolic logic describes the phallic function of the *Nom du Pere*. Having "gone out" of that frame, she is possessed by and possesses what is properly "out of mind" and beyond symbolization. Sexton projects confessional identity in "Her Kind" as a multiply in-flected "haunting" by a range of subject positions. Women's place in "Her Kind" is a locus of conflicted identifications: a structural impossibility and excluded middle where "a woman like that is not a woman, quite." In "Her Kind" the witch is pre-sented as "dreaming evil" insofar as she traditionally stands as the polar opposite to the procreative mother, whose appropriated womb serves to reproduce the nu-clear family. Yet within the circuit of women's experience, Sexton claims both roles, even as she notes that the latter's nurturing agency and domestic labor have been "misunderstood" under patriarchy.

On one level, the final stanza continues and escalates the previous stanzas' cul-tural critique of the confining domestic roles of the 1950s containment culture that Sexton herself both embraced as a housebound agoraphobic and rejected in her periodic hospitalizations for hysteric depression. Yet in a further, more radical move, Sexton opens that domestic pathology to a more ecstatic encounter with language's transformative agency. Here we witness the witch as scapegoat and abject other who must be periodically purged from the body politic. Sexton certainly acted out, hysterically so, the figure of the witch before the law in her performative public readings, in breaking the proscription against incest, adultery, and bisexuality in the contemporary domestic sphere, in courting critical controversy through her increasingly antipoetic verse after receiving the Pulitzer Prize (going so far as to describe her *Death Notebooks* as posthumous poems) and even in such nuanced, symptomatic behaviors as chain-smoking Salem cigarettes. Witch-hunting, as historians such as Juliet Mitchell, Norman Cohn, and Brian Levack have argued, "became one of the ways that people could maintain their equilibrium at a time of great stress."[45] In "Her Kind" Sexton stages herself as the object of such mass hysteria. She is "ridden" by the drive of the social Other and receives the sentence of its collective judgment where it is executed on the body. More than just a cultural icon of woman as martyr, "Her Kind" concludes with an allegory of how woman as confessional poet is marked by desire that is "hollowed within the demand," that is, by the movement of signification, which Lacan figures in the "mark of the iron of the signifier on the shoulder of the speaking subject." Desire, he says, "is not so much a pure passion of the signified as a pure action of the signifier that stops at the moment when the living being becomes sign, rendering it insignificant" (É, 265). Similarly "learning the last bright routes" that consume the body even as they are inscribed on the page, Sexton lives on as survivor precisely "where," she says "your flames still bite my thigh." There she is touched by the Real as it befalls the full discourse of the poet, whose witnessing reaches that moment where the truth of personal confession and public testimony "shall meet," as Audre Lorde has it, "and not be / one."[46]

Epilogue

Reading Abu Ghraib

Trauma, as we have seen, plays havoc with time. Haunting the new millennium, the legacy of loss bequeathed by modernity makes an uncanny claim upon the present. Modern genocide, total war, as well as modernism's unresolved social antagonisms of race, class, and sexual difference remain charged with the traumatic affect of histories that, because they cannot be fully known, are subject to endless repetition. Lacking sufficient representation, the traumatic events of the past century cannot be fixed in history's knowable archive but persist "out of joint" with conventional understandings of linear temporality. The traumatic edge of modernism—as we find it in the latest human rights violation, in the specter of terrorism, in the "shock and awe" of state reprisal, in the setbacks of continuing economic disparities and discriminations—intrudes upon the present as if from an unimaginable future. At the same time, that edgy horizon possesses us, paradoxically enough, as something strangely familiar from the past: an unsettling déjà vu where we encounter exactly what we once pledged would happen "never again." Increasingly in the post-modern public sphere, such revenants of atrocity, oppression, and political clash have come—in their seemingly ubiquitous recycling—to constitute "information" as such.

The productive task of democratic "nation building"—that belongs to the globalizing agenda of Empire—demands, paradoxically, the regulation and reproduction of everyday information in ways that extend the internal relations of power, law, and order sustaining imperial sovereignty. Yet the rule of Empire, as Giorgio Agamben, Antonio Negri, and Michael Hardt have argued, always already rests on a relation of exception whose authority suspends the internal juridical order of common law from a position outside the legal status quo.[1] Increasingly, such political exceptionalism has itself become the rule of the day sustained under the guises of perpetual war, police and security actions, and other, more contingent civil emergencies. The spectacular shock and awe belonging to martial forms of imperial exceptionalism find their counterpart in the obscure, covert, and—it must be said—criminal arts of persuasion and torture that involve certain long-standing communicative techniques of psychological warfare. As Agamben has shown, the regime of modern exceptionalism parts company with the "juridicopolitical foundation of classical politics" even as it produces the biopoliticization of "bare life." For Agamben, the biopolitical exceptionalism that increasingly defines modernism's extrinsic relation to the law leads to Auschwitz. The "camp," he writes, "is the space that is opened when the state of exception begins to become the rule."[2] Arguably, America's own relation of exception to international law has witnessed the spectral return of the camp environment in U.S. detention centers at Guantanamo Bay and Abu Ghraib prison. While no one would compare the scale of torture of Abu Ghraib to the genocidal novum of the Holocaust, the persistent iconicity of atrocity that otherwise links Auschwitz to Abu Ghraib nevertheless makes for an uncanny repetition of the traumatic past. Abu Ghraib prison, in particular, discloses an analogous locale at the heart of Empire: one whose psychological operations, or psyops, record a uniquely intimate witnessing to the arresting biopolitics of imperial exceptionalism as it assumes the status of the global norm.

As we have seen since 9/11, managing the ongoing crises of Empire entails a certain routinization of violence: one that also involves techniques for easing the latent side effects of considerable social trauma. Extending the reach of American Empire into the electromagnetic spectrum of broadcast news, the "embedded" media practices that link the frontline to the headline would regulate the "live feed" of the moment through networks of normalized sign exchange. That attempt to manage trauma in the public sphere involves not just repression and censorship but also the artful screening of images that buffer horror through propaganda, spectacle, and entertainment. Yet "it would be a mistake," as Judith Butler has argued, "to think that we only need to find the right and true images, and that a certain reality will then be conveyed. The reality is not conveyed by what is represented within the image, but through the challenge to representation that reality delivers."[3] Reversing the claim of state representation to "capture" through prosopopoeia the readable faces of patriot and terrorist, victim and perpetrator, Butler argues that the regard of the Other beheld in the face demands another kind of witnessing: one sensitive to what Emmanuel Levinas has described in terms of the "extreme precariousness of the other."[4] It is such "precarious life," Butler argues, that is effaced by the media's "occlusions," particularly in its ideological representation of the other by means of figurative personification. Supplementing Butler's salutary reading of Levinas, we may also discern via a return to Freud certain specters and revenants of modernism that haunt the contemporary representation of violence with the violence of representation. Just as the media coverage of Vietnam was ghosted by unauthorized images of atrocity, torture, and other violations of the human—most notably, in the indelible scenes of the My Lai massacre—similar, bootlegged photos have come to complicate the official state "picture" of the American presence in Iraq. In particular, what are we to make of the photographed psyops of Abu Ghraib prison? And more to the point, how does the psychic life of the digitally mediated photograph exceed the conscious communicative intent of its ideological production to engage and disseminate the more overdetermined political unconscious of Empire as such?

Not insignificantly, shortly after the photographs of torture at Abu Ghraib circulated in the global media, a *New York Times* editorial concluded that "[t]he invasion of Iraq, which has already begun to seem like a bad dream in so many ways, cannot get much more nightmarish than this."[5] That the photographic record of the Abu Ghraib interrogations should invoke the figure of nightmare and bad dream should come as no surprise. The power of these unregulated photographs communicates in analogous ways to what Freud theorized as the dreamwork's pictorial force: its reliance on the uncanny image to express wishes and thoughts that would otherwise be repressed by rational discourse. Unlike conceptual thought, "dreams," Freud wrote, "think essentially in images."[6] Similarly, Freud's "explanation of hallucinations in hysteria and paranoia and of visions in mentally normal subjects is that they are in fact regressions—that is, thoughts transformed into images" (ID, 583). Regression of thought into image, whether in the dream or hallucination, marks a return to the "psychical locality" of the unconscious: a locality shaped by impulses, wishes, fantasies and "thoughts cut off from consciousness and struggling to find expression" (ID, 585). Not insignificantly, Freud described the "mental apparatus" of regression by way of a figure "resembling a compound microscope or a photographic apparatus . . . [whose] psychic locality will correspond to a point inside the apparatus at which one of the preliminary stages of an image comes into being" (ID, 574). Curiously enough, the American interrogation center at Abu Ghraib served as a military special-access program (SAP) not just for gathering valued intelligence information. More provocatively, this "black" program—run by what Brigadier General Janis Karpinski described as the "disappearing ghosts" of CIA officers and anonymous contract intelligence operatives—became a kind of psychical locality in Freud's sense: one that—through digital photography—

literally brought into focus the repressed truth of American foreign policy other-wise "cut off from consciousness and struggling to find expression."

Belying America's altruistic mission of liberating Iraqi citizens from Saddam Hussein's tyranny, Abu Ghraib disclosed another more profoundly repressed coun-ternarrative. Tier 1-A—the hard-site, high-security zone of Abu Ghraib prison—revealed a fantasy of imperial domination that went to the heart of America's po-litical unconscious: one that found expression not in reasoned discourse but in vis-ceral images of atrocity. Such psychological operations acted out a profound re-gression, in Freud's sense, to primal scenes of classic sadomasochism, bondage, and domination as in Pfc. Lynndie England's photographed pose of walking a naked Iraqi detainee on a dog leash. "I was instructed," said England, "by persons in higher rank to stand there and hold this leash and look at the camera. . . . We thought that's how they did it. . . . We're not trained as MI or CIA—mind games, intimidation, it sounded pretty typical to us. . . . Well, I mean, they [the photos] were for psy-op reasons."[7]

As Seymour M. Hersh has convincingly demonstrated, Abu Ghraib represents the Defense Department's policy disaster of mixing the covert psyops of military intelligence and CIA information gathering with the ordinary military policing of Iraqi prisoners of war. Psyops have constituted a typical weapon in the arsenal of psychological warfare whose institutional base reaches back as far as World War I, when in 1917, President Woodrow Wilson appointed George Creel to lead the Committee of Public Information made up of the U.S. secretaries of War, Navy, and State. The rubric of psychological warfare actually derives from the German coinage of *Weltanshauungskrieg* (literally, worldview warfare) referring to new techniques of propaganda and covert acts of terror employed to secure ideological consensus during the Second World War. In America, Wild Bill Donovan was an early practitioner of psychological warfare within the Office of Strategic Services (OSS)—a forerunner program to the Central Intelligence Agency, whose Office of Policy Coordination was charged in 1948 with the covert tasks of "propaganda, eco-nomic warfare; preventative direct action, including sabotage, anti-sabotage, de-molition and evacuation measures; subversion against hostile states," and so on.[8]

The conjuncture of mass communication, persuasion, and terror that come to-gether by degrees in military psyops runs the gamut from overt or "white" propa-ganda through "gray" acts of media subversion to the "black" arts of covert ter-rorism and torture. Photography, of course, has a long history of mass persuasion reaching back to the Constructivist era of the former Soviet Union, and psyops that rely on the photographic image had tactical pertinence in the Iraq war. Major Harry Taylor, head of the 42nd Commando Royal Marines' Psyops offers an apt summary of the uses of photographic propaganda: "We use tactical and strategic methods. Tactically, on the first stage, we target the military by dropping leaflets stating the inevitability of their defeat, telling them they will not be destroyed if they play our game and exactly how they can surrender. On the second wave we show them pictures of Iraqi officers who complied. On the third wave we show them pictures of those people who did not."[9] It is the third category of retributive photography that, arguably, Lynndie England was "instructed" to produce in the black psyops of Abu Ghraib.

Yet, in performing imperial mastery, England's fantasy of domination goes beyond the Orientalist stereotypes that otherwise script Abu Ghraib's scenes of sexual humiliation, derived as they were from Raphael Patai's 1973 *The Arab Mind*: what Seymour Hersh cites as the "bible of the neocons on Arab behavior."[10] In this fantasy of imperial power, the abject Iraqi subdued at the end of England's leash counterbalances the regressive oral-sadism literally unleashed in the attack dogs that otherwise mutilated the bodies of Iraqi prisoners inside Abu Ghraib. Significantly, the psychic fantasy of the man/dog is not unlike the "loup garou" or werewolf that, as Agamben explains, is a figure for both the exilic status of *Homo sacer* and the sovereign's relation of exception to the juridicopolitical order.[11] Whether on or off the leash, the loup garou can be read here as a condensation for the mutual constitution of imperial subject and *Homo sacer* in extrinsic relation to the law. Similarly, the other definitive image of Abu Ghraib—the infamous thumbs-up sign—became a definitive marker of phallic posturing: one that instantiates imperial sovereignty precisely from the production of the Iraqi as *Homo sacer*.

The imperial aim of giving the thumbs-up to what George Bush and other neoconservatives hail as the "Iraqi people" nevertheless confronts the trauma of, in Agamben's phrase, a "biopolitical fracture" whose excess always already inhabits the civic populus in the bare life of *Homo sacer*. Indeed, it is only *Homo sacer*'s abjection that instantiates Empire's idealized imagined community. Thus, Agamben writes, "Paraphrasing the Freudian postulate on the relation between Es and Ich, one could say that modern biopolitics is supported by the principle according to which 'where there is bare life, there will have to be a People'—on the condition that one immediately adds that the principle also holds in its reverse formulation, which has it that 'where there is a People, *there* there will be bare life.'"[12] The digitally recorded psyops of Abu Ghraib were intended to manipulate the thinking, the psychology, and the aims of suspected and would-be terrorists, but perversely they actually came to shed more light on America and its disturbing production of *Homo sacer*.

Such arresting images of "bare life" broadcast an ironic "blowback" to the Defense Department's "shock and awe" war plans. "You read it," Secretary of Defense

Donald Rumsfeld stated in his Senate Armed Services Committee testimony, "as I say, it's one thing. You see these photographs and it's just unbelievable. . . . It wasn't three-dimensional. It wasn't video. It wasn't color. It was quite a different thing."[13] Symptomatic perhaps in the pattern of repetition marking Rumsfeld's perplexed attempt to account for what "it was" there in the image—and, equally important, what "wasn't" there in the readable report—is not just an unconscious truth "struggling to find expression" but, more to the point, the traumatic force of precarious life sacrificed to imperial fantasy. Indeed, the photographs of Abu Ghraib capture not just the psyops' scripted scenarios of humiliation, cruelty, and dehumanization. They not only frame what Roland Barthes describes as the photograph's *studium:* the cultural and ideological codes by which "the figures, the faces, the gestures, the settings, the actions" take on a readable historical meaning.[14] Neither can they be fully grasped as sociological documents in the manner of what Pierre Bourdieu defines as the "middle-brow art" of family portraitures and tourist snapshots: the photograph's "means of solemnizing those climactic moments of social life in which the group solemnly reaffirms its unity."[15] Certainly, the conventions of posing that belong to the family photo and tourist shot underwrite England's and Spc. Charles Graner's posturing as a couple for the camera. Graner and England oddly enough became lovers and even parents together at Abu Ghraib. Beyond any of these readable narratives, however, the photos of Abu Ghraib communicate what Roland Barthes describes as the *punctum,* whose force punctuates, pricks, and wounds the scene of its *studium* with the trauma of "what Lacan calls the Tuché, the Occasion, the Encounter, the Real in its indefatigable expression. . . . [P]hotographs are signs which don't take, which turn, as milk does. . . . In short, the referent adheres" (CL, 4, 6). If photography is spectral in its arrest of time and its punctuation of the referent, then the images produced at Abu Ghraib are doubly possessed by the *punctum* of the Real.

For it is the death imprint as such that shadows the infamous thumbs-up photos of Graner and Spc. Sabrina Harman taken beside an iced Iraqi corpse, subsequently identified by the *Guardian* magazine as Manadel al-Jamadi, otherwise inventoried as body E63 for months in the cold storage of a Baghdad mortuary.[16] Al-Jamadi was allegedly brought to Abu Ghraib in healthy condition only to die shortly thereafter under brutal CIA torture. The horror of this crime against humanity was psychically redoubled after his death in the grotesque photo taken of Graner and Harman giving the thumbs-up beside al-Jamadi's ice-packed corpse. Not insignificantly, the thumbs-up sign accompanies virtually every act of corporeal violation photographed at Abu Ghraib. "Two Thumbs Up" serves as a metonym for the imagined self-possession of the imperial subject produced out of its relational difference from *Homo sacer*'s lack of being. This defining fetish of American identity, more than any of the other images of Abu Ghraib, signifies Empire's biopolitical fracture and its symptomatic disavowal. It points redundantly and thus uncannily to what Barthes describes as the "pure deictic language" of the photo's invitation to the viewer to "'Look,' 'See,' 'Here it is'" (CL, 5). As an indexical sign, it both gestures to and disavows its grounding in the Real. The thumbs-up flashed at Abu Ghraib solely in proximity to prostrate Iraqi bodies and corpses instantiates the imperial subject through the symptomatic logic of the fetish. That is, its indexical sign of victory always already encrypts a reference rooted in the traumatic Real whose powers of abjection, annihilation, and death, paradoxically enough, it at once invokes and magically dispels.

What makes these photographs such a "different thing"—as Rumsfeld's testimony has it—is, arguably, not just the impact of such literal images of death and bodily violation but also the return of a certain specter of modernism haunting the photographic archive of American foreign policy. The gleeful and thoroughly banal sadism captured in the thumbs-up sign that Graner and Harman flash beside a desecrated and unburied corpse—the same thumbs-up that they sport in back of a human pyramid of naked and anonymous Iraqi bodies—surely conjures the phantoms of atrocity witnessed in the pictorial record and survivor accounts of the Holocaust and other modern genocides. For while Abu Ghraib's human pyramid of stripped prisoners invokes what former Defense Secretary James Schlesinger characterized as a "kind of 'Animal House' on the night shift," its image does not merely gloss fraternity hazing rituals. Such piles of nude prisoners also recall the heaps of naked bodies stacked like cordwood at the killing centers of Auschwitz and Treblinka.[17] Again, while the event of Abu Ghraib would surely not appear on any scale or continuum with the Holocaust, its iconicity nevertheless signifies on the conventional representations of what has come to define the modern biopolitics of bare life in the camps.

Yet in the photographs, what Hannah Arendt would define as Abu Ghraib's "crime[s] against the human status" seem strangely invisible to their American perpetrators.[18] Atrocities otherwise captured by the camera's lens inside Abu Ghraib elude the knowing eye and recede into what Walter Benjamin would characterize as the photograph's "optical unconscious."[19] Given the fact that Abu Ghraib's widely broadcast images seemingly had little impact on the American electorate, one might well question whether "ordinary Americans" can bear witness to their government's psychological operations. Here again, Freud's photographic figure for time as deferred action (*nachträglichkeit*) remains salutary: latency "seems so strange that we might try to make it easier to understand by a simile; the process may be compared to a photograph, which can be developed and made into a picture after a short or long interval."[20] Perhaps ordinary Americans are not unlike ordinary Germans, who similarly turned a blind eye on the production of bare life precisely because the imperial *Ich* only emerges where *Homo sacer*'s *Es* has been.

Like the overdetermined associations that ramify the dreamwork, digitized photographic representation is susceptible to iteration: to multiple citation beyond the psyops' performative intent. Such powers of symbolic articulation may well baffle the imperial chain of command so as to call in question Empire's fiction of the *bellum justum*. Mediated by the latency of time, such images of atrocity will perhaps prove susceptible to alternative counternarratives capable of a "just" witnessing to Empire's traumatic historicity. Such testimony will, no doubt, call for new modes of poetic expression, for the high modernists' aim of writing poems capable, as Pound had it, of "containing history" is complicated in the postmodern era by the return of modern traumas that remain—as Toni Morrison described them—"uncontained and uncontainable."[21] Indeed, such traumatic historicities can no longer be considered as somehow external to the verse medium but "first and foremost," as Marjorie Perloff has observed, "a condition of language."[22] Anticipating, perhaps, that postmodern horizon of poetic testimony, William Carlos Williams avowed late in his career that

> It is difficult
> to get the news from poems
> yet men die miserably every day
> for lack
> of what is found there.[23]

Set off in Williams's formal pattern of enjambment is the poet's passionate attention precisely to what much of contemporary verse has come to inscribe in its special field of discourse as a signifying "lack." Composed in the wake of the extreme event, poetry offers a "difficult" and necessarily belated linguistic response to what otherwise goes missing from the conventional regimes of representation regulating the breaking "news" of the day. That lack of authorized, consumable, and often coerced information—afforded by the poetry of traumatic witness—speaks to the heart of "what is found there," long deferred even now at the edge of modernism.

Notes

1. On this point see Dominick LaCapra, *Writing History, Writing Trauma* (Baltimore: Johns Hopkins University Press, 2001). Wary of both historical "facts" and textual undecidability, LaCapra proposed "writing trauma" through what Roland Barthes described in terms of the "interlocutions" of the "middle voice." See Roland Barthes, "To Write an Intransitive Verb?" in *The Languages of Criticism and the Sciences of Man: The Structuralist Controversy,* ed. Richard Macksey and Eugenio Donato (Baltimore: Johns Hopkins Press, 1970), 144.

2. On the resources of melancholia for new modes of representation and identification, see *Loss: The Politics of Mourning,* ed. David L. Eng and David Kazanjian (Berkeley: University of California Press, 2003), and Judith Butler, *The Psychic Life of Power: Theories in Subjection* (Stanford: Stanford University Press, 1997).

3. Kaja Silverman, *The Threshold of the Visible World* (New York: Routledge, 1996), 23. In this vein, Dominick LaCapra proposes a similar concept of traumatic "empathy" that, as he defines it, "should be understood in terms of an affective relation, rapport, or bond with the other recognized and respected as other." *Writing History, Writing Trauma,* 213.

4. See Shoshana Felman and Dori Laub, *Testimony: Crises of Witnessing in Literature, Psychoanalysis, and History* (New York: Routledge, 1992), and Geoffrey Hartman, *The Longest Shadow: In the Aftermath of the Holocaust* (Bloomington: Indiana University Press, 1996).

5. "This is another way of saying that the archive, as printing, writing, prosthesis, or hypomnesic technique in general is not only the place for stocking and for conserving an archivable content *of the past* which would exist in any case, such as, without the archive, one still believes it was or will have been. No, the technical structure of the *archiving* archive also determines the structure of the *archivable* content even in its very coming into existence and in its relationship to the future. The archivization produces as much as it records the event." Jacques Derrida, *Archive Fever: A Freudian Impression,* trans. Eric Prenowitz (Chicago: University of Chicago Press, 1996), 17.

6. Michel Foucault, *The Archaeology of Knowledge,* trans. A. M. Sheridan Smith (New York: Pantheon Books, 1972), 130.

7. On this point see Herman Rapaport, *Later Derrida: Reading the Recent Work* (New York: Routledge, 2002), and Derrida, *Archive Fever.*

8. "[T]he pathology," writes Cathy Caruth, "cannot be defined either by the event itself—which may or may not be catastrophic, and may not traumatize everyone equally—

nor can it be defined in terms of a *distortion* of the event, achieving its haunting power as a result of distorting personal significances attached to it. The pathology consists, rather, solely in the *structure of its experience* or reception: the event is not assimilated or experienced fully at the time, but only belatedly, in its repeated *possession* of the one who experiences it." "Introduction," in *Trauma: Explorations in Memory*, ed. Cathy Caruth (Baltimore: Johns Hopkins University Press, 1995), 4.

9. Sigmund Freud, "On the Psychical Mechanism of Hysterical Phenomena: Preliminary Communication" (1893) in *The Standard Edition of the Complete Psychological Works of Sigmund Freud*, trans. James Strachey (London: Hogarth Press and the Institute of Psycho-Analysis, 1953–1974), 2:6.

10. Michael Rothberg's important study of the Holocaust, *Traumatic Realism*, offers a cogent mapping of the event's relationship to realist, modernist, and postmodernist representation, defining the latter as "a framework that implies the conjuncture of new communications technologies, conflictual contemporary politics, the mass-marketing of genocide, and the obsession with traumatic memories." *Traumatic Realism: The Demands of Holocaust Representation* (Minneapolis: University of Minnesota Press, 2000), 184.

11. Peter Novick, *The Holocaust in American Life* (Boston: Houghton Mifflin, 1999), 11 (hereafter cited in the text as HAL).

12. For a discussion of *nachträglichkeit* as gap, silence, and the repressed event of Holocaust trauma, see Jean-François Lyotard, *Heidegger and "the jews,"* trans. Andreas Michel and Mark S. Roberts (Minneapolis: University of Minnesota Press, 1990).

13. Theodor Adorno, "Cultural Criticism and Society" (1965), in *Prisms*, trans. Samuel and Shierry Weber (Cambridge: MIT Press, 1981), 34.

14. Laura S. Brown, "Not Outside the Range: One Feminist Perspective on Psychic Trauma," in Caruth, *Trauma*, 100–112.

15. Cynthia Ozick, "A Liberal's Auschwitz," in *The Pushcart Prize: Best of the Small Presses*, ed. Bill Henderson (Yonkers, NY: Pushcart Book Press, 1975), 127. On this point see Edward Alexander, "Stealing the Holocaust," *Midstream* 26, no. 9 (1980): 50; and Al Strangeways, "'The Boot in the Face': The Problem of the Holocaust in the Poetry of Sylvia Plath," *Contemporary Literature* 37, no. 3 (Fall 1996): 376.

16. "Sylvia Plath," in *The Poet Speaks*, ed. Peter Orr (London: Routledge and Kegan Paul, 1966), 169.

17. Edward Butscher, *Sylvia Plath, Method and Madness* (New York: Seabury Press, 1976), 327.

18. Strangeways, "'The Boot in the Face,'" 373.

19. Jacqueline Rose, *The Haunting of Sylvia Plath* (London: Virago Press, 1991), 225 (hereafter cited in the text as HSP).

20. Eric Santner, *Stranded Objects: Mourning, Memory, and Film in Postwar Germany* (Ithaca: Cornell University Press, 1990), 6.

21. See Martin S. Bergmann and Milton E. Jucovy, eds. *Generations of the Holocaust* (New York: Basic Books, 1982), and Alexander and Margarete Mitscherlich, *The Inability to Mourn: Principles of Collective Behavior*, trans. Beverley R. Placzek (New York: Grove Press, 1975).

22. Sylvia Plath, "December 31, 1958, Journal entry," *The Journals of Sylvia Plath (1950–1962)*, ed. Karen V. Kukil (London: Faber and Faber, 2000), 453; cited in Rose, *The Haunting of Sylvia Plath*, 272.

23. Sylvia Plath, *The Collected Poems* (New York: Harper & Row, 1981), 293, n. 183.

24. Following Julia Kristeva and Jacques Lacan, Rose claims that what matters in "Daddy" is the way in which Plath acts out the loss of the *"Père Imaginaire."* "The poem," she writes, "seems to be outlining the conditions under which the celebrated loss of the symbolic function takes place . . . it is this crisis of representation in the place of the father which is presented by Plath as engendering—forcing even—her identification with the Jew." *The Haunting of Sylvia Plath*, 227.

25. Sigmund Freud, "Mourning and Melancholia," in *Collected Papers*, trans. Joan Rivière (London: Hogarth Press, 1956), 4:169.

26. Theodor Reik, "Freud and Jewish Wit," *Psychoanalysis* 2, no. 3 (1954): 18; quoted in Yoseff Hayim Yerushalmi, *Freud's Moses: Judaism Terminable and Interminable* (New Haven: Yale University Press, 1991), 1.

27. Sigmund Freud, *Moses and Monotheism*, in *The Standard Edition of the Complete Psychological Works of Sigmund Freud*, 23:136.

28. Ibid.

29. Ibid., 43.

30. "The truly fundamental thesis of *Moses and Monotheism* (1939) . . . is that Moses should have been assassinated, since it is in this *Agieren*, these acting-outs (the compulsive murder of the paternal figure, repeating in non-recognition that of the primal father, thematized in *Totem and Taboo* in 1913) that the Jews escape the general movement of the first murder's recognition and the religion of reconciliation, Christianity, which comes offering to the libido its formations of compromise. For the Jews, the son does not have to ask for and obtain a reconciliation with the father. There is between them an alliance, which is a pre-conciliation. . . . It could be shown, contrary to Freud's construction in *Moses and Monotheism*, that this figure corresponds to a mode of rejection that is not repression, but a foreclosure." Jean-François Lyotard, "Jewish Oedipus," trans. S. Hanson, *Genre* 10, no. 3 (1977): 405.

31. Elie Wiesel, "Trivializing the Holocaust: Semi-Fact and Semi-Fiction," *New York Times*, April 16, 1978; Novick, *The Holocaust in American Life*, 15.

32. See Geoffrey Hartman, "Shoah and Intellectual Witness," *Partisan Review* 65, no. 1 (1998), 47.

33. For a discussion of the Armenocide as a "total" genocide, as opposed to instances of "genocide-in-part," see Robert Melson, *Revolution and Genocide: On the Origins of the Armenian Genocide and the Holocaust* (Chicago: University of Chicago Press, 1992). For other discussions of the relations between the Armenocide and the Holocaust, see Leo Kuper, *Genocide: Its Political Uses in the Twentieth Century* (New Haven: Yale University Press, 1981); Helen Fein, "A Formula for Genocide: A Comparison of the Turkish Genocide (1915) and the German Holocaust (1939–1945)," *Comparative Studies in Sociology* 1 (1978): 271–93; Vahakn N. Dadrian, "The Convergent Aspects of the Armenian and Jewish Cases of Genocide: A Reinterpretation of the Concept of Holocaust," *Holocaust and Genocide Studies* 3, no. 2 (1988): 151–70; Hrair R. Dekmejian, "Determinants of Genocide: Armenians and Jews as

Case Studies," *The Armenian Genocide in Perspective*, ed. Richard G. Hovannisian (New Brunswick, NJ: Transaction Books, 1986), 85–96.

34. "It is crucial to stress," writes Geoffrey Hartman, "that the claim of exceptionality refers to the implementation of an ideology that singled out the Jews for extermination solely because they were Jews. All were to be killed, whether by shooting, gassing, or working them to death—including the children. It is this fact, not numbers, which made the Nazis war against the Jews an exceptional act of genocide, one we define by the special if inadequate term 'the Holocaust.'" *The Longest Shadow* (New York: Palgrave Macmillan, 2002), 138. Yet, as Ana Douglass and Thomas A. Vogler argue, such intentionalist arguments also pertain to other genocides: "As the Tasmanians were slaughtered because they were Tasmanians, the Armenians because they were Armenians, the Bosnians because they were Bosnians, so the Jews." "Introduction," in *Witness and Memory: The Discourse of Trauma*, ed. Ana Douglass and Thomas A. Vogler (New York: Routledge, 2003), 27.

35. Yehuda Bauer, "The Place of the Holocaust in Contemporary History," in *Holocaust: Religious and Philosophical Implications*, eds. John K. Roth and Michael Berenbaum (New York: Paragon House, 1989), 33–34.

36. See Martin S. Bergmann and Milton E. Jucovy, eds. *Generations of the Holocaust* (New York: Basic Books, 1982); Robert M. Prince, *The Legacy of the Holocaust: Psychohistorical Themes in the Second Generation* (Ann Arbor: UMI Research Press, 1985); John J. Sigal and Morton Weinfeld, *Trauma and Rebirth: Intergenerational Effects of the Holocaust* (New York: Praeger, 1989); Dina Wardi, *Memorial Candles: Children of the Holocaust*, trans. Naomi Goldblum (London: Tavistock / Routledge, 1992).

37. See Geoffrey Hartman, in "Holocaust and Intellectual Witness," *Partisan Review* 65 (1998): 37–48; Terrence Des Pres, *The Survivor* (New York: Oxford University Press, 1976); and Lawrence Langer, *Holocaust Testimonies: The Ruins of Memory* (New Haven: Yale University Press, 1991).

38. T. S. Eliot, *Collected Poems, 1909–1950* (New York: Harcourt, Brace and World, 1971), 133.

39. Lyotard, *Heidegger and "the jews,"* 16.

40. Gilles Deleuze, *Cinema 2: The Time-Image*, trans. Hugh Tomlinson and Robert Galeta (Minneapolis: University of Minnesota Press, 1989), 143.

41. Jacques Derrida, *Points . . . : Interviews, 1974–1994*, ed. Elisabeth Weber, trans. Peggy Kamuf et al. (Stanford: Stanford University Press, 1995), 383.

42. Judith Butler, "Afterward: After Loss, What Then?" in Eng and Kazanjian, *Loss*, 468.

43. Fredric Jameson, *Signatures of the Visible* (New York: Routledge, 1992), 87.

44. Jean Baudrillard, *The Transparency of Evil: Essays on Extreme Phenomena*, trans. James Benedict (New York: Verso, 1993), 90.

45. Pierre Nora, "Between Memory and History: Les Lieux de Mémoire," *History and Memory in African-American Culture*, ed. Geneviève Fabre and Robert O'Meally (New York: Oxford University Press, 1994), 284–300.

46. Ross Chambers, "Orphaned Memories, Foster-Writing, Phantom Pain: The *Fragments* Affair," in *Extremities*, ed. Nancy K. Miller and Jason Tougaw (Urbana: University of Illinois Press, 2002), 92.

47. For a discussion of the tensions in the Freudian field between theories of infantile sexuality and sexual seduction, see Jeffrey Masson, *The Assault on Truth: Freud's Suppression of the Seduction Theory* (New York: Farrar, Straus and Giroux, 1984).

48. Paul S. Appelbaum, Lisa A. Uyehara, and Mark R. Elin, eds. *Trauma and Memory: Clinical and Legal Controversies* (New York: Oxford University Press, 1997); Martin A. Conway, *Recovered Memories and False Memories* (New York: Oxford University Press, 1997); Kenneth Pope and Laura S. Brown, *Recovered Memories of Abuse: Assessment, Therapy, Forensics* (Washington, DC: American Psychoanalytic Association, 1996); Paul Antze and Michael Lambek, eds., *Tense Past: Cultural Essays in Trauma and Memory* (New York: Routledge, 1996).

49. Jane Gallop, "The Father's Seduction," in *Daughters and Fathers,* ed. Lynda E. Boose and Betty S. Flowers (Baltimore: Johns Hopkins University Press, 1989), 107.

CHAPTER I: HISTORY'S "BLACK PAGE"

1. For a critique of the normalizing denial of global catastrophe in the "end of history" rhetoric of Francis Fukuyama, see Jacques Derrida, *Specters of Marx: The State of the Debt, the Work of Mourning, and the New International,* trans. Peggy Kamuf (New York: Routledge, 1994).

2. W. B. Yeats, *The Collected Poems of W. B. Yeats* (New York: Macmillan, 1956), 292.

3. T. S. Eliot, *The Waste Land and Other Poems* (New York: Harcourt, Brace and World, Inc., 1962), 43. In lines 367–77, Eliot inflects Hermann Hesse's somewhat Orientalist fascination with the impending "chaos" of things "Asiatic" through a more apocalyptic register whose landscape of "falling towers" spreads westward in a domino effect into the heart of Europe: "Jerusalem Athens Alexandria / Vienna London" (44). After reading Hesse's *Blick ins Chaos* (1920), Eliot visited Hesse in Montagnola, Switzerland, in May 1922. "In your book *Blick ins Chaos,*" Eliot told Hesse, "I detect a concern with serious problems that has not yet penetrated to England, and I should like to spread its reputation." Quoted in Theodore Ziolkowski, "Introduction," in Herman Hesse, *My Belief: Essays on Life and Art,* ed. Theodore Ziolkowski (New York: Farrar, Straus and Giroux, 1974), ix.

4. See Christopher B. Ricks, *T. S. Eliot and Prejudice* (London: Faber, 1988).

5. Ezra Pound, "This Super-Neutrality," *New Age* 17, no. 25 (October 1915): 595.

6. See Marjorie Housepian Dobkin, "What Genocide? What Holocaust? News from Turkey, 1915–1923: A Case Study," *The Armenian Genocide in Perspective,* ed. Richard G. Hovannisian (New Brunswick, NJ: Transaction Books, 1986), 97–109.

7. See Viscount Bryce, *The Treatment of Armenians in the Ottoman Empire, 1915–16: Documents Presented to Viscount Grey of Fallodon,* ed. Arnold J. Toynbee (London: Sir Joseph Causton and Sons, Ltd., 1916).

8. *New York Tribune,* October 8, 1915, quoted in Arnold J. Toynbee, *Armenian Atrocities: The Murder of a Nation* (London: Hodder & Stoughton, 1915), 117.

9. See Tessa Hofmann, "German Eyewitness Reports of the Genocide of the Armenians, 1915–1916," in *A Crime of Silence: The Armenian Genocide,* ed. Gerard Libaridian (London: Zed Books, and Totowa, NJ: Biblio Distribution Center, 1985), 61–93.

10. *New York Times,* August 18, 1915; *New York Times,* August 27, 1915; *New York Times,* September 5, 1915; cited in Dobkin, "What Genocide?" 98.

11. For an account of the Turkish massacre of the Christian Armenian and Greek community of Smyrna, as well as Hemingway's journalistic accounts, see Marjorie Housepian Dobkin, *The Smyrna Affair* (New York: Harcourt Brace Jovanovich, 1972).

12. Ernest Hemingway, *The Short Stories of Ernest Hemingway* (New York: Macmillan, 1966), 87.

13. As Louis H. Leiter notes, the serial repetition that structures the officer's narrative "dramatizes the gradual numbing of human responses through repeated horrors." "Neural Projections in Hemingway's 'On the Quai at Smyrna.'" *Critical Essays on Ernest Hemingway's "In Our Time,"* ed. Michael S. Reynolds (Boston: Hall, 1983), 139.

14. John Dos Passos, *The Best Times* (New York: New American Library, 1966), 90 (hereafter cited in the text as BT).

15. John Dos Passos, *Orient Express* (New York: Harper & Brothers, 1927), 58–59.

16. Virginia Woolf, *Mrs. Dalloway* (New York: Harcourt Brace, 1997), 130.

17. Sigmund Freud, *Civilization and Its Discontents* (1930), in *The Standard Edition of the Complete Psychological Works of Sigmund Freud*, ed. James Strachey (London: Hogarth Press and the Institute of Psycho-Analysis, 1953–1974), 21:89; Robert Jay Lifton, *The Broken Connection: On Death and the Continuity of Life* (New York: Simon and Schuster, 1979), 173.

18. See Sigmund Freud, *Moses and Monotheism*, trans. Katherine Jones (New York: Vintage, 1939), 84. In her analysis of the latency phenomenon remarked by Freud, Cathy Caruth theorizes that "the fact of latency, would thus seem to consist, not in the forgetting of a reality that can hence never be fully known, but in an inherent latency within the experience itself. The historical power of the trauma is not just that the experience is repeated after its forgetting, but that it is only in and through its inherent forgetting that it is first experienced at all. And it is this inherent latency of the event that paradoxically explains the peculiarly temporal structure, the belatedness, of historical experience: since the traumatic event is not experienced as it occurs, it is fully evident only in connection with another place, and in another time." Cathy Caruth, "Trauma and Experience: Introduction," in *Trauma: Explorations in Memory*, ed. Cathy Caruth (Baltimore: Johns Hopkins University Press, 1995), 8.

19. *New York Times*, November 24, 1945, 7. *Office of the United States Chief of Council for Prosecution of Axis Criminality, Nazi Conspiracy and Aggression* (Washington, DC: Government Printing Office, 1946), 7:753.

20. See Annette Höss, "The Trial of Perpetrators by the Turkish Military Tribunals: The Case of Yozgat," in *The Armenian Genocide: History, Politics, Ethics*, ed. Richard G. Hovannisian (New York: St. Martin's Press, 1992), 208–21.

21. Letter to Admiral W. S. Sims, May 5, 1920, Naval Records; U.S. National Archives, Washington, DC, Subject file WT, Record Group 45; quoted in Dobkin, "What Genocide?" 105.

22. See Stephan H. Astourian, "Genocidal Process: Reflections on the Armeno-Turkish Polarization," in Hovannisian, *The Armenian Genocide: History, Politics, Ethics*, 53–79.

23. "Confidentially," wrote Dulles to Bristol in an April 21, 1922, letter, "the State Department is in a bind. Our task would be simple if the reports of the atrocities could be declared untrue or even exaggerated but the evidence, alas, is irrefutable and the Secretary of State wants to avoid giving the impression that while the United States is willing to intervene actively to protect its commercial interests, it is not willing to move on behalf of the Christian minorities. . . . I've been kept busy trying to ward off congressional resolutions of sym-

pathy for these groups [Greeks, Armenians, and Palestine Jews]." Quoted in Dobkin, "What Genocide?" 106.

24. *New York Times*, August 4, 1928; quoted in Dobkin, "What Genocide?" 107.

25. See Leo Kuper, *Genocide* (Middlesex: Penguin Books, 1981), 219.

26. For a detailed analysis of these congressional sessions, see Vigen Guroian, "The Politics and Morality of Genocide," in Hovannisian, *The Armenian Genocide: History, Politics, Ethics*, 311–39.

27. U.S. Congress, House, Congressman Downey speaking for H. J. Res. 238 providing for consideration of H. J. Res. 132, August 7, 1987, *Congressional Record*, 7332; cited in Guroian, "The Politics and Morality of Genocide," 321.

28. U.S. Congress, Senate, Senator Byrd speaking against a motion to proceed to S. J. Res. 212, 101 Congress, 2nd sess., February 20, 1990, *Congressional Record*, 1216. Cited in Guroian, "The Politics and Morality of Genocide," 328.

29. Ibid., February 21, 1990, Senator Exon speaking against a motion to proceed to S. J. Res. 212: 1336; February 22, 1990, Senator Simon speaking in favor of a motion to proceed to S. J. Res. 212: 1428. Cited in Guroian, "The Politics and Morality of Genocide," 330, 329.

30. See Stanford J. Shaw and Ezel Kural Shaw, *History of the Ottoman Empire and Modern Turkey*, vol. 2, *Reform, Revolution, and Republic: The Rise of Modern Turkey, 1808–1975* (Cambridge: Cambridge University Press, 1977); William L. Langer, *The Diplomacy of Imperialism* (New York: Alfred A. Knopf, 1935); and Bernard Lewis, *The Emergence of Modern Turkey* (Oxford: Oxford University Press, 1961).

31. See Robert Melson, *Revolution and Genocide: On the Origins of the Armenian Genocide and the Holocaust* (Chicago: University of Chicago Press, 1992), 151–59.

32. See Shaw and Shaw, *History of the Ottoman Empire and Modern Turkey*, 2:315–16.

33. Erich Feigl, *A Myth of Terror* (Salzburg: Edition Zeitgeschichte, 1988), 36.

34. See Deborah Lipstadt, *Denying the Holocaust: The Growing Assault on Truth and Memory* (New York: Free Press, 1993), 21–23.

35. Ronald Suny, *Looking toward Ararat: Armenia in Modern History* (Bloomington: Indiana University Press, 1993), 115.

36. Noting the obscurity of Lowry's publishers, Peter Balakian observed that his first book, a ninety-page diatribe entitled *The Story Behind Ambassador Morgenthau's Story*, "is in just 53 of the 20,000 academic and research libraries whose holdings are listed by the On-line Computer Library Center Inc. *Studies in Defterology* is held by 14 libraries, and *The Islamization of and Turkification of the City of Trabzon* is in one library." "Armenian Genocide and Turkish Studies," *Chronicle of Higher Education*, December 1, 1995, B5.

37. Roger W. Smith, Eric Markusen, and Robert Jay Lifton, "Professional Ethics and the Denial of the Armenian Genocide," *Holocaust and Genocide Studies* 9 (Spring 1995): 1–22.

38. Amy Magaro Rubin, "Critics Accuse Turkish Government of Manipulating Scholarship," *Chronicle of Higher Education*, October 27, 1995, A44.

39. Among the cosigners were Ben Bagdikian, Houston A. Baker, Robert N. Bellah, Isarael W. Charny, Rev. William Sloane Coffin, Jean Bethke Elshtain, Henry Louis Gates, Jr., Geoffrey Hartman, Seamus Heaney, Robert Jay Lifton, Deborah E. Lipstadt, Arthur Miller, Joyce Carol Oates, Harold Pinter, David Riesman, Nathan A. Scott, Susan Sontag, William Styron, Ronald Suny, John Updike, Kurt Vonnegut, Derek Walcott, and Howard Zinn.

40. John Yemma, "Turkish Largess Raises Questions," *Boston Globe*, November 25, 1995.

41. Terrence Des Pres, "On Governing Narratives: The Turkish-Armenian Case," *Writing Into the World* (New York: Viking, 1991), 258.

42. For a sophisticated discussion of genocide and its representation, see Dominick LaCapra, *Representing the Holocaust: History, Theory, Trauma* (Ithaca: Cornell University Press, 1994).

43. For a cogent set of discussions on the topic of reference and textual representation, see Cathy Caruth and Deborah Esch, eds. *Critical Encounters: Reference and Reponsibility in Deconstructive Writing* (New Brunswick, NJ: Rutgers University Press), 1994.

44. Sigmund Freud, "The Unconscious," in *The Standard Edition of the Complete Psychological Works of Sigmund Freud*, 14:194; quoted in Maria Torok, "Story of Fear: The Symptoms of Phobia—the Return of the Repressed or the Return of the Phantom?" Nicolas Abraham and Maria Torok, *The Shell and the Kernel: Renewals of Psychoanalysis*, trans. and ed. Nicholas T. Rand (Chicago: University of Chicago Press, 1994), 1:179.

45. "The presence of the phantom indicates the effects, on the descendants, of something that had inflicted narcissistic injury or even catastrophe on the parents." Nicolas Abraham, "Notes on the Phantom: A Complement to Freud's Metapsychology," in Rand, *The Shell and the Kernel*, 174, 171. Through their own clinical experience and in seminal rereadings of Freud's well-known case study of the Wolf Man, Abraham and Torok have theorized the phantom in terms of the narrative "gaps left within us by the secrets of others."

46. Torok describes the transmission of the phantom in terms of "either a fear whose actual victims are their parents or, alternatively, a fear that the parents themselves had inherited and now transmit willy-nilly to their own reluctant offspring." "Story of Fear," 181.

47. According to Carolyn Forché in her recent work on the poetry of witness, "A poem is itself an event, a trauma that changes both a common language and an individual psyche, it is a specific kind of event, a specific kind of trauma." Carolyn Forché, "Introduction," in *Against Forgetting: Twentieth-Century Poetry of Witness* (New York: Norton, 1993), 33. For her part, Forché distinguishes poetry as a "voluntary" experience from the real violence of historical trauma proper. "Unlike an aerial attack," she writes, "a poem does not come at one unexpectedly. One has to read or listen, one has to be willing to accept the trauma" (33). Yet, despite Forché's commonsensical contrast, there are special instances where the transmission of traumatic reference in poetry takes on a more active force.

48. For an applied theory of reading cryptonyms in psychoanalysis, see Nicolas Abraham and Maria Torok, *The Wolf Man's Magic Word: A Cryptonymy*, trans. Nicholas Rand (Minneapolis: University of Minnesota Press, 1986). "In short: It is the idea that words can be excluded from the Preconscious—thus also from the dream texts—and replaced, in the name and capacity of the return of the repressed, by cryptonyms or their visual representation that is required for a general preliminary conclusion to our inquiry" (20).

49. Insofar as the phantom presences trauma unconsciously in the staged word, it "constitutes an attempt at exorcism, an attempt, that is, to relieve the unconscious by placing the effects of the phantom in the social realm." Abraham, "Notes on the Phantom," 175.

50. Nadine Fresco, "Remembering the Unknown," *International Review of Psychoanalysis* 11, no. 4 (1984): 418.

51. Diana Der-Hovanessian, *Selected Poems* (Riverdale-on-Hudson, NY: The Sheep Meadow Press, 1994), 30 (hereafter cited in the text as SP).

52. As Ronald Suny points out, the belief in an essential core of Armenian identity is more an effect of, rather than a foundation for, nationalist political ideology. "The notion," he writes, "of a single explanatory formula for all Armenian history or a unifying theme or purpose . . . one suspects, is more a literary conceit than an accurate description of Armenia's complex, uneven, and fragmented history." *Looking toward Ararat*, 4.

53. Shoshana Felman has noted the staging of an involuntary choice that authors encounter as witnesses of trauma. "The contemporary writer," she says, "often dramatizes the predicament (whether chosen or imposed, whether conscious or unconscious) of a voluntary or an unwitting, inadvertent, and sometimes involuntary witness: witness to a trauma, to a crime or to an outrage; witness to a horror or an illness whose effects explode any capacity for explanation or rationalization." Shoshana Felman and Dori Laub, *Testimony: Crises of Witnessing in Literature, Psychoanalysis, and History* (New York: Routledge, 1992), 4.

54. See James J. Reid, "Total War, the Annihilation Ethic, and the Armenian Genocide, 1870–1918," in Hovannisian, *The Armenian Genocide: History, Politics, Ethics*, 26.

55. "The transition from a mouth filled with the breast to a mouth filled with words occurs by virtue of the intervening experiences of the empty mouth. Learning to fill the emptiness of the mouth with words is the initial model for introjection. . . . Introducing all or part of a love object or a thing into one's own body, possessing, expelling or alternately acquiring, keeping, losing it—here are varieties of fantasy indicating, in the typical forms of possession or feigned dispossession, a basic intrapsychic situation: the situation created by the reality of a loss sustained by the psyche. If accepted and worked through, the loss would require major readjustment. But the fantasy of incorporation merely simulates profound psychic transformation through magic; it does so by implementing literally something that has only figurative meaning. So in order not to have to 'swallow' a loss, we fantasize swallowing (or having swallowed) that which has been lost, as if it were some kind of thing." Nicolas Abraham and Maria Torok, "Mourning or Melancholia: Introjection versus Incorporation," in Rand, *The Shell and the Kernel*, 127–28.

56. "Since the phantom is not related to the loss of an object of love, it cannot be considered the effect of unsuccessful mourning, as would be the case with melancholics or with all those who carry a tomb in themselves. It is the children's or descendants' lot to objectify these buried tombs through diverse species of ghosts. What comes back to haunt are the tombs of others." Abraham, "Notes on the Phantom," 171–72.

57. Jacques Lacan defines the difference between "empty" and "full" speech in "The Function and Field of Speech and Language in Psychoanalysis," in *Écrits: A Selection*, trans. Alan Sheridan (New York: Norton, 1977), 30–113.

58. Pierre Vidal-Naquet, "By Way of a Preface and by the Power of One Word," *A Crime of Silence: The Armenian Genocide, The Permanent Peoples' Tribunal*, ed. Gerard Libaridian (London: Zed Books, 1985, and Totowa, NJ: Biblioi Distribution Center, 1985), 2–3.

59. Peter Balakian, *Sad Days of Light* (Pittsburgh: Carnegie Mellon University Press, 1993), 3 (hereafter cited in the text as SDL).

60. "Extracts from an Interview with Comm. G. Gorrini, Late Italian Consul-General at Trebizond, Published in the Journal '*Il Messaggero*,' of Rome, 25th August, 1915," quoted in Bryce, *The Treatment of Armenians in the Ottoman Empire,* 290–91.

61. Henry Morgenthau, *Ambassador Morgenthau's Story* (Plandome, NY: New Age Publishers, 1975), 321–32, 308; reprint of Doubleday, Page and Co., 1919; cited in Guroian, "The Politics and Morality of Genocide," 312.

62. Viscount Bryce, "Statement by a German Eye-Witness of Occurrences at Moush; Communicated by the American Committee for Armenian and Syrian Relief," in *The Treatment of Armenians in the Ottoman Empire,* 90; Viscount Bryce, "Record of an Interview with Roupen, of Sassoun, by Mr. A. S. Safrastian; Dated Tiflis, 6th November, 1915," in *The Treatment of Armenians in the Ottoman Empire,* 86.

63. Viscount Bryce, "Extract from a Letter Dated 16th September, 1915," in *The Treatment of Armenians in the Ottoman Empire,* 388.

64. "The Method of suicide in most instances was drowning in the Euphrates River. In fact, this practice was common enough that several survivors told us the words of a song which was sung in the orphanages that included the phrase 'Virgin girls holding each others' hands, threw themselves into the River Euphrates.' . . . Hundreds of girls often drowned themselves in a single day according to survivors' accounts. It appears that a form of group hysteria developed in which groups of young women elected to die together. As best we can reconstruct, these girls would link arms or hold each others' hands and leap from a bridge or cliff into the turbulent waters of the Euphrates or other rivers." Donald E. Miller and Lorna Touryan Miller, *Survivors: An Oral History of the Armenian Genocide* (Berkeley: University of California Press, 1993), 103, 104.

65. Dr. Martin Niepage, *The Horrors of Aleppo* (London: T. Fisher Unwin, Ltd., 1917), 12.

66. Dr. Armin T. Wegner, "Open Letter to the President of the United States of North America, Mr. W. Wilson, Regarding the Expulsion of the Armenian People to the Desert," *Pogrom* 72/73 (1980), 59ff; cited in Hofmann, "German Eyewitness Reports," 6.

67. See Lawrence L. Langer, *Holocaust Testimonies: The Ruins of Memory* (New Haven: Yale University Press), 1991.

68. "Our neighbor used to come over sometimes and say to my mother to come and listen to this poor Miriam Hanem. I, too, used to go to look. She would be sitting on the floor, crying and crying, pulling her hair. She would tell her story, over and over: 'I killed two of them. I killed two of them,' she would repeat. Apparently, she was walking, holding one child's hand and holding the other in her arms. On the way they would eat grass or nothing at all. From all of this, they had diarrhea and, meanwhile, they could not stop because the gendarme would beat them and make them walk. So she let go of one of the kids because he kept dragging her behind. She couldn't walk on with him pulling her back. So he was left behind. Meanwhile, she walked on and on until the child in her lap died. She buried this one, but then would cry to us, 'What happened to the one who was alive? The wolves ate him; the wolves ate him. One died, I know. The other one the wolves ate.'" Miller and Miller, *Survivors,* 100.

69. "Occasionally, mothers apparently acted collectively in deciding to part from their infants. Two survivors told us independently that in front of a khan (inn) in Urfa, perhaps dozens of mothers placed their infants under a tree and walked on." Ibid., 98.

70. Gleaned from the accounts of Anna Harlow Birge, a member of the American Board of Commissioners for Foreign Missions, are the harbingers of the Nazi death trains. In traveling by rail to Constantinople in the fall of 1915, Birge gives the testimony of witnessing "one train after another crowded, jammed with these poor people being carried away to some spot where no food could be obtained. . . . [T]he faces of the little children were looking out from behind the tiny barred windows of each car. . . . The side doors were wide open and one could plainly see old men, and old women, huddled together like so many sheep or pigs—human beings treated worse than cattle are treated. . . . [T]wenty babies had been thrown into a river as a train crossed, thrown by the mothers themselves who could not bear to hear their little ones crying for food, when there was none to give them. . . . [T]he crying of those babies and little children for food is still ringing in my ears." Letter, Birge to James L. Barton, November 22, 1915, 5, 6, American Board of Commissioners for Foreign Missions (ABCFM) archives; quoted in Suzanne Elizabeth Moranian, "Bearing Witness: The Missionary Archives as Evidence of the Armenian Genocide," in Hovannisian, The Armenian Genocide: History, Politics, Ethics, 120.

71. "Camp to Barton," December 21, 1915, 5 ABCFM archives; quoted in Moranian, "Bearing Witness," 120–21.

72. For a discussion of how Paul Virilio and Michel Foucault theorize the visible regime of torture and punishment to shore up monarchical power, see Nácunán Sáez, "Torture: A Discourse on Practice," Tattoo, Torture, Mutilation, and Adornment: The Denaturalization of the Body in Culture and Text, eds. Frances E. Mascia-Lees and Patricia Sharpe (Albany: State University of New York Press, 1992), 126–44.

73. See Leo Kuper, "The Turkish Genocide of Armenians, 1915–17," in Hovannisian, The Armenian Genocide in Perspective, 56.

74. See Astourian, "Genocidal Process," 59, 65.

75. "The body," Scarry writes, "tends to be brought forward in its most extreme and absolute form only on behalf of a cultural artifact or symbolic fragment or made thing (a sentence) that is without any other basis in material reality: that is, it is only brought forward when there is a crisis of substantiation." The Body in Pain (New York: Oxford University Press, 1985), 127.

76. Fresco, "Remembering the Unknown," 418.

77. On trauma's "speechless terror," see Bessel A. van der Kolk, Psychological Trauma (Washington, DC: American Psychiatric Press, 1987).

78. Bessel A. van der Kolk and Onno van der Hart, "The Intrusive Past: The Flexibility of Memory and the Engraving of Trauma," in Caruth, Trauma, 172 (hereafter cited in the text as IP).

79. See Abraham and Torok, "Mourning or Melancholia," 133.

80. Scarry, The Body in Pain, 35.

81. Peter Balakian, Black Dog of Fate: A Memoir (New York: Basic Books, 1997), 203.

82. Peter Balakian, Dyer's Thistle (Pittsburgh: Carnegie Mellon University Press, 1996), 29 (hereafter cited in the text as DT).

83. Caruth, "Trauma and Experience," 8.

84. Peter Balakian, "Arshile Gorky and the Armenian Genocide," Art in America 84 (February 1996): 108.

85. Hayden Herrera, *Arshile Gorky, His Life and Work* (New York: Farrar, Straus and Giroux, 2003), 152.

86. In discussing the conjuncture of death and eros in the mourning process, Maria Torok writes that "[a] measure of libidinal increase upon the object's death seems to be a widespread, if not universal phenomenon." "The Illness of Mourning and the Fantasy of the Exquisite Corpse," in Rand, *The Shell and the Kernel*, 110. The erotic and often manic nature of desire in the mourning process, for Torok, stems from a readjusting of the internal economy of libidinal desires that—formerly invested in the lost love object—must be redistributed and reinvested in other objects.

87. See introduction, n. 33, above.

CHAPTER 2: THE HOLOCAUST AT HOME

1. Claude Lanzmann, "Why Spielberg Has Distorted the Truth," *Le Monde*, March 3, 1994, reprinted in *Guardian Weekly*, April 3, 1994, 14; quoted in Geoffrey Hartman, *The Longest Shadow*, 84.

2. Irving Greenberg, "Cloud of Smoke, Pillar of Fire," *Holocaust: Religious and Philosophical Implications*, ed. Michael Berenbaum and John K. Roth (New York: Paragon House, 1989), 315.

3. See Jean Améry, *At the Mind's Limits: Contemplations by a Survivor on Auschwitz and Its Realities*, trans. Sidney Rosenfeld and Stella P. Rosenfeld (Bloomington: Indiana University Press, 1980).

4. See Nadine Fresco, "Remembering the Unknown," *International Review of Psycho-Analysis* 11 (1984): 417–27.

5. Elie Wiesel, "Testimony at the Barbie Trial," *From the Kingdom of Memory: Reminiscences* (New York: Summit Books, 1990), 182.

6. See Hans Blumenberg, "Light as a Metaphor for Truth: At the Preliminary Stage of Philosophical Concept Formation," *Modernity and the Hegemony of Vision*, ed. David Michael Levin (Berkeley: University of California Press, 1993), 30–62.

7. See Emmanuel Levinas, *Existence and Existents*, trans. Alphonso Lingis (The Hague: Martinus Nijhoff, 1978), 46ff.

8. Martin Heidegger, "The Age of the World Picture" (1938), *The Question Concerning Technology and Other Essays* (New York: Harper & Row, 1977), 143.

9. On the Real as incineration, see Jacques Lacan's classic reading of Freud's "dream of the burning child" from *The Interpretation of Dreams* in "Tuché and Automaton," in *The Four Fundamental Concepts of Psychoanalysis*, trans. Alan Sheridan (New York: Norton, 1998), 53–64.

10. Charlotte Delbo, *Le convoi du 24 janvier* (Paris: Èditions de Minuit, 1965), 66.

11. On witnessing to the "impossible" at Auschwitz, Emil Fackenheim writes, "More deeply immersed in the varieties and vicissitudes of historical change, only a human condition, which was considered permanent only insofar as beyond it was the humanly impossible. At Auschwitz, however, 'more was real than is possible,' and the impossible was done by some and suffered by others." Emil Fackenheim, "Holocaust," in *Contemporary Jewish Religious Thought*, ed. Arthur A. Cohen and Paul Mendes-Flohr (New York: Free Press, 1988), 402.

12. Elie Wiesel, *Night, Dawn, The Accident: Three Tales* (New York: Hill and Wang, 1972), 43.

13. This topos is something that LaCapra has explored in readings of Claude Lanzmann in "Lanzmann's 'Shoah': 'Here There Is No Why,'" *Critical Inquiry* 23, no. 2 (Winter 1997): 231–69. *Writing History, Writing Trauma* (Baltimore: Johns Hopkins University Press, 2001, hereafter cited in the text as WHWT), however, pays more sustained, analytic attention to this distinction in cogent readings of some of the leading theorists of Holocaust trauma working within the fields of history, literature, and documentary and video testimony.

14. Geoffrey Hartman, "The Book of Destruction," in *Probing the Limits of Representation: Nazism and the "Final Solution,"* ed. Saul Friedländer (Cambridge: Harvard University Press, 1992), 331.

15. Jean-François Lyotard describes Auschwitz as a "cleavage in Western thought" and a "crack in philosophical time" in "Phraser après Auschwitz," *Les Fins de l'homme: à partir du travail de Jacques Derrida* (Paris: Galilée, 1981), 189; the key terms "tremendum" and "caesura" are from Arthur A. Cohen, *The Tremendum: A Theological Interpretation of the Holocaust* (New York: Crossroad, 1981). Emil Fackenheim uses the term "impossibility" in "Holocaust," 399–408. "Rupture" is a term Fackenheim gives to the historical uniqueness of the Holocaust in *To Mend the World: Foundations of Future Jewish Thought* (New York: Schocken Books, 1982).

16. Cohen, *The Tremendum*, 78.

17. From the text of a television interview by Günter Gaus, broadcast by the German Channel 2 on October 28, 1964. Quoted in Philippe Lacoue-Labarthe, *Heidegger, Art and Politics: The Fiction of the Political*, trans. Chris Turner (Cambridge, MA: Basil Blackwell, Ltd., 1990), 34.

18. Maurice Blanchot, *The Writing of the Disaster*, trans. Ann Smock (Lincoln: University of Nebraska Press, 1986), 47 (hereafter cited in the text as WD).

19. George Steiner, *Language and Silence* (New York: Atheneum, 1967), 123; quoted in Berel Lang, *Act and Idea in the Nazi Genocide* (Chicago: University of Chicago Press, 1990), 151.

20. André Neher, "The Silence of Auschwitz," *Holocaust: Religious and Philosophical Implications*, ed. John K. Roth and Michael Berenbaum (New York: Paragon House, 1989), 10.

21. See Dan Bar-On, *Legacy of Silence: Encounter with Children of the Third Reich* (Cambridge: Harvard University Press, 1989). Gordon Wheeler notes that silence "actively prohibits speaking and telling" and in German perpetrator culture is psychically charged with the powerful emotional legacies of guilt, fear, and shame. "Translator's Introduction," in *The Collective Silence: German Identity and the Legacy of Shame*, ed. Barbara Heimannsberg and Christoph J. Schmidt, trans. Cynthia Oudejans Harris and Gordon Wheeler (San Francisco: Jossey-Bass, 1993), xix.

22. Alexander and Margarete Mitscherlich, *The Inability to Mourn: Principles of Collective Behavior*, trans. Beverley R. Placzek (New York: Grove Press, 1975).

23. Theodor W. Adorno, "What Does Coming to Terms with the Past Mean?" *Bitburg in Moral and Political Perspective*, ed. Geoffrey Hartman (Bloomington: Indiana University Press, 1986), 115.

24. Ronald Reagan, "Remarks of President Reagan at Bitburg Air Base, May 5, 1985," *Bitburg in Moral and Political Perspective*, 258–59 (hereafter cited in the text as B).

25. "Historikerstreit," *Die Dokumentation der Kontroverse um die Einzigartigkeit der nationalsozialistischen Judenvernichtung* (Munich: Piper Verlag, 1987), 32; quoted in Saul Friedländer,

Memory, History, and the Extermination of the Jews of Europe (Bloomington: Indiana University Press, 1993), 34.

26. See Deborah E. Lipstadt, "Deniers, Relativists, and Pseudo-scholarship," *Dimensions* 6, no. 1 (1991): 7; see also, *Denying the Holocaust: The Growing Assault on Truth and Memory* (New York: Free Press, 1993).

27. Fackenheim, "Holocaust," 399.

28. Jean-François Lyotard, *The Differend: Phrases in Dispute*, trans. Georges Van Den Abbeele (Minneapolis: University of Minnesota Press, 1988), 13 (hereafter cited in the text as D).

29. Dori Laub, "Truth and Testimony: The Process and the Struggle," in Shoshana Felman and Dori Laub, *Testimony: Crises of Witnessing in Literature, Psychoanalysis, and History* (New York: Routledge, 1992), 64–65 (hereafter cited in the text as TT).

30. See, for example, Sandor Goodhart, *Sacrificing Commentary: Reading the End of Literature* (Baltimore: Johns Hopkins University Press, 1996); and LaCapra, "Lanzmann's 'Shoah,'" 231–69.

31. See Terrence Des Pres, *The Survivor: An Anatomy of Life in the Death Camps* (New York: Oxford University Press, 1976).

32. Freud writes: "We describe as 'traumatic' any excitations from outside which are powerful enough to break through the protective shield [*Reizschutz*]. It seems to me that the concept of trauma necessarily implies a connection of this kind with a breach in an otherwise efficacious barrier against stimuli. Such an event as an external trauma is bound to provoke a disturbance on a large scale in the functioning of the organism's energy and to set in motion every possible defense measure. At the same time, the pleasure principle is for the moment put out of action. There is no longer any possibility of preventing the mental apparatus from being flooded with large amounts of stimulus, and another problem arises instead—the problem of mastering the amounts of stimulus which have broken in and of binding them, in the psychical sense, so that they can then be disposed of." "Beyond the Pleasure Principle" (1920), in *The Standard Edition of the Complete Psychological Works of Sigmund Freud*, ed. James Strachey (London: Hogarth Press and the Institute of Psycho-Analysis, 1953–1974), 18:29–30.

33. Shoshana Felman, "The Return of Voice; Claude Lanzmann's *Shoah*," in Felman and Laub, *Testimony*, 239.

34. Charles Bernstein, "The Second World War and Postmodern Memory," *Apoetics* (Cambridge: Harvard University Press, 1992), 193.

35. Ibid., 194. Similarly, Terrence Des Pres writes, "The Holocaust would seem to have no end. The destruction of Europe's Jews stopped in 1945, but the spectacle of the death camps continues to haunt us, and not merely as a fading memory or as a bad dream that lingers. The Holocaust happened. That in itself is the intractable fact that we can neither erase nor evade. And the more we think of it, the more it intrudes to occupy our minds, until *l'univers concentrationnaire* becomes a demonic anti-world that undermines our own." Terrence Des Pres, "Introduction," in Ellen S. Fine, *Legacy of Night: The Literary Universe of Elie Wiesel* (Albany: State University of New York Press, 1982), xi. In glossing this quote, Sandor Goodhart remarks that "[c]ontrary to what we have been led to expect, Des Pres sug-

gests, this memory does not fade. . . . Indeed the more distant we get from the event, the less easy it would seem to avoid or evade it." *Sacrificing Commentary,* 216.

36. See Fackenheim's "Holocaust" on this point.

37. Theodor W. Adorno, *Negative Dialectics,* trans. E. B. Ashton (New York: Seabury Press, 1973), 362.

38. Charles Olson, *The Collected Poems of Charles Olson,* ed. George Butterick (Berkeley: University of California Press, 1987), 89.

39. On the individual and societal responses to trauma, see Robert Jay Lifton, *The Broken Connection: On Death and the Continuity of Life* (New York: Simon and Schuster, 1979).

40. W. D. Snodgrass, "About the Author," in *The Fuehrer Bunker: The Complete Cycle* (Brockport, NY: BOA Editions, Ltd., 1995), 207.

41. "The Fuehrer Bunker poems," Snodgrass has said in his *Paris Review* interview, "may be my real confessional poems—an analysis of one's own evil." Alexandra Eyle, "Interview: W. D. Snodgrass: The Art of Poetry," *Paris Review* 35 (Spring 1994): 187 (hereafter cited in the text as PR).

42. T. S. Eliot, *Collected Poems, 1909–1950* (New York: Harcourt, Brace and World, 1971), 141. Eliot borrows here in "Little Gidding" from Stéphane Mallarmé, "Le Tombeau d'Edgar Poe," where he writes: "Donners un sens plus pure aux mots de la tribu." *Oeuvres Complètes* (Paris: Gallimard, 1945), 189. See Michael André Bernstein, *The Tale of the Tribe: Ezra Pound and the Modern Verse Epic* (Princeton: Princeton University Press, 1980), 7.

43. Roy Harvey Pearce, *The Continuity of American Poetry* (Princeton: Princeton University Press, 1961), 61.

44. See Sigmund Freud, *Moses and Monotheism,* trans. Katherine Jones (New York: Vintage, 1939), 84; and Cathy Caruth, "Trauma and Experience: Introduction," in *Trauma: Explorations in Memory,* ed. Cathy Caruth (Baltimore: Johns Hopkins University Press, 1995), 8.

45. Blanchot, *The Writing of the Disaster,* 3.

46. W.D. Snodgrass, *The Fuehrer Bunker* (Brockport, NY: BOA Editions, LTD., 1995), (hereafter cited in the text as FB).

47. See Susan Sontag, "Fascinating Fascism," *Under the Sign of Saturn* (New York: Farrar, Straus and Giroux, 1980), 73–105 (hereafter cited in the text as FF).

48. According to Otto Strasser in his OSS interview of May 13, 1943, Geli Raubal told him that "Hitler made her undress. . . . He would lie down on the floor. Then she would have to squat over his face where he could examine her at close range and this made him very excited. When the excitement reached its peak, he demanded that she urinate on him and that gave him his sexual pleasure. Geli said the whole performance was extremely disgusting to her and . . . it gave her no gratification." Quoted in Robert G. L. Waite, *The Psychopathic God Adolf Hitler* (New York: Basic Books, 1977), 238.

49. One of the rumors concerning Hitler's father Alois is that he was the illegitimate son of a Mr. Frankenberger, a Jew who employed Hitler's grandmother Maria Anna Schicklegruber in Graz as his domestic servant and later paid money for the support of Alois, his bastard son. See Waite, *The Psychopathic God Adolf Hitler,* 126ff.

50. Interview with Michel Foucault, *Cahiers du cinéma,* nos. 251–52 (July–August 1974): 10ff. Quoted in Saul Friedländer, *Reflections of Nazism: An Essay on Kitsch and Death* (New York: Harper & Row, 1984), 75–76.

51. Sontag, "Fascinating Fascism," 101. See also Lynda Hart, *Between the Body and the Flesh: Performing Sadomasochism* (New York: Columbia University Press, 1998).

52. See Christopher R. Browning, *Ordinary Men: Reserve Police Battalion 101 and the Final Solution in Poland* (New York: Harper Collins, 1992); and Daniel Jonah Goldhagen, *Hitler's Willing Executioners: Ordinary Germans and the Holocaust* (New York: Vintage Books, 1997).

53. Whether and what Albert Speer knew about the Final Solution is the subject of heated controversy among his biographers. In any event, Snodgrass simplifies the issue of Speer's innocence by leaving his own account uncontested. "When I met Albert Speer," Snodgrass has said, "he seemed very much a human being. I enjoyed talking with him. That doesn't mean I believe everything he said." Eyle, "Interview," 164–201. However skeptical, Snodgrass nevertheless presents Speer's version of his actions without contradiction. On the thorny issue of Speer's credibility as a perpetrator witness to the Holocaust, see Matthias Schmidt, *Albert Speer: The End of a Myth*, trans. Joachim Neugroschel (New York: St. Martin's Press, 1984); Gitta Sereny, *Albert Speer: His Battle with Truth* (New York: Alfred A. Knopf, 1995); and Dan van der Vat, *The Good Nazi: The Life and Lies of Albert Speer* (London: Weidenfeld & Nicolson, 1997).

54. For a discussion of other modes overidentification takes in secondary witness, see Geoffrey Hartman, *The Longest Shadow*.

55. Alicia Suskin Ostriker, *The Crack in Everything* (Pittsburgh: University of Pittsburgh Press, 1996), 29 (hereafter cited in the text as CIE).

56. Yevgeny Yevtushenko, "Babii Yar," trans. George Reavey, in *The Collected Poems, 1952–1990*, ed. Albert C. Todd and James Ragan (New York: John MacRae Books/Henry Holt and Company, 1991), 104.

57. Sigmund Freud, "Beyond the Pleasure Principle," in *The Standard Edition of the Complete Psychological Works of Sigmund Freud*, 18:29.

58. See Fresco, "Remembering the Unknown," 417–27. "The silence," Fresco writes of repressed Holocaust memory, "was all the more implacable in that it was often concealed behind a screen of words, again, always the same words, an unchanging story, a tale repeated over and over again, made up of selections from the war" (419).

59. Ibid., 420.

60. Susan Gubar, *Poetry after Auschwitz: Remembering What One Never Knew* (Bloomington: Indiana University Press, 2003), 259.

61. Sharon Olds, "That Year," *Satan Says* (Pittsburgh: University of Pittsburgh Press, 1993), 6–7.

62. See Al Strangeways, "'The Boot in the Face': The Problem of the Holocaust in the Poetry of Sylvia Plath," *Contemporary Literature* 37, no. 3 (Fall 1996): 370–90; James E. Young, "'I May Be a Bit of a Jew': The Holocaust Confessions of Sylvia Plath," *Philological Quarterly* 66, no. 1 (Winter 1987): 127–47; Jacqueline Rose, *The Haunting of Sylvia Plath* (London: Virago Press, 1991); Jahan Ramazani, "'Daddy, I Have Had to Kill You': Plath, Rage, and the Modern Elegy," *PMLA* 108, no. 5 (October 1993): 1142–56.

63. Sharon Olds, "That Year," *Satan Says* (Pittsburgh: University of Pittsburgh Press, 1995), 6–7.

64. "Audiences," Lawrence Langer writes, "have little difficulty dealing with heroic gestures where the agent is in control of the choice—episodes of sharing and support and even of self-sacrifice, all of which occurred in rare favorable circumstances in the usually hostile camp environment. Such gestures feed the legends on which the myths of civilizations have been built. But few witnesses mention them in their testimony, where, unflattering as it may sound, spiritual possibility turns out to be a luxury for those not on the brink of starvation. To understand and to sympathize with *unheroic* gestures . . . withholding endorsement or blame but finding instead an admissable frame for them in the moral discourse of our culture—this is one of the burdensome but crucial challenges that still lie before us in this study." *Holocaust Testimonies: The Ruins of Memory* (New Haven: Yale University Press, 1991), 26–27.

65. Charles Reznikoff, excerpt from "Mass Graves," *Holocaust* (Los Angeles: Black Sparrow Press, 1975), 80–81.

66. William Heyen, "Kotov," in Louis Daniel Brodsky and William Heyen, *Falling from Heaven: Poems of a Jew and a Gentile* (St. Louis: Time Being Books, 1991), 38.

67. See Charlotte Delbo, *Auschwitz and After,* trans. Rosette C. Lamont (New Haven: Yale University Press, 1995). Similarly, Lawrence Langer describes testimony as split by "disruptive memory" and narrative "continuity": "Testimony is a form of remembering. The faculty of memory functions in the present to recall a personal history vexed by traumas that thwart smooth-flowing chronicles. Simultaneously, however, straining against what we might call disruptive memory is an effort to reconstruct a semblance of continuity in a life that began as, and now resumes what we would consider, a normal existence." Langer, *Holocaust Testimonies,* 2–3.

68. Similarly, in theorizing the trauma of survival, Cathy Caruth notes, "What is enigmatically suggested, that is, is that the trauma consists not only in having confronted death but in *having survived, precisely without knowing it.* . . . Repetition, in other words, is not simply the attempt to grasp that one has almost died but, more fundamentally and enigmatically, the very *attempt to claim one's own survival.* If history is to be understood as the history of a trauma, it is a history that is experienced as the endless attempt to assume one's survival as one's own." *Unclaimed Experience: Trauma, Narrative, and History* (Baltimore: Johns Hopkins University Press, 1996), 64.

69. "Reserving itself, not exposing itself, in regular fashion it [*différance*] exceeds the order of truth at a certain precise point, but without dissimulating itself as something, as a mysterious being, in the occult of a nonknowledge or in a hole with indeterminable borders (for example, in a topology of castration). In every exposition it would be exposed to disappearing as disappearance. It would risk appearing: disappearing. . . . Différance is not only irreducible to any ontological or theological—ontotheological—reappropriation, but as the very opening of the space in which ontotheology—philosophy—produces its system and its history, it includes ontotheology, inscribing it and exceeding it without return." Jacques Derrida, "Différance," *Margins of Philosophy,* trans. Alan Bass (Chicago: University of Chicago Press, 1982), 6.

70. Jacques Derrida, "The Retrait of Metaphor," *Enclitic* 2 (Fall 1978): 29; "le retrait de la métaphore," in *Psyche: Inventions de l'autre* (Paris: Galilée, 1987), 88–89; quoted in Ned Lukacher, "Introduction," in *Cinders,* trans. Ned Lukacher (Lincoln: University of Nebraska Press, 1991), 2.

71. On Derrida's reinscription of Heidegger's visual metaphorics, see Herman Rapaport, "Time's Cinders," *Modernity and the Hegemony of Vision*, ed. David Michael Levin (Berkeley: University of California Press, 1993): 218–33; and Elaine Marks, "Cendres juives: Jews Writing in French 'after Auschwitz,'" in *Auschwitz and After: Race, Culture, and "the Jewish Question" in France*, ed. Lawrence D. Kritzman (New York: Routledge, 1995), 35–46.

72. Philippe Lacoue-Labarthe, *Heidegger, Art and Politics: The Fiction of the Political*, trans. Chris Turner (Cambridge, MA: Basil Blackwell, Ltd., 1990), 35.

73. "But with Auschwitz," Lyotard observes, "something new has happened in history (which can only be a sign and not a fact), which is that the facts, the testimonies which bore the traces of *here's* and *now's*, the documents which indicated the sense or senses of the facts, and the names, finally the possibility of various kinds of phrases whose conjunction makes reality, all this has been destroyed as much as possible. Is it up to the historian to take into account not only the damages, but also the wrong? Not only the reality, but also the meta-reality that is the destruction of reality? Not only the testimony, but also what is left of the testimony when it is destroyed (by dilemma), namely, the feeling? Not only the litigation, but also the differend, that a differend is born from a wrong and is signaled by a silence, that the silence indicates that phrases are in abeyance of their becoming event, that the feeling is the suffering of this abeyance" (*The Differend*, 57).

74. Jacques Derrida, *Cinders*, trans. and ed. Ned Lukacher (Lincoln: University of Nebraska Press, 1991), 39.

75. Anthony Hecht, "The Book of Yolek," in *The Transparent Man* (Alfred A. Knopf, 1990), 73–74.

76. Anthony Hecht, "Commentary" on "The Book of Yolek," in *Jewish American Poetry: Poems, Commentary, and Reflections*, ed. Jonathan N. Barron and Eric Murphy Selinger (Hanover, NH: Brandeis University Press, 2000), 81.

77. Sigmund Freud, "The Uncanny" (1919), in *The Standard Edition of the Complete Psychological Works of Sigmund Freud*, 17:225 (hereafter cited in the text as U).

78. Brodsky and Heyen, *Falling from Heaven*, 22 (hereafter cited in the text as FFH).

79. Barbara Heimannsberg and Christoph J. Schmidt, "Psychological Symptoms of the Nazi Heritage, Introduction to the German Edition," in Heimannsberg and Schmidt, *The Collective Silence*, 3.

80. "The Federal Republic did not succumb to melancholia; instead, as a group, those who had lost their 'ideal leader,' the representative of a commonly shared ego-ideal, managed to avoid self-devaluation by breaking all affective bridges to the immediate past." Mitscherlich and Mitscherlich, *The Inability to Mourn*, 26.

81. "One fairly common strategy of circumventing this complex layering of mourning tasks (and thereby remaining within the closure of narcissism) was to identify with the victim, to become the one who helplessly and innocently suffered the deceptions and ravages of the fascist utopia as well as the destruction wrought by the allied forces." Eric L. Santner, *Stranded Objects: Mourning, Memory, and Film in Postwar Germany* (Ithaca: Cornell University Press, 1990), 6.

82. William Heyen, *My Holocaust Songs* (Concord, NH: William B. Ewert, 1980), 15 (hereafter cited in the text as MHS).

83. Hilda Schiff, "William Heyen (Biographical Details of Poets)," *Holocaust Poetry* (London: Fount, 1995), 212.

84. Adrienne Rich, "Split at the Root: An Essay on Jewish Identity," in *Blood Bread and Poetry: Selected Prose, 1979–1985* (New York: Norton, 1986), 105 (hereafter cited in the text as SR).

85. Adrienne Rich, *Your Native Land, Your Life, Poems* (New York: Norton, 1986), 18 (hereafter cited in the text as YNL).

86. Susan Gubar provides the most nuanced reading of prosopopoeia in post-Holocaust poetry. On the one hand, Gubar acknowledges the force of identification at work in prosopopoeia and credits poets who express the "sense of personal connectedness to events not experienced firsthand, their visceral but also aesthetic reaction to what Marianne Hirsch has called 'postmemory.'" On the other hand, employing the trope of prosopopoeia would seem an improbable strategy of poetic witness. One that, according to Gubar, "dramatizes precisely the sorts of empathic imaginative acts that the Shoah itself called into question. . . . In the process, it unmasks the rhetoric of identification as a ruse." *Poetry after Auschwitz*, 181, 194.

87. Emmanuel Levinas, *Totality and Infinity: An Essay on Exteriority*, trans. Alphonso Lingis (Pittsburgh: Duquesne University Press, 1992), 195–96, 199.

88. On the disruption of "ekphrasis"—verbal art's representation of a visual artwork—see Susan Gubar's comments on what she calls "antimorphosis" in *Poetry after Auschwitz*, 101ff.

89. Rachel Blau DuPlessis, *Drafts 1–38, Toll* (Middletown, CT: Wesleyan University Press, 2001), 121 (hereafter cited in the text as T).

90. Wallace Stevens, from "Of Modern Poetry," in *The Collected Poems of Wallace Stevens* (New York: Vintage Books, 1982), 240.

91. Wallace Stevens, from "The Snow Man," in *The Collected Poems of Wallace Stevens*, 10.

92. Rachel Blau DuPlessis, "Letter to Lynn Keller, 4 February 1995," quoted in Keller, *Forms of Expansion: Recent Long Poems by Women* (Chicago: University of Chicago Press, 1997), 242.

93. Keller cites Bernstein's article "Robert Duncan: Talent and the Individual Tradition," *Sagetrieb* 4 (Fall–Winter 1985): 177–90, as well as Michael Davidson's *The San Francisco Renaissance: Poetics and Community at Mid-century* (Cambridge: Cambridge University Press, 1989) on the issue of Duncan's own literary influences.

94. Keller, *Forms of Expansion*, 244–51.

95. Adorno, *Negative Dialectics*, 365. On this issue, see Susan Gubar's *Poetry after Auschwitz*.

96. Theodor W. Adorno, *Prisms*, trans. Samuel and Shierry Weber (Cambridge: MIT Press, 1981), 34.

97. Edmond Jabès, *The Book of Margins*, trans. Rosmarie Waldrop (Chicago: University of Chicago Press, 1993), ix.

98. Jean-François Lyotard, *Heidegger and "the jews,"* trans. Andreas Michel and Mark S. Roberts (Minneapolis: University of Minnesota Press, 1990), 3.

99. Rachel Blau DuPlessis, "Circumscriptions: Assimilating T. S. Eliot's Sweeneys," in *People of the Book: Thirty Scholars Reflect on Their Jewish Identity* (Madison: University of Wisconsin Press, 1996), 135 (hereafter cited in the text as C).

100. My reading differs from Keller's position, which ascribes DuPlessis's poetic innovations more to literary tradition than to traumatic extremity. "DuPlessis's serial work," Keller claims, "less an exploration of psychological depths and Freudian methodologies, was from the start more self-consciously positioned within and against the modernist tradition of the encyclopedic long poem. . . . Given that *Drafts* is haunted by such 'monumental works of modernism,' it is hardly surprising that DuPlessis should be grappling quite deliberately with the question, 'still fresh after eighty years or more: What to do about the long poem?'" Keller, *Forms of Expansion*, 277.

101. Rachel Blau DuPlessis, "On Drafts: A Memorandum of Understanding," in *Onward: Contemporary Poetry and Poetics*, ed. Peter Baker (New York: Peter Lang, 1996).

102. Elaine Marks draws this distinction in her reading of French literature on the Holocaust: "Jews writing in French 'after Auschwitz'" may be divided roughly into two groups: those who write about Auschwitz, and those who write about how to write about Auschwitz. "Cendres juives," 35.

103. Walter Benjamin, *The Origin of German Tragic Drama*, trans. John Osborne (London: NLB, 1977), 160.

104. Susan Handelman, *Fragments of Redemption: Jewish Thought and Literary Theory in Benjamin, Scholem, and Levinas* (Bloomington: Indiana University Press, 1991), 156.

105. Walter Benjamin, "Theses on the Philosophy of History," in *Illuminations*, ed. Hannah Arendt; trans. Harry Zohn (New York: Schocken Books, 1969), 261 (hereafter cited in the text as I).

106. T. S. Eliot, "*Ulysses*, Order, and Myth," in *Selected Prose of T. S. Eliot*, ed. Frank Kermode (New York: Harcourt, 1975), 177.

107. Walter Benjamin, excerpt from "Theses on the Philosophy of History," quoted in Carolyn Forché, *The Angel of History* (New York: Harper Perennial, 1994), n.p. (hereafter cited in the text as AH).

108. Thus, Don Bogen writes that Forché's book "takes its title from Walter Benjamin's 'Theses on the Philosophy of History,' in which history is seen as a growing pile of debris from what appears to the observing angel to be one single catastrophe. . . . His situation, of course, parallels that of the poet, and the fragmentary units with which Forché works have a rubblelike combination of specificity and disconnectedness." "Muses of History," *Nation*, October 24, 1994, 464.

109. For a definitive reading of Benjamin's angel from 1921 to 1940, see O. K. Werckmeister, "Walter Benjamin's Angel of History, or The Transfiguration of the Revolutionary into the Historian," *Critical Inquiry* 22 (Winter 1996): 239–67.

110. Walter Benjamin, "Agesilaus Santander," in *Gesammelte Schriften*, ed. Rolf Tiedemann and Hermann Schweppenhäuser (Frankfurt am Main: Suhrkamp, 1972–89), 6:523; quoted in Werckmeister, "Walter Benjamin's Angel of History," 246.

111. On this point, see Michael Greer, "Politicizing the Modern: Carolyn Forché in El Salvador and America," *The Centennial Review* 30, no. 2 (Spring 1986): 160–80.

112. Carolyn Forché, "Introduction," in *Against Forgetting: Twentieth-Century Poetry of Witness*, ed. Carolyn Forché (New York: Norton, 1993), 31.

113. Gershom Scholem, excerpt from "Gruss vom Angelus," trans. Harry Zohn, cited in Walter Benjamin, *Illuminations*, 257.

114. Walter Benjamin, "Karl Kraus," in *Reflections: Essays, Aphorisms, Autobiographical Writings*, trans. Edmund Jephcott (New York: Schocken Books, 1986), 273.

115. Geoffrey Hartman, *Criticism in the Wilderness* (New Haven: Yale University Press, 1980), 78–79; quoted in Handelman, *Fragments of Redemption*, 170.

116. See Lacan, "Tuché and Automaton," 53–64.

117. Ibid., 57–58.

118. On the repetition of failed vision in the dream, see Cathy Caruth: "If the words of the child—*Father, don't you see I'm burning?*—can be read, in this light, as a plea by the child to see the burning *within* the dream, the response of the father in this awakening dramatizes the story of a repeated *failure* to respond adequately, a failure to see the child in its death. To see the child's living vulnerability as it dies, the father has to go on dreaming. In awakening, he sees the child's death too late, and thus cannot truly or adequately respond. . . . In awakening, the father's response repeats in one act a double failure of seeing: a failure to see adequately inside and a failure to see adequately outside." "Traumatic Awakenings," in *Violence, Identity, and Self-Determination*, ed. Hent De Vries and Samuel Weber (Stanford: Stanford University Press, 1997), 216–17.

119. Lacan, "The Split between the Eye and the Gaze," in *The Four Fundamental Concepts of Psychoanalysis*, 69 (hereafter cited in the text as FFC).

120. "Repetition in Warhol," Foster writes, "is not reproduction in the sense of representation (of a referent) or simulation (of a pure image, a detached signifier). Rather, repetition serves to *screen* the real understood as traumatic. But this very need also *points* to the real, and at this point the real *ruptures* the screen of repetition. . . . It works less through content than through technique, especially through the 'floating flashes' of the silkscreen process, the slipping and streaking, blanching, and blanking, repeating and coloring of the images." Hal Foster, *The Return of the Real: Art and Theory at the End of the Century* (Cambridge: MIT Press, 1996), 132, 134.

121. Adorno, *Negative Dialectics*, 362.

122. W. B. Yeats, "The Second Coming," in *The Collected Poems of W. B. Yeats* (New York: Macmillan Publishing Co., Inc., 1974), 185.

CHAPTER 3: HARLEM DANCERS AND THE MIDDLE PASSAGE

1. See Judith Butler, *Bodies that Matter* (New York: Routledge, 1993); Homi Bhabha, *The Location of Culture* (New York: Routledge, 1994, hereafter cited in the text as LC); and Fredric Jameson, *Postmodernism, or, The Cultural Logic of Late Capitalism* (Durham: Duke University Press, 1991).

2. Coco Fusco, "It is also part of the legacy of these prohibitions and of the internalization of racist notions of aesthetic value that the 'authenticity' of our work continues to be measured against the most reductive and stereotypical notions of the popular. For example, black conceptual artist Adrian Piper does not focus on the famed orality of African-American culture and as a result is often labeled 'less black' than those who do. And the *Two Undiscovered Amerindians* performance that Guillermo Gómez-Pena and myself carried out in 1992 generated enormous controversy for audiences and sponsoring institutions precisely because we were not 'real' representatives of the culture we displayed." "Performance and the

Power of the Popular," in *Let's Get It On: The Politics of Black Performance*, ed. Catherine Ugwu (Seattle: Bay Press, 1995), 161 (hereafter cited in the text as LGIO).

3. bell hooks, "Performance Practice as a Site of Opposition," in Ugwu, *Let's Get It On*, 219.

4. Peggy Phelan, *Unmarked: The Politics of Performance* (London: Routledge, 1993), quoted in hooks, "Performance Practice as a Site of Opposition," 214.

5. Benedict Anderson, *Imagined Communities: Reflections on the Origin and Spread of Nationalism* (London: New York: Verso, 1983).

6. Pierre Nora, "Between Memory and History: Les Lieux de Mémoire," in *History and Memory in African-American Culture*, ed. Geneviève Fabre and Robert O'Meally (New York: Oxford University Press, 1994), 284–300 (hereafter cited in the text as HM).

7. Alain Locke, "The New Negro," in *The New Negro*, ed. Alain Locke (New York: Albert and Charles Boni, 1925), 7.

8. Paul Gilroy, *The Black Atlantic: Modernity and Double Consciousness* (Cambridge: Harvard University Press, 1993), 194.

9. Paul Gilroy, "'To Be Real': The Dissident Forms of Black Expressive Culture," in Ugwu, *Let's Get It On*, 14, 15, 13.

10. Lorenzo Thomas, *Extraordinary Measures: Afrocentric Modernism and Twentieth-Century American Poetry* (Tuscaloosa: University of Alabama Press, 2000), 100 (hereafter cited in the text as EM).

11. Nnamdi Azikiwe, *Liberia in World Politics* (Westport, CT: Negro Universities Press, 1943), 396; quoted in ibid., 113.

12. Melvin Dixon, "The Black Writer's Use of Memory," in Fabre and O'Meally, *History and Memory in African-American Culture*, 23.

13. Quoted in Nathan Huggins, *Harlem Renaissance* (New York: Oxford University Press, 1971), 191–95; and Alan R. Shucard, *Countée Cullen* (Boston: Twayne, 1984), 90.

14. Gerald L. Early, ed. *My Soul's High Song: The Collected Writings of Countée Cullen, Voice of the Harlem Renaissance* (New York: Doubleday, 1991), 59–60.

15. Countée Cullen, "Heritage," in *On These I Stand: An Anthology of the Best Poems of Countée Cullen* (New York: Harper & Row, 1947), 24 (hereafter cited in the text as H).

16. In this vein, Paul Gilroy writes that "[d]iaspora accentuates *becoming* rather than *being*. . . . Foregrounding the tensions around origins and essences that diaspora brings into focus, allows us to perceive that identity should not be fossilised or venerated in keeping with the holy spirit of ethnic absolutism. Identity too becomes a noun of process and placed on ceaseless trial. Its almost infinite openness provides a timely alternative to the authoritarian implications of mechanical—clockwork—solidarity based on outmoded notions of 'race.'" Gilroy, "'To Be Real,'" 25.

17. Frantz Fanon, *Black Skin, White Masks*, trans. Charles Lam Markmann (New York: Grove Weidenfeld, 1991), 188 (hereafter cited in the text as BSWM).

18. *Report to the House of Lords on the Abolition of the Slave Trade* (2 vols; London, 1789), quoted in Lynne Fauley Emery, *Black Dance from 1619 to Today* (Princeton, NJ: Princeton Book Company, 1988), 6 (hereafter cited in the text as BD).

19. Fanon, *Black Skin, White Masks*, 161. "It would be interesting," Fanon speculates, "on the basis of Lacan's theory of the mirror period, to investigate the extent to which the imago

of his fellow built up in the young white at the usual age would undergo an imaginary aggression with the appearance of the Negro. . . . Only for the white man The Other is perceived on the level of the body image, absolutely as the not-self—that is, the unidentifiable, the unassimilable" (ibid.).

20. Gwendolyn B. Bennett, "Heritage," in *Shadowed Dreams: Women's Poetry of the Harlem Renaissance*, ed. Maureen Honey (New Brunswick, NJ: Rutgers University Press, 1989), 103.

21. Sterling Brown, "Contemporary Negro Poetry, 1914–1936," *An Introduction to Black Literature*, ed. Lindsay Patterson (New York: Publishers Co., 1969), 146.

22. Langston Hughes, "The Negro Speaks of Rivers," in *The Collected Poems of Langston Hughes*, ed. Arnold Rampersad (New York: Alfred A. Knopf, 1994), 23.

23. See James Clifford, "Negrophilia: February, 1933," in *A New History of French Literature*, ed. Denis Hollier (Cambridge: Harvard University Press, 1989), 904. For a discussion of modern primitivism and Josephine Baker as a modern *sauvage*, see James Clifford, *The Predicament of Culture: Twentieth-Century Ethnography, Literature, and Art* (Cambridge: Harvard University Press, 1988), 197–200 (hereafter cited in the text as PC).

24. Tristan Tzara, *Seven Dada Manifestos and Lampisteries*, trans. Barbara Wright (London: J. Calder, 1992), 57–58.

25. bell hooks, "Selling Hot Pussy," in *Black Looks: Race and Representation* (Boston: South End Press, 1992), 61–77.

26. Ruth G. Dixon, "Epitome," in Honey, *Shadowed Dreams*, 83.

27. Carl Van Vechten, *Nigger Heaven* (New York: Alfred A. Knopf, 1926), 256 (hereafter cited in the text as NH).

28. Michel Fabre describes Josephine Baker as a "cultural beacon" whose artistry makes her a lasting *lieu de mémoire*. See "International Beacons of African-American Memory: Alexandre Dumas Père, Henry O. Tanner, and Josephine Baker as Examples of Recognition," in *History and Memory in African-American Culture*, 122–49.

29. Helene Johnson, "Bottled," in Honey, *Shadowed Dreams*, 97–98.

30. Josephine Baker, quoted in Josephine Baker and Jo Bouillon, *Josephine* (New York: Harper & Row, 1976), 51–52 (hereafter cited in the text as J).

31. On negrophilia, see Clifford, "Negrophilia: February, 1933," and Petrine Archer-Straw, *Negrophilia: Avant-Garde Paris and Black Culture in the 1920s* (New York: Thames & Hudson, 2000).

32. Jacques Lacan, *The Four Fundamental Concepts of Psychoanalysis*, trans. Alan Sheridan (New York: Norton: 1998), 59.

33. Claude McKay, *Selected Poems of Claude McKay* (New York: Bookman Associates, 1953), 61.

34. Phyllis Rose, *Jazz Cleopatra: Josephine Baker in Her Time* (New York: Doubleday, 1989), 53.

35. *St. Louis Republic*, July 3, 1917, quoted in Elliott Rudwick, *Race Riot at East St. Louis, July 2, 1917* (Urbana: University of Illinois Press, 1982), 46.

36. Gilroy, "'To Be Real,'" 14.

37. Slavoj Žižek, *The Sublime Object of Ideology* (London and New York: Verso Press, 1989), 163–64.

CHAPTER 4: SPECTERS OF COMMITMENT IN MODERN
AMERICAN LITERARY STUDIES

1. For a discussion of the anthology market between the wars and its relation to the high modern canon, see Craig S. Abbott, "Modern American Poetry: Anthologies, Classrooms, and Canons," *College Literature* 17 (1990): 209–22.

2. Cary Nelson, *Repression and Recovery: Modern American Poetry and the Politics of Cultural Memory, 1910–1945* (Madison: University of Wisconsin Press, 1989), 21.

3. See Barbara Foley, *Radical Representations* (Durham: Duke University Press, 1993); Michael Denning, *The Cultural Front* (New York: Verso, 1996); Walter Kalaidjian, *American Culture between the Wars: Revisionary Modernism and Postmodern Critique* (New York: Columbia University Press, 1994); Paul Lauter, *Canons and Contexts* (New York: Oxford University Press, 1991); Cary Nelson, *Repression and Recovery* (Madison: University of Wisconsin Press, 1989) and *Revolutionary Memory* (New York: Routledge, 2002); Paula Rabinowitz, *Labor and Desire* (Chapel Hill: University of North Carolina Press, 1991) and *They Must Be Represented* (New York: Verso, 1994); Alan Wald, *The Revolutionary Imagination* (Chapel Hill: University of North Carolina Press, 1983) and *Exiles from a Future Time* (Chapel Hill: University of North Carolina Press, 2002), among others.

4. Jacques Derrida, *The Specters of Marx: The State of the Debt, the Work of Mourning, and the New International*, trans. Peggy Kamuf (New York: Routledge, 1994), 11, 99.

5. Michael Davidson takes Stevens's phrasing from "Sunday Morning" for his book *Ghostlier Demarcations: Modern Poetry and the Material World* (Berkeley: University of California Press, 1997).

6. Through their own clinical experience and readings of Freud's well-known case study of the Wolf Man, Nicolas Abraham and Maria Torok have marked the discursive crypts of phantom signifiers in terms of narrative "gaps left within us by the secrets of others." Nicolas Abraham, "Notes on the Phantom: A Complement to Freud's Metapsychology," in *The Shell and the Kernel: Renewals of Psychoanalysis*, trans. and ed. Nicholas T. Rand (Chicago: University of Chicago Press, 1994), 1:171. For an extended analysis of cryptonyms, see Abraham and Torok, *The Wolf Man's Magic Word: A Cryptonymy*, trans. Nicholas Rand (Minneapolis: University of Minnesota Press, 1986). Building on the work of Abraham and Torok, Derrida has adapted his discussion of the "hauntology" of cryptonyms to the philosophy of political economy in *The Specters of Marx*.

7. Ross Chambers, "Orphaned Memories, Foster-Writing, Phantom Pain: The *Fragments* Affair," in *Extremities*, ed. Nancy K Miller and Jason Tougaw (Urbana: University of Illinois Press, 2002), 92.

8. Patricia Yaeger, "Consuming Trauma; or, The Pleasures of Merely Circulating," in Miller and Tougaw, *Extremities*, 35.

9. Karl Marx, *The Eighteenth Brumaire of Louis Bonaparte*, in Karl Marx, Frederick Engels, *Collected Works*, vol. 11 (New York: International Publishers, 1970), quoted in Jacques Derrida, *The Specters of Marx*, 108.

10. "'The conjuration,'" Derrida writes, "is anxiety from the moment it calls upon death to invent the quick and to enliven the new, to summon the presence of what is not yet there (*noch nicht Dagewesenes*). The anxiety in the face of the ghost is properly revolution-

ary. . . . The paradox must be sharpened: the more the new erupts in the revolutionary crisis, the more the period is in crisis, the more it is 'out of joint,' then the more one has to convoke the old, 'borrow' from it." *The Specters of Marx*, 109.

11. Hugh Kenner, "The Making of the Modernist Canon," *Canons*, ed. Robert von Hallberg (Chicago: University of Chicago Press, 1984), 374 (hereafter cited in the text as MMC).

12. On this point, see Kalaidjian, *American Culture between the Wars*.

13. For a cogent discussion of the New Right's assault on progressive academic culture through such organizations as the Institute for Educational Affairs (IEA), the National Association of Scholars (NAS), and Accuracy in Academia (AIA), as well as in such generalist publication venues as the *Partisan Review*, the *American Scholar*, *Commentary*, and the *New York Review of Books*, see Michael Bérubé, "Winning Hearts and Minds," *Yale Journal of Criticism* 5 (Spring 1992): 1–25.

14. See Elizabeth Cullingford, *Yeats, Ireland and Fascism* (New York: New York University Press, 1981); Tim Redman, *Ezra Pound and Italian Fascism* (New York: Cambridge University Press, 1991); Robert Casillo, *The Genealogy of Demons: Anti-Semitism, Fascism, and the Myths of Ezra Pound* (Evanston: Northwestern University Press, 1988); Lucy McDiarmid, *Saving Civilization: Yeats, Eliot , and Auden between the Wars* (New York: Cambridge University Press, 1984); John Fekete, *The Critical Twilight: Explorations in the Ideology of Anglo-American Literary Theory from Eliot to McLuhan* (Boston: Routledge and Kegan Paul, 1977); Alexander Karanikas, *Tillers of a Myth: Southern Agrarians as Social and Literary Critics* (Madison: University of Wisconsin Press, 1966).

15. Donald Davidson, "A Mirror for Artists," in *I'll Take My Stand* (New York: Harper & Row, 1962), 28 (hereafter cited in the text as ITS).

16. See Hans Magnus Enzensberger, "The Industrialization of the Mind" (3–14) and "Constituents of a Theory of the Media" (46–76), in *Critical Essays*, trans. Reinhold Grimm and Bruce Armstrong (New York: Continuum, 1982).

17. Antonio Gramsci, "Americanism and Fordism," in *Selections from the Prison Notebooks*, ed. and trans. Quintin Hoare and Geoffrey Nowell-Smith (New York: International Publishers, 1971), 302.

18. For a discussion of the growth of what Daniel Bell, B. Bruce-Briggs, Everett Carll Ladd, Jr., Norman Podhoretz, and others have discussed as the postwar "new class," see B. Bruce-Briggs, ed., *The New Class?* (New York: McGraw Hill, 1979), and Alvin W. Gouldner, *The Future of Intellectuals and the Rise of the New Class* (New York: Oxford University Press, 1979).

19. Henry Ford, *My Life and Work* (New York: Garden City Publishing Co., 1926), 263.

20. Buttressed by the pervasive spectacle of advertising, Fordism, according to Michel Aglietta, "marks a new state in the regulation of capitalism, the regime of intensive accumulation in which the capitalist class seeks overall management of the production of wage-labour by the close articulation of relations of production with the commodity relations in which the wage earners purchase their means of consumption. Fordism is thus the principle of *an articulation between process of production and mode of consumption.*" Michel Aglietta, *A Theory of Capitalist Regulation: The US Experience*, trans. David Fernbach (London: NLB, 1979), 116–17.

21. *American Review* 3 (April 1934): 124; cited in Karanikas, *Tillers of a Myth*, 179.

22. Karanikas, *Tillers of a Myth*, 42.

23. Hoffman Nickerson, "Property and Tactics," *American Review* 5 (April–October 1935): 568–69.

24. Ross J. S. Hoffman, "The Totalitarian Regimes: An Essay in Essential Distinctions," *American Review* 9 (September 1937): 336.

25. Nickerson, "Property and Tactics," 565.

26. As just one example of this tendency, Richard J. Gray's *American Poetry of the Twentieth Century* not only represses the Southern Agrarian dimension of modern American verse but obscures and deflects its political subtexts through a more narrow focus on the symptomatic themes, say, of the individual's dissociation of sensibility and nostalgia for "unity of being." See Richard J. Gray, *American Poetry of the Twentieth Century* (New York: Longman, 1990), 101–25.

27. See, for example, "A Note on Symbol and Conceit," *American Review* 3 (May 1934): 201–11; and "The Christianity of Modernism," *American Review* 6 (February 1936): 435–46.

28. Cleanth Brooks, "Metaphysical Poetry and Propaganda Art," *Modern Poetry and the Tradition* (Chapel Hill: University of North Carolina Press, 1939), 50–51.

29. With this major setback to socialist culture in the United States, Fekete argues, "[T]he New Criticism was able to move in, not to combat a strong left-wing position, but rather to occupy the vacuum left by the failure of socialist criticism to realize its opportunities. . . . In other words, the cultural politics of the New Criticism are linked with the political culture of the period, and, as in the rest of the modern critical tradition, the cultural methodology reveals its politics directly." *The Critical Twilight*, 49.

30. F. Scott Fitzgerald, *The Great Gatsby* (New York: Simon and Schuster, 1992), 99.

31. Edwin Rolfe, "Poetry," *Partisan Review* 2, no. 7 (April–May 1935): 36, 38.

32. Joseph Freeman, "They Find Strength," *New Masses* 18, no. 11 (March 1936): 23.

33. Edwin Rolfe, *The Collected Poems of Edwin Rolfe*, ed. Cary Nelson and Jefferson Hendricks (Urbana: University of Illinois Press, 1993), 59 (hereafter cited in the text as CP).

34. For a discussion of lyricism as the dominant poetic mode in the postwar era, see Walter Kalaidjian, *Languages of Liberation: The Social Text in Contemporary American Poetry* (New York: Columbia University Press, 1989).

35. Jerome McGann defines the aesthetics of sincerity "as one of the touchstones by which Romantic poetry originally measured itself. In a poem's sincerity one observed a deeply felt relation binding the poetic Subject to the poetic subject, the speaking voice to the matter being addressed. Romantic truth is inner vision, and Romantic knowledge is the unfolding of the truths of that inner vision. . . . [T]hey are the positions that will dominate the theory of poetry for 150, 175 years or more, even to our own day." "Private Poetry, Public Deception," in *The Politics of Poetic Form: Poetry and Public Policy*, ed. Charles Bernstein (New York: Roof Books, 1990), 121, 141.

36. "That is to say, to make the terrible mistake of trying to present in political practice an Idea of Reason. To be able to say, 'We are the proletariat,' or 'We are the incarnation of free humanity,' and so on." Jean-François Lyotard, "Complexity and the Sublime," in *Postmodernism*, trans. Geoffrey Bennington (London: Institute of Contemporary Arts, 1986), 11.

37. See Barbara Herrnstein Smith, *Contingencies of Value: Alternative Perspectives for Critical Theory* (Cambridge: Harvard University Press, 1988).

38. Thomas McGrath, "Foreword," reprinted in Rolfe, *The Collected Poems of Edwin Rolfe*, 207.

39. Alexander Kluge and Oskar Negt, *Public Sphere and Experience: Toward an Analysis of the Bourgeois and Proletarian Public Sphere*, trans. Peter Labanyi, Jamie Owen Daniel, and Assenka Oksiloff (Minneapolis: University of Minnesota Press, 1993), 95 (hereafter cited in the text as PSE).

40. See, for example, Robert Penn Warren, "The Present State of Poetry in the United States," *Kenyon Review* 1 (August 1939): 393.

41. For example, in the National Poetry Foundation's call for papers for its 1996 annual conference on "American Poetry in the 1950s," some sixty poets are suggested as figures for discussion. Here Rolfe's legacy was registered in his conspicuous absence from the list.

42. See Edward Dmytryk, *Odd Man Out: A Memoir of the Hollywood Ten* (Carbondale: Southern Illinois University Press, 1996), 59, n. 3.

43. On family life and the containment of social identity in the fifties, see Elaine Tyler May, *Homeward Bound: American Families in the Cold War Era* (New York: Basic Books, 1988).

44. The text of the "Long Telegram" is reprinted in *Containment: Documents on American Policy and Strategy, 1945–1950*, ed. Thomas H. Etzold and John Lewis Gaddis (New York: Columbia University Press, 1978), 50–63.

45. For a discussion of the parallels between American foreign policy and domestic identity containment, see David Campbell, *Writing Security: United States Foreign Policy and the Politics of Identity* (Minneapolis: University of Minnesota Press, 1992).

46. See Benedict Anderson, *Imagined Communities: Reflections on the Origin and Spread of Nationalism* (London: Verso, 1983), 16. "Communities," in Anderson's signal formulation, "are to be distinguished, not by their falsity/genuineness, but by the style in which they are imagined" (15).

47. On the use of nationalism to resist modernization, John Breuilly has written that "some writers have linked nationalism to the maintenance of order, which might involve the avoidance of rapid modernisation." *Nationalism and the State* (Chicago: University of Chicago Press, 1985), 34. See also Gerald Heeger, *The Politics of Underdevelopment* (New York: St. Martin's Press, 1974), 15–46.

48. T. S. Eliot, "Tradition and the Individual Talent," in *Selected Essays* (New York: Harcourt, Brace and World, 1960), 6.

49. Anonymous author, "Introduction: A Statement of Principles," in *I'll Take My Stand*, xxvi.

50. W. E. B. Du Bois, "Worlds of Color: The Negro Mind Reaches Out," in *The New Negro*, ed. Alain Locke (New York: Albert and Charles Boni, 1925), 407.

51. "Williams," writes John Dittmer, "was a cousin of the Jasper County sheriff. Justice Department agents visited Williams's farm on February 23, 1921, to investigate allegations of peonage. They did not file charges. Several weeks later a black hired hand, Clyde Manning, confessed that after the initial investigation he and Williams destroyed evidence by murdering eleven blacks. Williams and Manning shot one victim, killed four others with an ax, and bound and weighted the other six men with stones before throwing them into the river. . . . Recalling conditions during his administration in the 1940s, former governor

Ellis Arnall, admitted that 'the Georgia penal system was bad; it was evil; it was inhuman.'" *Black Georgia in the Progressive Era, 1900–1920* (Urbana: University of Illinois Press, 1977), 81, 87.

52. See Stewart E. Tolnay and E. M. Beck, "Rethinking the Role of Racial Violence in the Great Migration," in *Black Exodus: The Great Migration from the American South,* ed. Alferdteen Harrison (Jackson: University of Mississippi Press, 1991), 20–35.

53. John Dittmer, *Black Georgia in the Progressive Era,* 132.

54. For an account of this burning, see ibid., 134.

55. Allen Tate, "A View of the Whole South," *American Review* 2 (February 1934): 424; cited in Karanikas, *Tillers of a Myth,* 90.

56. Cleanth Brooks and Robert Penn Warren, *Understanding Poetry,* 3d ed. (New York: Farrar, Straus and Giroux, 1958), xvii.

57. See Pierre Bourdieu and Jean Claude Passeron, *Reproduction in Education, Society, and Culture,* trans. Richard Nice (London: Sage, 1990); and Bourdieu, *Distinction: A Social Critique of the Judgement of Taste,* trans. Richard Nice (Cambridge: Harvard University Press, 1984).

58. Cleanth Brooks and Robert Penn Warren, *Understanding Poetry: An Anthology for College Students* (New York: Henry Holt and Company, 1938), iv.

59. For a detailed reading of race in the makeup of English studies between the wars, see Lauter, *Canons and Contexts,* 22–47.

60. James Weldon Johnson, "Preface to the First Edition," in *The Book of American Negro Poetry* (New York: Harcourt, Brace and Co., 1922, rev. ed. 1931), 9 (hereafter cited in the text as ANP).

61. Countée Cullen, "Foreword," in *Caroling Dusk: An Anthology of Verse by Negro Poets,* ed. Countée Cullen (New York: Harper & Brothers Publishers, 1927), x (hereafter cited in the text as CD).

62. "I have the conviction," Cheney said, "that great literature, no matter whom it is written by, speaks to transcendent values that we all share, no matter what our time and circumstance. In the West the first responsibility is to ground students in the culture that gave rise to the institutions of our democracy." Quoted in Richard Bernstein, "Academia's Liberals Defend Their Carnival of Canons against Bloom's 'Killer B's,'" *New York Times,* September 25, 1988, E26; and in Eve Kosofsky Sedgwick, "Nationalism and Sexualities in the Age of Wilde," in *Nationalisms and Sexualities,* ed. Andrew Parker et al. (New York: Routledge, 1992), 237–38. Similarly, Bennett's famous manifesto "To Reclaim a Legacy" incorporates "culture" under the rubric of Eurocentrism, which in his metaphor, is the "glue that binds together our pluralistic nation." "That our society was founded upon such principles as justice, liberty, government with the consent of the governed, and equality under the law is the result of ideas descended directly from great epochs of Western civilization—Enlightenment England and France, Renaissance Florence, and Periclean Athens." William Bennett, "To Reclaim a Legacy: Text of Report on Humanities in Education," *Chronicle of Higher Education,* November 28, 1984, 21.

63. Cleanth Brooks, "The Remaking of the Canon," *Partisan Review* 58 (Spring 1991): 351, 353.

64. Ibid., 355. As a respondent to Brooks's paper, Gertrude Himmelfarb concurred with him. In a similar defense of such contemporary institutions of "close reading" as the "great"

books program at St. John's College, she betrayed New Criticism's hidden ideological agenda by discriminating between the representation of multicultural diversity and "merit"— her code word for canonical distinction. "I do not recognize," she proclaimed, "representation as a legitimate criterion. The final judgment has to do with merit—the worth and greatness of the idea or book. This was the criterion of the learned and wise in the past, and it seems to me we cannot do better than that." Gertrude Himmelfarb, "Response to Cleanth Brooks," *Partisan Review* 58 (Spring 1991): 379. Resting her definition of a work's "greatness" on David Hume's criterion of "durable admiration," Himmelfarb implicitly discounted the materialist "contingencies of value" theorized in, say, Barbara Herrnstein Smith's critique of canonicity. See Smith, *Contingencies of Value*.

CHAPTER 5: THE ENIGMA OF WITNESS

1. Hank O'Neal, *"Life Is Painful, Nasty & Short . . . In My Case It Has Only Been Painful & Nasty"* (New York: Paragon House, 1990), 131 (hereafter cited in the text as LP).

2. Andrew Field, *Djuna: The Formidable Miss Barnes* (Austin: University of Texas Press, 1985), 24 (hereafter cited in the text as D).

3. Roland Barthes, *Image-Music-Text,* trans. Stephen Heath (New York: Hill and Wang, 1977), 155.

4. Shari Benstock, *Women of the Left Bank: Paris, 1900–1940* (Austin: University of Texas Press, 1986), 233.

5. Susan Sniader Lanser, "Speaking in Tongues: *Ladies Almanack* and the Discourse of Desire," in *Silence and Power,* ed. Mary Lynn Broe (Carbondale: Southern Illinois University Press, 1991), 168.

6. See Karla Jay, "The Outsider among the Expatriates: Djuna Barnes' Satire on the Ladies of the Almanack," in Broe, *Silence and Power,* 184–94; and Elizabeth Meese, *(SEM)-erotics: Theorizing Lesbian: Writing* (New York: New York University Press, 1992).

7. Simone de Beauvoir, *The Second Sex,* trans. E. M. Parshley (New York: Vintage, 1973), 301.

8. Djuna Barnes, *Ryder* (New York: Horace Liveright, 1928), 223 (hereafter cited in the text as R).

9. Marie Ponsot, "A Reader's *Ryder,*" in Broe, *Silence and Power,* 108.

10. James B. Scott, *Djuna Barnes* (Boston: Twayne Publishers, 1976), 66.

11. Judith Butler, *Gender Trouble: Feminism and the Subversion of Identity* (New York: Routledge, 1990), 37.

12. See Lynda Curry, "'Tom, Take Mercy': Djuna Barnes' Drafts of *The Antiphon,*" in Broe, *Silence and Power,* 290 (hereafter cited in the text as SP).

13. Alice Miller, *Thou Shalt Not Be Aware: Society's Betrayal of the Child* (New York: Farrar, Straus and Giroux, 1986), 160–61.

14. Gilles Deleuze and Félix Guattari, *Kafka: Toward a Minor Literature,* trans. Dana Polan (Minneapolis: University of Minnesota Press, 1986), 13.

15. Anne Sexton, quoted in Diane Middlebrook, *Anne Sexton: A Biography* (Boston: Houghton Mifflin, 1991), 158 (hereafter cited in the text as M).

16. M. L. Rosenthal, *The New Poets* (New York: Oxford University Press, 1967), 79.

17. See Helen Vendler, *The Given and the Made: Strategies of Poetic Redefinition* (Cambridge: Harvard University Press, 1995), 49.

18. Anne Sexton, *The Complete Poems* (Boston: Houghton Mifflin, 1981), 34.

19. Michel Foucault, *History of Sexuality*, vol. 1: *An Introduction*, trans. Robert Hurley (New York: Pantheon, 1978), 59 (hereafter cited in the text as HS).

20. Martin T. Orne, "Foreword," in Middlebrook, *Anne Sexton*, xiii.

21. Jacques Lacan, *Écrits: A Selection*, trans. Alan Sheridan (New York: Norton, 1977), 269 (hereafter cited in the text as É).

22. See M. T. Orne, D. A. Soskis, et. al., "Hypnotically Induced Testimony," in *Eyewitness Testimony: Psychological Perspectives*, ed. G. L. Wells & E. F. Loftus (New York: Cambridge University Press, 1984), 171-213.

23. Maxine Kumin, "How It Was," foreword to *Anne Sexton: The Complete Poems* (Boston: Houghton Mifflin, 1981), xxiv (hereafter cited in the text as CP).

24. Robert Lowell, "Anne Sexton," in *Anne Sexton: Telling the Tale*, ed. Steven E. Colburn (Ann Arbor: University of Michigan Press, 1988), 24.

25. Barbara Swan, "A Reminiscence," in Colburn, *Anne Sexton*, 40.

26. Alicia Ostriker, "Anne Sexton and the Seduction of the Audience," in *Sexton: Selected Criticism*, ed. Diana Hume George (Urbana: University of Illinois Press, 1988), 9 (hereafter cited in the text as SC).

27. Jeffrey Masson, *The Assault on Truth: Freud's Suppression of the Seduction Theory* (New York: Farrar, Straus and Giroux, 1984).

28. J. D. McClatchy, "Anne Sexton: Somehow to Endure," in George, *Sexton: Selected Criticism*, 63.

29. Cassie Premo Steele, *We Heal from Memory: Sexton, Lorde, Anzaldua, and the Poetry of Witness* (New York: Palgrave, 2000), 15.

30. Jane Gallop, "The Father's Seduction," in *Daughters and Fathers*, ed. Lynda E. Boose and Betty S. Flowers (Baltimore: Johns Hopkins University Press, 1989), 102, 107.

31. Anne Sexton, Letter to Anne Clark, July 3, 1964, in *Anne Sexton: A Self Portrait in Letters*, ed. Linda Gray Sexton and Lois Ames (Boston: Houghton Mifflin, 1977), 244-45.

32. Michel Foucault, "Maurice Blanchot: The Thought from Outside," in *Foucault / Blanchot*, trans. Brian Massumi (New York: Zone Books), 25.

33. Jacques Lacan, *Séminaire VIII: Le Transfert, 1960-61* (Paris: Seuil, 1991), 229, quoted in Vincente Palomera, "On Counter-Transference," *The Klein-Lacan Dialogues*, ed. Bernard Burgoyne and E. Mary Sullivan (New York: Other Press, 1999), 148.

34. By staying within the frame of the poem's address of student-to-male mentor, Sexton's critics all too often read the poem as an early apology for confessionalism and thus swerve from the "fear" otherwise encoded in the work. For example, Steven E. Colburn writes, "For Sexton's Oedipus, however, no appalling horror attends the speaker's 'enquiry' into the 'narrow diary' of her mind." "The Troubled Life of the Artist," in George, *Sexton: Selected Criticism*, 290. Similarly, J. D. McClatchy downplays the trauma at the heart of the poem when he writes, "The sympathy she can afford for Holmes . . . recalls Freud's sense of the repulsion with the self and others that art overcomes. Her cautious justification is modeled on her psychiatrist's plea. . . . And the standard she sets herself is simply making sense." McClatchy, "Anne Sexton: Somehow to Endure," 38. "Whatever truth the speaker seeks,"

concludes Diana Hume George, "it will not be available in 'lovelier places' than the private mind speaking its halting language to another private mind, trying to make contact." *Oedipus Anne* (Urbana: University of Illinois Press, 1987), 11 (hereafter cited in the text as OA).

35. Suzanne Juhasz, "Seeking the Exit or the Home: Poetry and Salvation in the Career of Anne Sexton," in George, *Sexton: Selected Criticism*, 304.

36. Sigmund Freud, *Introductory Lectures on Psycho-Analysis* (1916–1917), in *The Standard Edition of the Complete Psychological Works of Sigmund Freud*, trans. James Strachey (London: Hogarth Press and the Institute of Psycho-Analysis, 1953–1974), 16:337.

37. Melanie Klein, "Infantile Anxiety Situations Reflected in a Work of Art and in the Creative Impulse" (1929), in *Love, Guilt, and Reparation, and Other Works, 1921–1917* (New York: Free Press, 1975), 217 (hereafter cited in the text as LGR).

38. Barbara Kevles, "The Art of Poetry XV: Anne Sexton," *Paris Review* 13 (Summer 1971): 159–91, reprinted in *No Evil Star: Selected Essays, Interviews, and Prose* (Ann Arbor: University of Michigan Press, 1985), 86 (hereafter cited in the text as PR).

39. Sigmund Freud, "On Transformations of Instinct as Exemplified in Anal Eroticism," in *The Standard Edition of the Complete Psychological Works of Sigmund Freud*, 17:128.

40. Paul de Man, "Autobiography as De-Facement," in *The Rhetoric of Romanticism* (New York: Columbia University Press, 1984), 75–76 (hereafter cited in the text as RR).

41. Hanna Segal, *Introduction to the Work of Melanie Klein* (London: Karnac and the Institute of Psycho-Analysis, 1988), ix.

42. Judith Butler, "Moral Sadism and Doubting One's Own Love: Kleinian Reflections on Melancholia," in *Reading Melanie Klein*, ed. Lyndsey Stonebridge and John Phillips (London: Routledge, 1998), 179–89.

43. Jacqueline Rose, "Negativity in the Work of Melanie Klein," in Stonebridge and Phillips, *Reading Melanie Klein*, 146.

44. "The passage toward the society of control involves a production of subjectivity that is not fixed in identity but hybrid and modulating. As the walls that defined and isolated the effects of the modern institutions progressively break down, subjectivities tend to be produced simultaneously by numerous institutions in different combinations and doses. Certainly in disciplinary society each individual had many identities, but to a certain extent different identities were defined by different places and different times of life: one was mother or father at home, worker in the factory, student at school, inmate in prison, and mental patient in the asylum. In the society of control, it is precisely these places, these discrete sites of applicability, that tend to lose their definition and delimitations. A hybrid subjectivity produced in the society of control may not carry the identity of a prison inmate or a mental patient or a factory worker, but may still be constituted simultaneously by all of their logics. It is factory worker outside the factory, student outside school, inmate outside prison, insane outside the asylum—all at the same time." Michael Hardt and Antonio Negri, *Empire* (Cambridge: Harvard University Press, 2000), 331.

45. Brian Levack, *The Witch Hunt in Early Modern Europe*, 2d ed. (New York: Longman, 1995), 59, quoted in Elaine Showalter, *Hystories: Hysterical Epidemics and Modern Culture* (New York: Columbia University Press, 1997), 24; see also Norman Cohn, *The Pursuit of the Millennium* (London: Secker & Warburg, 1957); Juliet Mitchell, *Women: The Longest Revolution: Essays on Feminism, Literature and Psychoanalysis* (London: Virago, 1984).

46. Audre Lorde, "From the House of Yemanjá," in *The Black Unicorn* (New York: Norton, 1995), 7.

EPILOGUE

1. See Giorgio Agamben, *Homo Sacer: Sovereign Power and Bare Life*, trans. Daniel Heller-Roazen (Stanford: Stanford University Press, 1998); Michael Hardt and Antonio Negri, *Empire* (Cambridge: Harvard University Press, 2000).

2. Giorgio Agamben, "The Camp as Nomos of the Modern," in Agamben, *Homo Sacer*, 168–69.

3. Judith Butler, *Precarious Life: The Powers of Mourning and Violence* (London: Verso, 2004), 146.

4. Emmanuel Levinas, "Peace and Proximity," in *Emmanuel Levinas: Basic Philosophical Writings*, ed. Adriaan T. Peperzak, Simon Critchley, and Robert Bernasconi (Bloomington: Indiana University Press, 1996), 167; cited in Butler, *Precarious Life*, 134.

5. Bill Keller, "The Nightmare at Abu Ghraib," *New York Times*, May 4, 2004.

6. Sigmund Freud, *The Interpretation of Dreams* (New York: Avon, 1980), 82 (hereafter cited in the text as ID).

7. Lynndie England, "Interview with Brian Maass," May 12, 2004, CBS News: <http://www.cbsnews.com/stories/2004/05/12/iraq/main616921.shtml>.

8. See Christopher Simpson, *Science of Coercion: Communication Research and Psychological Warfare, 1945–1960* (New York: Oxford University Press, 1994), 40.

9. Richard Edwards, "The Propaganda War in Iraq," *Guardian*, March 26, 2003, quoted in David Miller, "The Propaganda Machine," in *Tell Me Lies: Propaganda and Media Distortion on Iraq*, ed. David Miller (London: Pluto Press, 2004), 99.

10. Seymour M. Hersh, *Chain of Command: The Road from 9/11 to Abu Ghraib* (New York: Harper Collins, 2004), 39.

11. Agamben defines *Homo sacer* in terms of the "sacred man" of antiquity "who may be killed and yet not sacrificed. . . . An obscure figure of archaic Roman law, in which human life is included in the juridical order [*ordinamento*] solely in the form of its exclusion (that is, of its capacity to be killed), has thus offered the key by which not only the sacred texts of sovereignty but also the very codes of political power will unveil their mysteries." *Homo Sacer*, 8. See also "The Ban and the Wolf," in Agamben, *Homo Sacer*, 104–15.

12. Giorgio Agamben, "The Camp as Nomos of the Modern," in Agamben, *Homo Sacer*, 179.

13. Donald Rumsfeld, Senate Armed Services Committee testimony, quoted in Seymour M. Hersh, "The Gray Zone: How a Secret Pentagon Program Came to Abu Ghraib," *New Yorker*, May 24, 2004, 43–44.

14. Roland Barthes, *Camera Lucida: Reflections on Photography*, trans. Richard Howard (New York: Vintage, 1981), 26 (hereafter cited in the text as CL).

15. Pierre Bourdieu, *Photography: A Middle-Brow Art*, trans. Shaun Whiteside (Stanford: Stanford University Press, 1990), 21.

16. Luke Harding, "How Abu Ghraib Torture Victim Faces Final Indignity: An Unmarked Grave," *Guardian*, June 1, 2004. <http://www.guardian.co.uk/Iraq/Story/0,2763, 1228666,00.html>.

17. Quoted in Eric Schmitt, "Abuse Panel Says Rules on Inmates Need Overhaul," *New York Times*, August 25, 2004, <http://www.nytimes.com/2004/08/25/politics/25abuse.html>.

18. Hannah Arendt, *Eichmann in Jerusalem* (New York: Viking, 1964), 268.

19. See Walter Benjamin, "A Small History of Photography," in *One-Way Street and Other Writings*, trans. Edmund Jephcott and Kingsley Shorter (London: Verso, 1992), 243.

20. Sigmund Freud, *Moses and Monotheism*, trans. Katherine Jones (New York: Vintage, 1939), 162.

21. In Pound's definition "an epic is a poem containing history." See *Literary Essays of Ezra Pound*, ed. T. S. Eliot (New York: New Directions, 1968), 86; and Toni Morrison, "Unspeakable Things Unspoken: The Afro-American Presence in American Literature," *Michigan Quarterly Review* 28 (Winter 1989): 1–34.

22. Marjorie Perloff, "'A Small Periplus along an Edge': Rosmarie Waldrop's Auto-Graph," *How2* 1, no. 8 (Fall 2002): n.p. <http://www.scc.rutgers.edu/however/vi_8_2002/current/readings/perloff.shtm>.

23. William Carlos Williams, "Asphodel That Greeny Flower," in *The Collected Poems of William Carlos Williams*, ed. Christopher MacGowan (New York: New Directions, 1988), 2:318.

Index

Merleau-Ponty, Maurice, 102
Merrill, James, *The Changing Light at Sandover*, 58
Metro-Goldwyn-Mayer (MGM), 22
Michaelis, Karin, "The Empty Space," 177
Middlebrook, Diane, 173, 174–75
Middle Passage, 110, 127. *See also* Black Atlantic
Millay, Edna St. Vincent, 131
Miller, Alice, 164
Miller, Donald E., and Lorna Touryan, 34;
    suicide, 206nn64, 68–69
Mitchell, Juliet, 160, 186–87
Mitscherlich, Alexander and Margarete: *The
    Inability to Mourn*, 54, 79, 214n80
Morgenthau, Henry, 33
Morrison, Toni, 196
Mott, John R., 17
Mourning, process of, 208n86, 214nn80–81
Multiple personality syndrome (MPS), 167–68
My Lai Massacre. *See* Vietnam

Nancy, Jean-Luc, 7
National Endowment for the Humanities, 155
NATO, 22, 54
Nazis' ideology, 9; *Einsatzgruppen*, 60, 65;
    Nazism, 61, 63, 80
Negri, Antonio, 185, 189–90, 227n44
Negt, Oskar, 140
Neher, André, 53
Nelson, Cary, 128, 139
New Critics/Criticism, 13, 128–29, 131, 135–36,
    140, 147–48, 152–55, 222n29, 224–25n64
New Left, 139
New Right, 221n13
New Social Movements, 139
Niepage, Dr. Martin, 34
Nietzsche, Friedrich, 15–16, 59
Nigger Heaven (van Vechten), 119–20
Night (Weisel), 50–51
9/11, 190
Nolte, Ernst, 54–55, 63
Nom du Pere. See Lacan, Jacques
Nora, Pierre, 12, 109–11
Novick, Peter, 3–4, 8
Nuremberg, 64

Oedipal myth. *See* Barnes, Djuna; Sexton, Anne
Old Left, poetics, 140
Olds, Sharon, "That Year," 68–70
Olson, Charles: *The Maximus Poems*, 3; "The
    Kingfishers," 57

O'Neal, Hank, 158
Oppen, George, 88
Opportunity, 116–17
Orne, Dr. Martin. *See* Sexton, Anne
Ostriker, Alicia, 65–67, 94; on Anne Sexton, 169,
    171; "The Eighth and Thirteenth," 65–67
Ottoman Empire, Tanzimat, 35
Owsley, Frank, 133–34, 149–50
Ozick, Cynthia, 5

Parapraxis, 73
Partisan Review, 156
Patai, Raphael, *The Arab Mind*, 193
Pearce, Roy Harvey, 58
Pearl Harbor, 37, 39
Performance: art, 108; African-American, 113,
    124, 126; black skin, 12; performative confes-
    sionalism, 165; poetry, 112; ritual of, 109
Perloff, Marjorie, 196
Phantom, 204n49. *See also* Abraham, Nicholas
Phelan, Peggy, 109
Photography, 195; in Abu Ghraib, 192–96; and
    Empire, 191; propaganda, 193; role in warfare,
    192
Piper, Adrian, 108
Plantation Buck and Wing, 12
Plath, Sylvia: BBC interview, 6–7; "Daddy," 5–8,
    69; Electra complex, 7; German identity, 6–7;
    Holocaust, 8; Jewish subject, 7; "Lady
    Lazarus," 8; nationalist narration, 6; Nazism, 5;
    poetic response to trauma, 8; "The Shadow," 6;
    Ted Hughes, 7
Plato, allegory of the cave, 49–50
Plimpton, George, 17
Poe, Edgar Allan, "The Raven," 51
Poetry, African-American, 154. *See also*
    cryptonyms; trauma
Ponsot, Marie, 161
Popular Front, 138–39, 142, 148
Pornography, 60
Post-traumatic stress disorder (PTSD), 5, 56
Pound, Ezra, 128, 155, 158, 196; on the Armenian
    Genocide, 16–17; Bollingen controversy, 130
Primitivism, 12, 116–22, 124, 149
Princeton University, 24
Prosopopoeia, 182–83, 190, 215n86
Psychoanalysis, 13, 57, 204n48; and literature, 14,
    168
Psychological Operations (Psyops), 190–96; in
    World War I, 192